D0312611

The Concise Dinosaur Encyclopedia

KINGFISHER
a Houghton Mifflin Company imprint
222 Berkeley Street
Boston, Massachusetts 02116
www.houghtonmifflinbooks.com

First published as *The Kingfisher Illustrated Dinosaur Encyclopedia*
by Kingfisher Publications Plc in 2001

Reprinted in a revised format in 2004
4 6 8 10 9 7 5 3

3TR/0705/C&C/SF/"RD(PICA)/157MA/C

LIBRARY OF CONGRESS CATALOGING-IN-PUBLICATION DATA
has been applied for.

ISBN 0-7534-5754-7
ISBN 978-07534-5754-2

Printed in China

Cover design by Jo Brown

Consultant   Tim Batty, Curator of The Dinosaur Museum,
Dorchester, England
Managing editor   Miranda Smith
Senior designer   Malcolm Parchment
Picture researchers   Juliet Duff, Jane Lambert
DTP manager   Nicky Studdart
Production manager   Caroline Hansell

Additional illustrations
Julian Baker, Richard Bonson, Mike Davis, James Field,
Chris Forsey, Ray Grinaway, Gary Hinks, David Holmes, Mark Iley, Ian Jackson,
Steve Kirk, Terrence Lambert, Bernard Long, Kevin Maddison,
Shirley Mallinson, Bernard Robinson, Tim Slade, Guy Smith, Mike Taylor

THE CONCISE
DINOSAUR
ENCYCLOPEDIA

WRITTEN BY DAVID BURNIE

ILLUSTRATED BY JOHN SIBBICK

KINGFISHER

BOSTON

Colony-forming graptolites from the Silurian Period, drifting in the sea

CONTENTS

Eldonia ludwigi, a primitive echinoderm from the Burgess Shale

Oryctocephalus matthewi, an early trilobite from the Burgess Shale

Aysheaia—an ancestor of velvet worms—feeding on sponges during the Cambrian Period

Acanthostega (left) and *Ichthyostega* (right and above), two of the earliest four-legged vertebrates

Heleosaurus, a Late Permian reptile

The fossilized
skeleton of
Parasaurolophus,
a duck-billed
dinosaur

Skeletal muscles
of the plant eater
Brachiosaurus,
one of the tallest
sauropods

Deinosuchus, a giant crocodilian
from the Late Cretaceous, attacking
Corythosaurus, a duck-billed dinosaur

FOREWORD

This book is about a group of extraordinary animals—the dinosaurs. These reptiles dominated the natural world for more than 160 million years, and from the middle of the 1800s, when the first fossil skeletons were excavated, they have captured the imaginations of generations of people—children and adults alike. Through the patient work of paleontologists and other scientists, we are finding out more and more about these remarkable creatures, the continents they roamed, what they ate, the way they lived.

The work of a paleontologist is painstaking and backbreaking, but sometimes it is unbelievably rewarding. On August 12, 1990, in the Badlands of South Dakota, many miles from any human habitation, I found three articulated vertebrae, some ribs, and a large bone weathering out of a cliff face. I was almost certain that the bones belonged to a *Tyrannosaurus rex*, but I had no idea that the find, "Sue," would prove a record breaker. She is the largest and most complete skeleton of a *Tyrannosaurus* yet discovered—she is 42 feet (12.8m) long and stands 13 feet (4m) high at the hips. *And* she was not alone. She was found with the remains of other tyrannosaurs—a baby, a juvenile, and a young adult.

On May 17, 2000, at the Field Museum in Chicago, Sue's mounted skeleton was unveiled to the world for the first time in 66 million years, and she, like so many dinosaur fossils worldwide, has been attracting millions of visitors ever since. It has taken more than 4.5 billion years for the earth to reach its present state, and we are finding out details about its prehistoric beginnings all the time. Dinosaurs are a significant part of that prehistory. The more we discover about dinosaurs like Sue, the more we find out about the world we live in today.

Sue Hendrickson

Sue Hendrickson

LIFE IN THE DISTANT PAST

If the earth's entire history could be crammed into a single hour, animal life would not appear until the final 15 minutes was well underway. Land animals would make their entrance when the hour had just six minutes left to go, and the Age of Reptiles—one of the most dramatic periods—would run for just over two minutes, when the hour was almost at an end. This chapter looks at the first few minutes of this story and explains some of the processes that have shaped animal life and the evidence that prehistory has left behind.

THE BEGINNING OF LIFE

WHEN EARTH FORMED, ABOUT 4.6 BILLION YEARS AGO, ITS AVERAGE TEMPERATURE WAS AS HOT AS THE SURFACE OF THE SUN. BUT JUST 700 MILLION YEARS LATER LIFE WAS ALREADY UNDERWAY.

E arth is the only place where life definitely exists, although it is possible that elsewhere in the universe other planets have living things of their own. As far as scientists can tell, life arose on Earth through a long series of chemical "accidents" that took place in watery surroundings. Driven by solar and chemical energy, these created the complex substances that form the machinery of all living things.

These rocky mounds are stromatolites growing in Shark Bay, Western Australia. They are formed by cyanobacteria (blue-green algae), which are simple microbes that collect energy from sunlight. Cyanobacteria form mounds by trapping sediment, which becomes cemented together. Shark Bay's stromatolites are several thousand years old, but some fossilized stromatolites are 3.4 billion years old—making them among the earliest signs of life on Earth.

WHAT IS LIFE?

Over 99.99999 percent of our planet is made up of inanimate matter—matter that is not alive. Unlike living things, inanimate matter cannot grow or use energy, and it cannot respond to the world around it. Most important, it cannot reproduce. So how did this unpromising starting point generate things that were alive four billion years ago?

The answer, most scientists believe, is by a series of random chemical reactions that took place between carbon-containing substances dissolved in the sea. Some of these reactions formed microscopic bubbles surrounded by oily membranes that contained tiny drops of fluid shielded from the water outside. Others formed substances that could copy themselves by attracting simpler chemicals from their surroundings.

Somehow the two came together and produced the first self-copying cells. When those cells started to use energy, life began.

POWERING UP

The first living things were bacteria. These would have gotten their energy from dissolved chemicals, but as they multiplied, supplies of this chemical food started to dwindle, and a struggle for survival began. This struggle is a feature of life, because living things outstrip their resources. But there are hidden benefits, because this makes living things evolve.

One early result of evolution was that some bacteria evolved a new way of life three billion years ago. They developed the ability to collect energy directly from sunlight. This process, called photosynthesis, was a major step forward, because sunlight delivers energy in vast amounts.

LIFE IN THE FAST LANE

When photosynthesis began, Earth's atmosphere contained nitrogen and carbon dioxide, but hardly any oxygen. Unlike earlier forms of life, photosynthetic bacteria

released oxygen as a waste product. The atmosphere's oxygen level began to creep up to 21 percent—today's level.

Oxygen is a highly reactive substance—for many primitive bacteria, a deadly poison—so they had to retreat into mud and sediment where oxygen could not be found. As oxygen became abundant more complex forms of life evolved that used oxygen to their advantage. These organisms could use oxygen to "burn" reserves of fuel stored inside their cells, which meant that they could release energy exactly when they needed it. Life was beginning to speed up.

The first of these "aerobic" organisms were single-celled aquatic microbes, larger than bacteria and much more complex. Called protists, they teem in freshwater and the sea today. But their place at the top was not destined to last, because over a million years ago plants and animals began to evolve.

◁ *This microscopic fossil is from a type of rock called Gunflint Chert, which is found in western Ontario. This rock layer formed about two billion years ago, and it contains some of the earliest known remains of microbes that lived by photosynthesis.*

◁ *The long filaments shown here are strands of* Anabaena, *a present-day cyanobacterium, or blue-green alga.* Anabaena *lives in shallow water and on damp ground. Its way of life is not very different from that of the earliest photosynthetic bacteria.*

◁ *When Earth's crust was newly formed, volcanic eruptions (far left) occurred on a colossal scale. These eruptions actually helped create suitable conditions for life, because they gave off steam, which eventually condensed to form the oceans. They also produced minerals that early bacteria could use as sources of energy.*

EARTH'S FIRST ANIMALS

THE MOST ANCIENT TRACES OF ANIMAL LIFE ARE UP TO ONE BILLION YEARS OLD, BUT THE OLDEST FOSSILS OF ANIMALS THEMSELVES DATE FROM ONLY ABOUT 600 MILLION YEARS AGO, DURING THE VENDIAN PERIOD.

Wilpena Pound, a giant bowl of sandstone 10.6 miles (17km) wide, lies in South Australia's Flinders Ranges—the same geological formation where the first Ediacaran fossils were found. The sandstone that makes up these hills formed over 540 million years ago, before animals with hard body parts appeared. The discovery that these rocks can contain animal fossils has changed ideas about evolution.

When the first animals evolved, they were soft-bodied and microscopic and lived on or in the seabed. Creatures like these hardly ever fossilized, and the only clues they left behind were indirect ones, such as the remains of burrows and tracks. But despite their tiny size, early animals must have flourished, because they gave rise to Earth's first visible animals: the Ediacarans.

△ *Measuring less than 0.8 in. (2cm) across, this fossil Ediacaran,* Medusina mawsoni, *looks like the remains of a jellyfish. Many think this animal, or others like it, were the direct ancestors of jellyfish that appeared during the Cambrian Period.*

A CHANCE DISCOVERY

The Ediacarans get their name from the Ediacara Hills, in South Australia. In 1946 an Australian geologist noticed some unusual fossils in slabs of ancient sandstone. Some of the fossils seemed to have been left by corals, jellyfish, and worms, but others were like nothing alive today.

At first the Ediacarans were thought to be animals from the Cambrian Period (page 28)—a time when nature produced a huge burst of animal life, starting about 540 million years ago. But a closer look showed that the Ediacaran fossils were older than this and came from the period now known as the Vendian, immediately before the Cambrian. Until this find the

Vendian had seemed to be a biological black hole, containing almost no trace of animal life.

Since the 1940s Ediacaran animals have been found in several different parts of the world, including Greenland, Russia, and Namibia. As more fossils are discovered biologists are trying to decide how these animals lived and what happened to them when the Vendian Period came to a close.

THE EDICARAN WORLD

Unlike most of today's animals, the ones from the Ediacaran did not have heads, tails, or limbs, and they did not have mouths or organs for digesting their food. Instead of pursuing food, they probably absorbed nutrients from the water around them. Some may also have harbored algae—a living partnership that gave them a share of the energy the algae collected from sunlight. Many Ediacarans were fastened to the seabed and looked almost like plants, but others simply lay in the shallows, waiting for nutrients to waft their way.

The plantlike species included *Charnia*, which looked like a feather made of jelly, and *Swartpuntia*, an even stranger animal with four semicircular combs. But the giant of them all was *Dickinsonia*, which could grow to the size of a doormat. Like all other Ediacarans, its body was barely more than paper-thin—essential for an animal that absorbed food through its outer skin.

Compared to the animals that followed them, the Ediacarans led uneventful lives. They had no weapons or defensive armor, nor any other way of resisting attack. There was no need—the Vendian sea was a safe place, because predators had not yet evolved.

A FAILED EXPERIMENT?

Over 50 years after the first Ediacarans were discovered, scientific arguments continue about their place in the animal world. Some scientists have suggested that they were not animals at all, but organisms that were more like today's lichens. Others claim that they were members of a completely separate kingdom of living things—the Vendobionts—which died out as the Cambrian Period began. Supporters of this theory point to the Ediacarans' strange body plan, which was like a fluid-filled mattress divided by partitions. They claim that Vendobionts were an evolutionary experiment, one that worked successfully until more energetic and aggressive animals appeared in the Cambrian.

MIXED FORTUNES

Because there is so little detailed evidence, neither of these theories has convinced all the experts working on ancient life. Instead, many researchers believe that the Ediacarans were genuine animals, but that they experienced very different fortunes as the Vendian Period approached its final stages. Some gave rise to more familiar animals that became widespread in Cambrian times, but others died out, and their strange features disappeared forever from the animal world.

▽ *This imaginary scene shows a collection of Ediacaran animals from different parts of the world. In the center is* Dickinsonia, *the largest member of the group, which sometimes grew to 3.3 ft. (1m) in length. To its left three featherlike* Charnia *project from the sediment, while a trio of brick-colored* Swartpuntia *are visible farther behind.* Spriggina —*the small animal in front of* Dickinsonia— *resembled a primitive trilobite, although like all Ediacarans, it had no hard body parts.*

How animals evolve

EVER SINCE ANIMALS FIRST APPEARED, THEY
HAVE GRADUALLY DEVELOPED DIFFERENT
SHAPES AND WAYS OF
LIFE. THIS PROCESS—
CALLED EVOLUTION—
IS A KEY FEATURE OF
ALL LIVING THINGS.

Cambrian trilobite

Ordovician trilobite

Silurian trilobite

Devonian trilobite

Before the scientific study of
fossils began, people believed
that the world was created
intact, together with all the forms
of life that now exist. That would
mean, for example, that the world
always had two kinds of elephants,
about 3,700 kinds of lizards, and
about 9,450 kinds of birds. But as
fossils of prehistoric animals began
to surface, this idea began to look
more and more improbable.

ADAPTING TO SURVIVE
Where do prehistoric animals
fit into the living world, and why
do they no longer exist? Evolution
provides the answers. If living things
always produced young that were
identical to themselves, each different

◁ *Trilobites existed for over 300 million years,
and during that time thousands of different species
evolved. Each species had its own characteristic
shape, with a range of adaptations that
suited its particular way of life on the
sea floor. Paleontologists are often
able to date rocks simply by looking
at the trilobites that they contain.*

kind—or species—would never change.
Young animals would grow up to be exactly
the same size and shape as their parents,
and they would also behave in exactly the
same way. But this is not how nature works.
Living things are variable, and they pass
on their variations when they breed.

These variations are often tiny, but
they can have some far-reaching effects.
For example, a lizard that has slightly
better-than-average eyesight will be
better at catching food. Compared to
an average lizard, it is more likely to stay
well fed and healthy, which means that it is
also more likely to attract a mate and breed.
Many of its young will have better-than-
average eyesight as well, and they will pass
on this variation in their turn. Sharp-eyed
lizards will gradually become more common,
and eventually better-than-average eyesight
will become a feature of the species as
a whole. The species will have evolved.

The driving force behind this kind of
change is called natural selection, because
nature sorts out individuals that have the
best features for survival. Natural selection
started when life began and has been
picking out useful variations ever since.

HOW NEW SPECIES FORM
Evolution works very slowly, so it takes
a long time for small variations to have
any noticeable effect. (A rare exception
to this rule occurs with simple organisms,
such as bacteria, because these can breed
extremely rapidly.) Over the long term
even the smallest variations start to add
up, creating major changes in the way
animals look and behave. As the
generations succeed each
other these changes
can become so

Phiomia

great that an entirely new species comes into being. Alternatively, differences can make the original species split into more than one line. If these lines remain separate by breeding only among themselves, two or more new species will take the original's place.

In nature different species compete with each other for needed resources, such as food and space to breed. If two species have similar lifestyles, the struggle between them becomes intense. It may continue for centuries or millennia, but the outcome is always the same: one species gets the upper hand; the other declines and may eventually become extinct.

Extinction is a natural feature of life. Usually it occurs very slowly and is balanced by the new species that evolve. But extinction can also occur in sudden waves, when an unexpected change in living conditions wipes out thousands or even millions of species in a short space of time. Many biologists think that we are living through one of these waves today.

TRIED AND TESTED

The study of evolution dates back to the 1800s, with the work of English naturalist Charles Darwin. Darwin collected a mass of evidence showing that evolution occurs, and he identified the driving force behind it. During his lifetime many people imagined that evolution followed a set path, steadily improving living things in the same way that designers improve machines. But today biologists take a different view. The reason

for this is that, unlike a human designer, natural selection cannot plan ahead. Instead, it works like an impartial judge, testing every tiny variation and rejecting any that do not have an immediate use. It cannot select anything that simply might prove useful in the future.

This way of selecting features means that complicated structures, such as eyes, legs, or feathers, have to evolve through a succession of stages and that each of these stages has to bring benefits of its own. Primitive feathers, for example, would have been useless for flight, so they must have served some other function when they first arose. Paleontologists believe that they know what this function was—a discovery that has had a major impact on our understanding of dinosaurs as well as birds (page 132).

Another feature of evolution is that it can never go back to the beginning. Instead, natural selection works with living things as they currently exist, encouraging features that help them make the most of their way of life. But no matter how much living things change on the outside, their bodies still contain the evidence of their long-distant evolutionary past. For paleontologists, this evidence is a treasure trove of information about how living things have evolved.

▽ *Elephants and their relatives arose from a single species, which lived over 40 million years ago. Fossils show that since that time at least 350 different species evolved. From left to right this illustration shows* Phiomia, *which stood about 8.2 ft. (2.5m) tall,* Gomphotherium, *which also had a short trunk and tusks, and* Deinotherium, *which had backward-curving tusks in its lower jaw.* Platebelydon *had lower tusks that worked like a shovel. The imperial mammoth,* Mammuthus imperator, *looked more like a modern elephant, with a long trunk and forward-curving tusks. These animals belonged to several different branches of the elephant line.*

Mammuthus imperator

Gomphotherium   *Deinotherium*   *Platybelodon*

EVIDENCE FROM THE PAST

BURIED IN SEDIMENT, TRAPPED FOREVER
IN AMBER, OR FROZEN IN ICE—THESE ARE
JUST SOME OF THE WAYS THAT PREHISTORIC
ANIMAL REMAINS HAVE WITHSTOOD
THE TEST OF TIME.

B ecause most prehistoric animals are now extinct,
our knowledge of them comes entirely from the
remains they have left behind. With species that died
out relatively recently—which in geological terms can mean
thousands of years—these remains can include actual body
parts, or even entire animals. But with species that lived much
further back in time, no body parts are left.
Instead, scientists study something else:
remains that have literally turned into stone.

*This enormous egg—carefully pieced
together from broken fragments—was laid
by* Aepyornis, *a giant flightless bird that lived
in Madagascar until perhaps 500 years ago.
Although* Aepyornis *is extinct, its eggs are still
occasionally found on the island, usually when
heavy rain reveals them by washing away the
soil. The oldest specimens are fossilized, but
this one consists of original shell.*

△ *This remarkable
fossil shows a predatory*
Coelophysis *with the
remains of a young*
Coelophysis *in its
stomach. Rare finds
like these give an insight
into how prehistoric
animals behaved.*

THE PAST PRESERVED

When an animal dies, its remains
rarely stay in one piece for long. On
land scavengers soon home in on the corpse
and tear off flesh and bones. Insects lay their
eggs in the remains, producing maggots that
burrow through what is left. Anything left
behind is broken down by bacteria, the
most useful natural recyclers. Within days,

or weeks if the weather is cold or dry,
all that is left is a few scattered bones.

On rare occasions an animal's body
is preserved. If the corpse is smothered
by something that excludes air, such
as volcanic ash and seabed sediment,
scavengers and decomposing bacteria
are not able to do their work. The corpse
remains intact and gradually disappears as
further layers of sediment or ash build up.
The remains may then be fossilized (pages
18–19)—the ultimate form of preservation,
because it can save the shape of living
things for several billion years.

STICKY MOMENTS

For biologists interested in the earth's
past, fossils are by far the most useful kind
of evidence. But prehistoric animals and plants
can also be preserved in other ways. When an
unlucky insect or small animal encounters a
blob of sticky resin oozing from a tree, it can
become trapped and then enveloped, sealed
inside a transparent tomb, which

hardens as it dries. The animal's internal organs decompose, but its outer structure is preserved. Resin itself can fossilize, turning into a glassy substance called amber. Some beads of amber, and the animals locked up inside them, are over 50 million years old.

Resin is not a hazard for large animals, but sticky asphalt, or tar, is. This natural substance seeps up to the surface of the ground, creating treacherous pools that can engulf an animal that ventures across it. The animal becomes impregnated with oily fluids from the tar, which make it very hard for decomposers to attack its remains. The flesh gradually breaks down, but the original unfossilized bones often remain. These relics have been found in several parts of the world, but the most famous is Rancho La Brea, in California. Here an incredible variety of animals has been preserved from Ice Age times (page 212).

▷ *Trapped in amber, this grasshopper, found in Russia, is about 40 million years old.*

STOPPING THE CLOCK

Some kinds of preservation stop the clock for thousands of years. Mummification is one of these. When a corpse becomes mummified, it dries out completely, which prevents it from bacterial attack. In nature such remains are usually found in deserts and dry caves. The ancient Egyptians used artificial mummification to preserve their dead.

Being frozen is another way of putting decay on hold. In parts of the world such as northern Siberia, where the ground is permanently frozen, remains of Ice Age mammals are often preserved in this way.

▽ *A 10,000-year-old baby mammoth is lifted from frozen ground in northern Russia. The mammoth has been flattened by the weight of the ice above it, but it is completely preserved.*

HOW FOSSILS FORM

FOR A DEAD ANIMAL TO TURN INTO A FOSSIL, CIRCUMSTANCES HAVE TO BE EXACTLY RIGHT. MANY ANIMALS BEGIN TO FOSSILIZE, ONLY TO DISAPPEAR WITHOUT A TRACE.

The word "fossil" originally meant any rock or mineral that was dug up out of the ground. Today it means something much more precise: the remains of plants or animals, which have been preserved in the earth's crust. Unlike the original remains, fossils are tough, and they are also chemically stable, which means that they can survive for incredible lengths of time. Most fossils are at least 10,000 years old, but some date back to the very early days of life on Earth.

FOSSIL EVIDENCE

As well as preserving animals, fossils can also preserve traces that they leave behind. These traces include footprints—like these dinosaur prints from Utah—and also burrows, leftover food, stomach stones (or gastroliths), and fossilized droppings (or coprolites). Trace fossils are interesting because they reveal details of animal behavior, but matching them up with their makers is often a difficult task.

DEAD AND BURIED

The process of fossilization begins when something dies and is quickly covered up, for example by sediment or by an avalanche of underwater mud. Sediment consists of very fine particles, which form a soft blanket over the remains. This blanket protects the remains from scavengers, and it also keeps oxygen out, making it hard for microbes to break down the remains in the normal way.

In many cases this is where the story ends, because waves and currents often disturb remains in water, and wind and rain do

△ Ammonites and their relatives often formed fossils because they had hard shells and because they lived in shallow seawater—an ideal environment for being buried after death. Like trilobites, their detailed anatomy changed as they evolved, and this allows them to be used as a fossil calendar to determine the age of particular layers of rock.

1

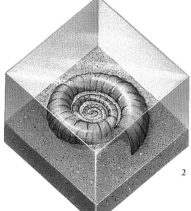

2

the same on land. But if the dead animal lies undisturbed for long enough, more sediment builds up above it. This burial may take place at a rate of just a few millimeters a year, but as time goes by the stage is set for fossilization to begin.

TURNED TO STONE
Hidden away beneath the surface, the minerals that make up any hard body parts, like bones and shells, often dissolve and recrystallize, becoming harder than before. Alternatively underground water may seep through the body parts, dissolving their minerals and washing them away. New minerals are deposited, a process that is often described as turning to stone. These changes occur very slowly, and the remains keep their original shape.

As sediment continues to pile up, the remains become even more deeply buried. Time and increasing pressure do the rest, turning the remains into a fossil and the sediment around it into solid rock.

BACK TO THE SURFACE
Even at this stage things can go wrong. During the thousands or millions of years that it takes a fossil to form, the rock around it may change. The layers may buckle and bend, while extreme pressure may crush the

fossil flat. Heat is another factor. If too much warmth reaches the rock from the crust below, the rock may partly melt, and any fossils that it contains will be destroyed. If a fossil manages to escape these hazards, it then has to resurface to be found. This occurs when sedimentary rock is eroded, usually by wind or rain. Then someone has to find the fossil before it falls away from the surrounding rock, breaks up, and finally disappears.

GAPS IN THE RECORD
Because fossilization is so chancy, the earth's fossil record gives a patchy view of prehistoric life. Some animals, such as trilobites and ammonites, fossilized in huge numbers because they had hard shells or body cases and because they lived on the seabed. In the case of trilobites, these animals grew by shedding their skins. Each shed skin formed a perfect trilobite replica, which could also turn into a fossil.

But for some groups—even ones that had bones—fossilization was an uncommon event. This is particularly true of early primates and other mammals that lived in trees. When they died, their bodies dropped to the ground, where scavenging animals fed on them, scattering the remains. Fossil hunters occasionally discover solitary bones or teeth, but complete skeletons are very rare.

◁ *A fossilized* Archaeopteryx, *one of the earliest birds. Unusually, this contains the outline of feathers. Soft body parts usually disappear during fossilization.*

▽ *The diagram below shows typical steps in fossilization.*
1 *An ammonite sinks to the seabed, where it dies.*
2 *The ammonite's shell rests on the seabed, where it is soon covered by fine particles of sediment that drift down from the water above.*
3 *During a process known as diagenesis, the shell's minerals are altered and replaced.*
4 *Further layers of rock form above the fossil.*
5 *Geological movements tilt the rock layers, tipping the fossil onto its edge. Erosion gradually exposes the fossil at the surface.*

3

4

5

19

STUDYING FOSSILS

WITHOUT FOSSILS OUR KNOWLEDGE OF THE EARTH'S LIVING PAST WOULD STRETCH BACK ONLY A FEW THOUSAND YEARS. BUT WITH THEM SCIENTISTS CAN INVESTIGATE THE ANIMALS THAT LIVED FAR BACK IN TIME.

Fossils are fascinating objects, which explains why many people enjoy collecting them. For paleontologists, the scientists who study the earth's living past, they are also a crucial source of information. They reveal when and how animals lived, what they ate, and sometimes how they reproduced. They also show how different species were linked by evolution. Gathering this information starts with fossil hunting, and it ends when a specimen is cleaned, studied, and assembled and ready to go on view.

FOSSIL-BEARING ROCKS

Fossil finding is partly a matter of luck and partly a matter of knowing where fossils are likely to be found. It is necessary to be able to recognize the three main types of rock because two of them never contain fossils. The first fossil-free type, igneous rock, includes granite and basalt—rocks that are crystalline and very hard. They develop from molten rock, or magma, which obliterates the remains of any living things. The second type, metamorphic rock, includes marble and slate. These rocks have been transformed by pressure or heat so that any fossils they may have contained will have been destroyed. The third category, sedimentary rock, includes limestone, sandstone, and chalk. Sedimentary rocks are always laid down in layers—a key feature of all fossil-finding sites.

SEARCHING THE GROUND

Some of the world's most interesting fossils have been discovered in places where sedimentary rock is quarried or mined. Many fossils of flying reptiles have come from quarries in Germany, and some of the largest sauropod fossils have been discovered in quarries in the United States. Many other fossils are found by amateurs and professionals searching rocky outcrops where remains have been brought to the surface by erosion. These outcrops include the dry, flat-topped hills in desert areas and coastal cliffs where the rock is undermined by the sea. The softer the rock, the faster it erodes and the more quickly fossils are exposed.

Sometimes fossils are intact when they are found, but wind or rain often separate skeleton bones. Real skill is needed to work out how the bones may have moved and where the rest of the skeleton is likely to be. This kind of hunt often leads up slopes of crumbling rock until the parent material is spotted high above.

△ *These sedimentary rocks at Ghost Ranch, New Mexico, are rich in dinosaur fossils. The red rock was laid down during the Triassic, when the Age of Reptiles began.*

▷ *Here fossilized bones of an allosaur are being removed at Utah's Dinosaur National Monument. Care is taken to prevent fossils from breaking.*

UP AND AWAY

Once a fossil has been found,
it is usually extracted so that it can be taken
away and studied. For something as small
as a trilobite, this can involve little more than
a few taps with a hammer to free it from the
surrounding matrix or bedrock. But when
the fossil is a complete dinosaur skeleton,
with individual bones that may be over
3.3 ft. (1m) long, removing the fossil is a
major operation that may take several years.

One of the difficulties with this kind of
work is that fossilized bones often break up
once they are exposed to rain and sunshine.
To keep them intact, the bones are wrapped
in jackets of quick-setting plaster before
they are carried or winched away.

BACK IN THE LAB

Once a fossil has arrived in the lab,
it often needs further work so that it can
be fully revealed. Delicate specimens, such
as insects or small fish, are cleaned using
metal probes, brushes, and machines that
resemble dentists' drills. The specimen may
also be dipped in a bath of acetic acid, the
substance that gives vinegar its sharp smell.
This loosens any surrounding rock, which
eventually falls away. Fragile bones are
hardened by treating them with a plastic,
which holds any loose fragments in place.

When the fossil has been cleaned and
treated, the process of studying it can
begin. The tiniest irregularities or marks
can reveal important details, so anything
that looks unusual is given a closer look,
sometimes with a microscope. This kind
of work often resembles forensic science,
and in some cases the examination turns
up tooth marks or fractured bones,
showing how the animal met its end.

Paleontologists can also use medical
scanners—a technique that allows them
to look at the bony structures beneath the
surface. This new
way of studying fossils has been used with
several kinds of dinosaurs to investigate their
brain size (page 129) and to try to work

out whether or not they were
warm-blooded (page 148).

JOINING UP

Museums have a limited
amount of space, so many
fossils end up in storerooms
where they can be examined
by experts carrying out
research. The most important
and impressive fossil
specimens—particularly of
dinosaurs and prehistoric
mammals—are reassembled to
show what they would have looked like
in real life. This process, called articulation,
involves arranging the bones so that they are
in the correct position and then supporting
the entire skeleton so that it does not
collapse. Articulation is a complex operation,
and even the experts can make mistakes.
During the 1800s, for example, the great
American fossil hunter Edward Drinker
Cope put the skull of the marine reptile
Elasmosaurus on the end of its tail!

△ *Before large bones
can be removed, they have
to be channeled out of the
surrounding bedrock (top
left). The bones are then
covered with a protective
layer of plaster before being
raised with a pulley. Once
in the laboratory (left) the
plaster is removed. Here the
skull of a large allosaur is
being examined.*

△ *Laid out on a
laboratory bench, the
fossilized remains of a
plesiosaur are examined
by two paleontologists.
The fossil was found near
Coober Pedy, a mining
town in Australia, and
its pink color comes from
a form of silica found in
that part of the world.*

▷ *These six views of the earth show how the continents have moved during the last 245 million years. This part of our planet's history has been dominated by the breakup of Pangaea, the supercontinent that existed when the Age of Reptiles began. Until about 100 million years ago today's southern continents were joined to form a giant fragment of Pangaea called Gondwana, which slowly broke apart.*

CONTINENTS ON THE MOVE

EVERY YEAR SOME OF THE WORLD'S
CONTINENTS DRIFT FARTHER APART,
AND OTHERS CREEP CLOSER TOGETHER.
THESE MOVEMENTS HAVE CHANGED
THE FACE OF THE EARTH.

W hen continental drift was first suggested, nearly 100 years ago, most geologists found it impossible to believe. But today continental drift is an accepted scientific fact, and it is not only continents that are on the move—the earth's entire outer crust is in motion. New oceans open up and force continents apart, and old oceans disappear as continents collide. Because continents carry their wildlife with them, these changes have had a tremendous effect on animal evolution.

ONE WORLD
Today there are seven continents scattered unevenly across the face of the globe. A journey from North America to Europe or from Africa to Australia involves crossing thousands of miles of open sea. But 245 million years ago, at the start of the Age of Reptiles, the world could hardly have

looked more different. All the earth's land was joined together to form a single supercontinent called Pangaea, and the rest of the globe was covered by the vast Panthalassic Ocean. In theory an animal could have walked around the world as long as it could negotiate the mountains and rivers in its way.

Continental drift started when dry land first formed, a time millions of years before Pangaea came into being. Little is known about the continents for most of that time, but it is clear that they also drifted and that giant supercontinents formed several times. One of these ancient landmasses, called Pannotia, existed during the Vendian Period, about 650 million years ago. It broke apart after about 100 million years, creating the separate pieces from which Pangaea was made.

JOINING UP
Continents move at the rate of just an inch or so each year, which adds up to only a tiny distance during an animal's lifetime. Even in the lifetime of an entire species, the positions of the continents barely change. But over millions of years the effects of this movement can be great. It can split up some groups of animals as continents separate and bring others together when they collide.

South America is a perfect example of how this can affect animal life. Until about three million years ago it was an island—one that had been cut off from the rest of the world for nearly 100 million years. During this long period of isolation it

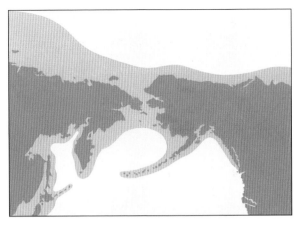

Continental drift also shapes the world's climate. It can do this by altering the path of ocean currents, which deliver warm water from the tropics to other parts of the world. Drifting continents also control the world's ice cover, because ice caps can only form over land. If there are no continents near the poles, the polar sea may freeze, but deep ice caps do not form.

For animals the earth's ice cover is important. The more ice there is in ice caps, the cooler and drier the world's climate becomes. At the same time, the world's sea levels fall, because so much of the world's water is in a frozen form. If the sea level falls far enough, it exposes parts of the seabed, and allows animals to travel between nearby continents without leaving dry land. This happened during the last Ice Age, when animals traveled from Asia to North America across the floor of the Bering Sea.

◁ *This map shows how low sea levels allowed animals (and people) to travel from Asia to North America toward the end of the last Ice Age. The dark brown areas show dry land as it exists today; the light brown areas show regions of the seabed that were dry land in Ice Age times.*

developed a wide range of unique animals, including some strange marsupials and the largest rodents that have ever lived. But when South America collided with North America, animals could move between the two continents, and many of South America's native mammals found themselves losing out in the struggle to survive. Three million years on, however, signs of South America's island past are not hard to find—its mammals and birds still include many families that do not exist anywhere else on Earth.

PARTING COMPANY

Further back in time continental drift had an even bigger impact on the way reptiles evolved. When the Age of Reptiles began, Pangaea still existed, so many families of reptiles were found over huge areas of the earth. But after Pangaea split up, some groups evolved in particular parts of the world. One example of these local reptiles was the ceratopsids—a group of armored dinosaurs that were restricted to North America. Another group was the segnosaurs—a little-known family whose remains have been found only in Asia and the Far East.

▽ *Continental drift explains why the remains of some prehistoric land animals can be found in widely scattered regions of the world. The map below shows fossil finds of* Lystrosaurus, *which lived across much of Pangaea over 220 million years ago. After it became extinct its home was broken up by continental drift.*

▷ Lystrosaurus *was a mammal-like reptile that lived in the Late Permian and Early Triassic Periods.*

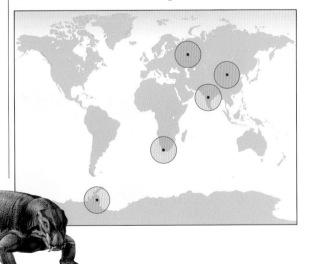

SETBACKS AND DISASTERS

THE FOSSIL RECORD SHOWS THAT LIFE ON EARTH IS A HAZARDOUS AND UNPREDICTABLE BUSINESS. ON SEVERAL OCCASIONS HUGE NUMBERS OF SPECIES HAVE BEEN WIPED OUT IN RELATIVELY SHORT SPACES OF TIME.

Extinction is a natural feature of life on Earth, and it normally happens at a slow and rather unsteady rate. But from time to time external events can trigger off extinctions on a truly colossal scale, and life can take several million years to recover. At least five mass extinctions have taken place in the distant past, with many smaller waves of extinction between them. Each one has rocked the living world and changed the course of animal evolution. The most famous extinction wiped out the dinosaurs, but even greater catastrophes hit animal life further back in time.

TRIGGERING A CRASH

Mass extinctions are extremely rare and are spaced millions of years apart. Abrupt changes in the fossil record show that the last one occurred 66 million years ago, and the previous one happened over 140 million years before that. But although geologists can say when these catastrophes struck, deciding exactly what triggered them is a much more difficult matter.

In the case of the Cretaceous extinction, which swept away the dinosaurs, the most likely explanation is the sudden impact of a meteorite from space (page 204). Meteorite impacts happen all the time, but most of them involve small objects that either burn up in the earth's atmosphere or reach the ground but do little harm. The one that arrived 66 million years ago was a deadly exception—its explosive crash landing obliterated huge areas of natural habitats, and brought the Age of Reptiles to an end.

WHEN LIFE GETS TOUGH

The Cretaceous extinction seems to have been exceptional, and no convincing evidence of giant meteorite strikes has been found for earlier mass extinctions.

Ordovician mass extinction 438 million years ago
Likely cause: climate change
50% of all species wiped out, mainly in the seas

Devonian mass extinction 360 million years ago
Likely cause: climate change
40% of all species wiped out

Permian mass extinction 245 million years ago
Likely causes: volcanic activity, climate change, formation of Pangaea
70% of all land species wiped out

Triassic mass extinction 208 million years ago
Likely cause: climate change
45% of all species wiped out

Cretaceous mass extinction 66 million years ago
Likely causes: meteorite impact, volcanic eruptions
45% of all species wiped out

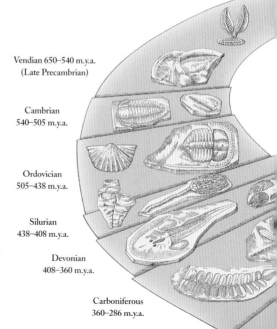

Vendian 650–540 m.y.a.
(Late Precambrian)

Cambrian
540–505 m.y.a.

Ordovician
505–438 m.y.a.

Silurian
438–408 m.y.a.

Devonian
408–360 m.y.a.

Carboniferous
360–286 m.y.a.

Instead, most experts believe that these biological disasters were caused by natural processes taking place on Earth.

Volcanic eruptions have a lethal effect on almost all forms of life, and there is plenty of evidence from ancient lava flows that they were more common and more violent in the past. Changes in sea level have more subtle effects, but in the long term they can be almost as deadly. When sea levels are high, the world's continental shelves are flooded, creating shallow seas that are rich habitats for marine life. When levels fall again, these shallow seas disappear, along with many of their animal inhabitants. Sea levels fell to record low levels 245 million years ago and probably played a part in the mass extinction at the end of the Permian Period—the greatest setback for life ever known (page 56).

THE SIXTH EXTINCTION?

Climate change is a factor that we are all too familiar with today. In the past the main danger to life was global cooling rather than global warming, but any rapid change in weather patterns in either direction can interfere with plant life and make it harder for animals to find food. Today, there is a final factor to be added to the list: the spiraling rate at which humans use up resources and space. Many biologists think that this is now triggering a sixth mass extinction—one that is caused not by natural events, but by ourselves.

◁ *Immense lava flows, covering hundreds of thousands of square miles, are evidence of huge bursts of volcanic activity in prehistory.*

△ *Climate change, ice formation, and changes in sea levels are connected factors that may have triggered off waves of extinctions.*

These are the major mass extinctions since the Cambrian. Other mass extinctions most likely happened further back in Earth's past but, because early animals were soft-bodied, they did not leave any fossil evidence.

Precambrian

4.5 b.y.a.   12 b.y.a.   3.5 b.y.a.

Permian   Triassic
286–245 m.y.a. 245–208 m.y.a.   Jurassic
                                 208–144 m.y.a.   Cretaceous
                                                  144–66 m.y.a.

Tertiary and
Quaternary
66 m.y.a. – present

DIVIDING UP TIME

One way to study the earth's past is to split it into equal intervals—billions of years, for example. But instead of doing this, geologists divide it into intervals that can be seen in layers of sedimentary rock. These layers have built up over millions of years, and they form a permanent record of the earth's past, complete with fossils of plants and animals that were alive when the rock was formed. The boundaries between the layers mark times when conditions on the earth changed rapidly. The changes altered the type of rock that was laid down, and they often made many existing forms of life extinct. The table below shows the names of these intervals, or layers, with the most recent times at the top, working backward into the past. The largest intervals—eons—are divided into smaller ones called eras and periods. These, in turn, are often divided into epochs (only the most recent epochs are shown here). The dates shown for each time interval are approximate. M.Y.A. = million years ago and Y.A. = years ago.

EON	ERA	PERIOD	EPOCH	DATES
PHANEROZOIC	CENOZOIC	QUATERNARY	Holocene Pleistocene	0–10,000 Y.A. 10,000–1.6 M.Y.A.
		TERTIARY	Pliocene Miocene Oligocene Eocene Paleocene	1.6–5.3 M.Y.A. 5.3–23 M.Y.A. 23–36 M.Y.A. 36–58 M.Y.A. 58–66 M.Y.A.
	MESOZOIC	CRETACEOUS		66–144 M.Y.A.
		JURASSIC		144–208 M.Y.A.
		TRIASSIC		208–245 M.Y.A.
	PALEOZOIC	PERMIAN		245–286 M.Y.A.
		CARBONIFEROUS		286–360 M.Y.A.
		DEVONIAN		360–408 M.Y.A.
		SILURIAN		408–438 M.Y.A.
		ORDOVICIAN		438–505 M.Y.A.
		CAMBRIAN		505–540 M.Y.A.
PRECAMBRIAN	PROTEROZOIC	VENDIAN PRE-VENDIAN		540–650 M.Y.A. 650–2,500 M.Y.A.
	ARCHAEAN HADEAN			2,500–3,800 M.Y.A. 3,800–4,600 M.Y.A.

THE AGE OF ANCIENT LIFE

L asting over 350 million years, the Paleozoic Era, meaning "ancient life," was a momentous time in the animal world. It started in the Cambrian Period with a surge of evolution that has still not been fully explained. At this stage in Earth's history animal life was confined to the seas, but as the era continued some animals made the transition to dry land. By the late stages of the Paleozoic, reptiles and mammallike animals appeared, but the era ended with the greatest mass extinction that the world has ever known.

CAMBRIAN PERIOD

BEGINNING ABOUT 540 MILLION YEARS AGO, IN AN EXPLOSIVE BURST OF EVOLUTION, THIS DISTANT PART OF THE EARTH'S PAST SAW THE APPEARANCE OF THE FIRST ANIMALS WITH HARD BODY PARTS.

Because the Cambrian Period was so far back in time, little is known about how the earth looked. There was one major continent and several smaller ones, but for animal life the habitable world lay in the sea. During Cambrian times the climate was warm, and sea levels rose, flooding large areas of low-lying land. These shallow seas created ideal conditions for new kinds of animal life, ones reinforced by shells, body cases, or internal skeletons. These all fossilize easily, so unlike earlier soft-bodied animals, Cambrian animals left a vast store of remains.

▷ *The Cambrian Period was known as the Age of the Trilobites because these animals played such an important part in seabed life. Here several species of trilobites crawl over an ocean floor studded with vaselike archaeocyathan sponges, while jellyfish drift overhead. Most trilobites had well-developed eyes, but* Acadagnostus *(the small species in the foreground) was blind and could roll up in a ball for self-defense.* Paradoxides *(the large trilobite in the center) was usually 8 in. (20cm), but could be 3 ft. (1m) long.*

SHELLS AND SKELETONS

Fossils show that Cambrian animals evolved hard body parts relatively quickly, over a period of perhaps 20 million years. A question that puzzles biologists is why this happened, when animals had been soft-bodied for so long. One possibility concerns the earth's atmosphere. Because of the work of cyanobacteria and algae (pages 10–11), the air's oxygen level had been rising steadily. By the time the Cambrian Period began, it may have been high enough for animals to lead more energy-intensive lives. Extra oxygen would have helped animals to "burn" more food, giving them energy to build new body parts, such as shells and flexible cases.

WHY BE TOUGH?

Animals evolve new features only if they are useful, so these new body parts must have served some essential purpose. For stationary animals there were advantages to growing hard body parts. For example, spongelike animals called archaeocyathans lived by filtering tiny particles of food from the Cambrian seas. They developed internal skeletons, which allowed them to grow a few millimeters off the seabed. Although not a great height, it would have been better for collecting food.

For animals that moved around, a hard covering could be useful in different ways. For Cambrian mollusks a shell, or exoskeleton, provided a mobile shelter that could be used in case of attack. It also acted as an anchor for the soft body parts to develop. For arthropods—which included trilobites and other animals with jointed limbs—hard parts played two separate roles. Their covering, a body case made of separate plates, provided protection, but because it could bend, it also helped them move.

THE CAMBRIAN EXPLOSION

The Cambrian Period saw a huge expansion in animal life—the evolutionary equivalent of the Big Bang. These new animals included some that did not survive beyond the end of the Cambrian, such as those that were first identified as fossils in the famous Burgess Shale (pages 32–35). The Cambrian Period also produced all the main animal groups that are alive today, including the chordates, the group to which we belong.

Known as the Cambrian explosion, this astonishing burst of evolution is difficult to explain. Nothing like it has happened since, so why did it take place? Scientists do not know, but many ideas have been put forward. One is that the explosion was not quite as explosive as it seems. According to this theory many different kinds of animals may have existed before the start of the explosion, but if they were soft-bodied, they would have left few traces. Many scientists believe that this is true. They also think that the Cambrian explosion did happen, although not quite as abruptly as it first seemed. It may have been triggered by changes in oxygen levels or in the layout of the seabed. Or life may have reached a critical point, triggering off a chain reaction in which many new body types were formed.

THE AGE OF ANCIENT LIFE

CAMBRIAN ANIMALS

A lthough Cambrian animals lived in the sea, few of them were creatures of open water. Instead, animal life hugged the seabed. Worms burrowed their way through the sediment, while snaillike mollusks crept across the surface, feeding on decaying remains. Trilobites also crawled across this surface layer, sometimes leaving telltale tracks that later became fossilized. The water itself was the territory of the fast movers of the Cambrian world: animals such as *Anomalocaris* (pages 32–33) and also—scientists have recently discovered—some of the earliest vertebrates.

△ *Brachiopods, or lampshells, became widespread in the Cambrian. These animals have shells like cockles and other bivalves, but they often grow on stalks.*

△ Myllokunmingia *sucked up food through its tiny, jawless mouth. This protofish had a skeleton of flexible cartilage.*

▷ *Some Cambrian mollusks, such as* Pleurotomaria *(center), had spiral shells—a strong design that has lasted until the present day.*

▷ *This fossil-rich rock from Australia shows the remains of spongelike archaeocyathans that date back 500 million years to Cambrian times.*

VERTEBRATES AND INVERTEBRATES
Biologists divide the animal world into two overall groups—the vertebrates and invertebrates. Vertebrates are animals that have backbones, and invertebrates are animals that do not. Today vertebrates include all of the largest and fastest animals, but invertebrates are far more varied and much more common, making up about 97 percent of all animal species on Earth.

Invertebrates were undoubtedly the first

animals to evolve. Fossils of Ediacaran invertebrates, for example, date back more than 50 million years before the Cambrian began (pages 12–13). During the Cambrian Period a huge range of hard-bodied invertebrates appeared, including sponges and their relatives, arthropods, mollusks, and look-alike animals called brachiopods. But the group the vertebrates belong to, the chordates, is more ancient than was thought.

The first chordates would have been soft-bodied, so have left very few remains. But when chordates began to develop hard body parts made of cartilage and bone, the fossil record becomes more clear. In 1999 scientists in China announced that they had found two fossilized vertebrates in rocks 530 million years old—close to the time the Cambrian Period began. These two animals, named *Myllokunmingia* and *Haikouichthys*, are the world's oldest known fossil fish. Measuring less than 1.2 in. (3cm) long, they were a step along the evolutionary road that was to lead to amphibians and reptiles, including the giants of the dinosaur age.

△ *This cross section shows a reef from the Early Cambrian, 535 million years ago. A variety of archaeocyathan sponges are growing on the reef's surface. In crevices below, tracks reveal the presence of small animals hiding away for safety.*

1. **SURFACE LAYER OF LIVING CYANOBACTERIA**
2. **BRANCHING ARCHAEOCYATHAN**
3. **RADIOCYATHAN**
4. *CHANCELLORIA*
5. *OKULITCHICYATHUS*
6. **ARTHROPOD TRACKS**
7. **CEMENTED REEF BASE**

SPONGES ON A REEF

In Cambrian times, just as today, the shallow seabed was often carpeted with life, much of it fixed permanently in place. The most ancient of these seabed dwellers were cyanobacteria—microorganisms that first appeared over 3 billion years ago. Just like their distant ancestors, many Cambrian cyanobacteria collected calcium carbonate from the water and laid this hard mineral down around themselves. The result was a hard mat that built up to form a reef.

When cyanobacteria first evolved, animal life did not exist. But by Cambrian times these crustlike reefs attracted animals that needed a safe anchorage so that they could collect their food. Foremost among them were archaeocyathans—spongelike animals that grew into a wide variety of shapes, although few were more than 4 in. (10cm) high. Like the cyanobacteria,

archaeocyathans collected calcium carbonate from the water, and they used it to build up their meshlike skeletons. Many looked like small vases, with a central hollow, while others resembled mushrooms or a collection of branching twigs. Most of these animals lived on the surface of the reef, but some hid in crevices and cavities, sifting food that drifted down from above. As they grew upward in the light and warmth their dead remains became cemented together, steadily adding to the reef. Just like true sponges, archaeocyathans belonged to an unusual offshoot of the animal world. Instead of swallowing food through a mouth, as most animals do, they collected it by pumping water through tiny holes, or pores, in their bodies. As the water flowed through the pores anything edible was filtered out and digested.

Archaeocyathans grew in warm, tropical waters, but unlike true sponges, their reign was relatively short. A few species survived into the closing stages of the Cambrian Period, but at that point the entire group became extinct.

31

A SEABED GRAVEYARD

*Rearing up over its prey, Anomalocaris—
a giant shrimplike predator from the Cambrian
Period—moves in to make a kill. Its intended
victim, an animal called* Marella, *speeds away by
beating its slender legs. These two animals, like all
the ones shown here, were found as fossils in the
legendary Burgess Shale. (See key on page 34.)*

33

DOMINANT ARTHROPODS

The largest fossils in the Burgess Shale belong to arthropods—animals with a hard outer case that bends at flexible joints. Today the most common arthropods include insects, spiders, and crustaceans. In Cambrian times, these different groups did not exist yet. Instead, Cambrian arthropods included trilobites and some remarkable animals found in the Burgess Shale.

The top predator of the Burgess Shale was *Anomalocaris*, a name that means "unusual shrimp." The specimens in the Burgess Shale are up to 2 ft. (60cm) long. Ones found more recently, from Cambrian rocks in China, are over twice as large as this. *Anomalocaris* swam by rippling flaps along its sides, and it attacked its prey with a pair of fearsome mouthparts that looked like legs. Its mouth was disk-shaped and had a ring of teeth that it used to crush hard-bodied prey. Other predatory arthropods included *Sanctacaris*, which looked like a smaller version of *Anomalocaris* with a blunter head.

The most common Burgess Shale animal, called *Marella*, was another arthropod, but a much more delicate and graceful animal. It had long head spines sweeping back in elegant curves and two pairs of feelers or antennae. Rarely more than 0.8 in. (2cm) long, it had many pairs of legs and probably fed by picking up small animals or dead remains on the surface of the seabed.

BURGESS SHALE

DISCOVERED IN 1909, IN CANADA'S ROCKY MOUNTAINS, THE BURGESS SHALE CONTAINS TENS OF THOUSANDS OF FOSSILS, MANY WELL PRESERVED. TOGETHER, THEY PAINT A VIVID PICTURE OF LIFE IN THE CAMBRIAN SEAS.

The Burgess Shale fossil formation was found by the American paleontologist Charles D. Walcott during a fossilhunt in northwest Canada. The animals in the shale lived on or near the seabed and were victims of underwater avalanches, which trapped them almost instantly in fine-grained mud. Because the mud was soft and contained very little oxygen, it preserved its victims remarkably well.

The Burgess Shale also includes many trilobites—a group of arthropods whose bodies were divided lengthwise into three lobes. Trilobites went on to become some of the most successful invertebrates of the Paleozoic Era, and they were among the most important casualties during the mass extinction that brought it to a close.

SOFT-BODIED ANIMALS
The Burgess Shale also contains much rarer fossils, showing the complete outlines of soft-bodied animals. A typical example is *Ottoia*, a burrowing worm up to 6 in. (15cm) long. Its burrow was U-shaped, and it lurked inside it, feeling for prey on the surface with a spike-tipped proboscis that could be extended like a trunk. When the trunk made contact with anything edible, it was swallowed whole. Fossils of *Ottoia* contain food remains—including chunks of other *Ottoia* worms, suggesting that the animal was cannibalistic.
   The shale includes fossils of *Pikaia*, a soft-bodied animal with a reinforcing rod running down its body. This feature means that it was probably an early chordate—the group to which vertebrates also belong.

MYSTERY ANIMALS
Some Burgess Shale animals have no modern equivalent, leaving scientists guessing about how they were related to the rest of the animal world. Animals such as *Hallucigenia*, *Opabinia*, and *Wiwaxia* now seem bizarre. The original fossils of *Hallucigenia* showed what seemed to be two rows of spiny legs and a set of short tentacles emerging from the back. These were all attached to a short, wormlike body without an obvious head. Working from these remains, *Hallucigenia* was reconstructed

with the animal walking on its spines and its tentacles waving above it. However, since then further fossils have shown that researchers had mistakenly put the animal upside down. There are actually two sets of tentacles, and it is these that are *Hallucigenia*'s legs.
   Opabinia looked like a shrimp, but had a bizarre claw-tipped snout, and *Wiwaxia* was like an armored cushion that cruised across the seabed. Their ancestry remains a mystery, hidden in undiscovered fossils.

◁ With its eccentric snout, Opabinia captures Amwiskia. Opabinia had five eyes, a body divided into segments, and rows of swimming flaps. Amwiskia had a flattened body and a horizontal tail.

△ When Anomalocaris died its body often broke up. For many years, its mouth disks were thought to be the remains of a jellyfish and its forelimbs parts of a shrimp. Their true identity was established in 1985.

◁ Sanctacaris used its crushing mouthparts to attack animals on the seabed. Here one pursues an animal called Leanchoilia (far left), while behind it, another attacks a Wiwaxia.

ORDOVICIAN PERIOD

WHEN THE ORDOVICIAN PERIOD STARTED, 505 MILLION YEARS AGO, ANIMAL LIFE WAS FOUND ONLY IN THE SEA. BY THE TIME IT ENDED, ANIMALS HAD TAKEN THEIR FIRST TENTATIVE STEPS ONTO LAND.

During the Ordovician Period almost all the world's land was south of the equator. Africa lay over the South Pole, joined to South America, Antarctica, and Australia, and together these land masses made up a giant continent called Gondwana. Ordovician animals thrived in the shallow seas, but climate change eventually brought these good times to a close. Ancient scratch marks created by glaciers show that a large ice cap developed over Gondwana and, at the close of the Ordovician Period, conditions became so cold that over half of the world's animal species became extinct.

▷ *Nautiloids were the largest animals in the Ordovician seas. Forms with straight and coiled shells, like the ones shown here, hunted over an underwater landscape carpeted with algae, corals, and crinoids—distant relatives of starfish. Drifting or planktonic animals were common, but most animals still fed on or near the seabed. Here, a snaillike mollusk crawls across the reef in the foreground, flanked by brachiopods that are filtering their food from the water.*

FILLING THE GAP

Like all major chapters in Earth's history, the Ordovician started with animals recovering from a round of extinctions. Compared to the mass extinction that ended the Ordovician, these were small, but they particularly affected the trilobites, which had become the most important arthropods of the time. So the Ordovician Period opened with a large number of biological vacancies—ones that evolution soon started to fill.

One group of animals that moved into this gap were the nautiloids—mollusks related to today's pearly nautiluses and more distantly to octopuses and squids. Unlike earlier mollusks, which lived on the seabed, nautiloids were able to swim. They could hover motionless above the seabed, watching for prey with well-developed eyes, or dart quickly through the sea by squirting a jet of water backward from their body cavity.

This new way of life was made possible by the unusual design of nautiloid shells. They were conical, or coiled, but instead of having a single internal chamber, like a snail's shell, they had a whole series of them, separated by thin partitions. The animal's body filled only the largest and most recent chamber, and the chambers behind it were hollow and filled with gas. A nautiloid could control the amount of gas in the chambers, allowing it to rise and fall like a submarine.

This new shell design was a sign of the times. Instead of hugging the seabed, more and more animals were starting to venture into the open water above.

VACUUM-CLEANER FISH

Although fishlike animals have been found from the Cambrian Period, the Ordovician is the point when they become widespread as fossils. Compared to nautiloids, these early vertebrates were small animals, and their downward-pointing mouths suggest that they fed on the seabed. They did not have jaws, although they probably could have moved their lips. At first most of them were like living vacuum cleaners, sucking up sediment and particles of food.

These fish—known as heterostracans—relied for survival on a bony shield that covered the front of their bodies. This reinforced plating became a common feature in early vertebrates, and it marked the start of an underwater arms race that was to continue for hundreds of millions of years.

REFUGE ON LAND

As the seas became more populated and more dangerous some animals sought refuge in fresh water and in the marshy shallows along the shore. Food grew here, in the form of simple matlike plants, but air quickly dries out living cells, so for most soft-bodied animals, emerging from damp mud and onto dry land would have been hazardous. Arthropods already had allover body cases that would have helped stop them from drying out. There are no direct remains of these pioneering animals, but tracks in fossilized mud show that they were probably the first to emerge on land, 450 million years ago.

THE AGE OF ANCIENT LIFE

ORDOVICIAN ANIMALS

The Ordovician Period was a time when invertebrates were still the unchallenged rulers of the ocean floor. Like today's invertebrates, some were able to move around, but many others lived alone or in groups, anchored to the seabed. These anchored animals gathered food that drifted within reach. They did not need eyes or large brains. But for moving animals, life was more demanding and more dangerous. They relied on sharp senses to find food, and quick reactions to avoid being attacked by other predators.

△ Discovered in South Africa in the early 1990s, Promissum was a giant conodont measuring 15.7 in. (40cm) in length. Its bulbous eyes suggest that it was an active hunter.

▽ Early horseshoe crabs crawled across the seabed on five pairs of legs. Today there are four species of these living fossils on the east coasts of North America and Asia.

ARMORED ARTHROPODS
When arthropods first appeared, in Early Cambrian times, their bodies were small, and their body cases, or exoskeletons, were paper-thin. But by the beginning of the Ordovician several lines of arthropods had evolved their body cases into suits of armor to protect themselves from attack. One group of armored arthropods common in Ordovician times was the horseshoe crabs.

Despite their name, these animals were not true crabs, but members of a line that later produced spiders and scorpions. The front of their body was protected by a domed shield, or carapace, which completely hid their mouth and legs. The back of the

△ Arandaspis was a heterostracan, or armored, jawless fish. Like other early fish, it swam by flicking its tail, and did not have any fins.

body was protected by a second, smaller shield and ended in a long, spiny tail. This unusual design is clearly shown by fossils, but there is a much easier way of seeing how the horseshoe crab's body worked, because these animals still survive today. They are not the same species that lived in Ordovician times, but amazingly they have changed very little in over 400 million years.

Ordovician horseshoe crabs fed on small seabed animals using pincer-tipped legs to pick up their food. Their pincers were hidden away underneath their head shields, which limited their size. Some close relatives of horseshoe crabs—eurypterids, or sea scorpions—carried their pincers out in the open. In the Ordovician Period most sea scorpions were relatively small, but during the Silurian Period, which followed, they became the largest arthropods of the time.

MYSTERIOUS CONODONTS
For over a century scientists collected and cataloged huge numbers of tiny, toothlike fossils that date back to the Ordovician and sometimes beyond. Known as conodonts (because they are often cone-shaped), these

ORDOVICIAN ANIMALS

△ *This view of an Ordovician reef is based on Newfoundland fossils almost 500 million years old. Two nautiloids scan the seabed, while trilobites and gastropods (snaillike mollusks) creep over the surface below them. Clusters of crinoids, bent over by the current, filter out small particles of food.*

1. **STRAIGHT-SHELLED NAUTILOID**
2. **COILED NAUTILOID**
3. **TRILOBITE**
4. **GASTROPOD**
5. **CORAL**
6. **CRINOID**

main vertebrate line that went on to produce four-legged animals, the conodonts did not last. By the end of the Triassic, when the first dinosaurs appeared, conodont teeth vanish from the fossil record, showing that this group of animals had become extinct.

objects clearly belonged to animals because their shapes evolved as time went by. These shapes are so characteristic that geologists could often estimate the age of rocks simply by looking at the conodonts that they contain. Despite years of searching, the animals that grew these miniature teeth were never found.

A breakthrough came in 1993 when fossils were discovered in Scotland of complete conodont animals with their teeth. Further fossils have been found in North America and South Africa, including one species, *Promissum*, which dates back to Ordovician times. The mystery animals turned out to be creatures with slender, snakelike bodies and well-developed eyes. Some fossils show traces of V-shaped muscle blocks and a notochord—features that are found in vertebrates and their relatives.

Many scientists think that conodonts were vertebrates, which would make them some of the earliest to have evolved. But, unlike the

PLANT LOOK-ALIKES

During the Ordovician a rare event occurred: a completely new group of animals appeared —one of the very few to appear after the Cambrian explosion (page 28). Known as bryozoans, these were tiny invertebrates protected by boxlike skeletons. They grew side by side in colonies, forming shapes that often looked like plants. Bryozoans proved to be a very successful addition to the animal world and are still widespread today.

The Ordovician seabed was also home to a collection of much larger plantlike animals, the crinoids, or sea lilies. Belonging to the same group of animals as starfish and sea urchins, they had a long stalk made of chalky disks and a crown of brittle arms that gathered food. Later some crinoids broke free from this static existence and took up a free-ranging life in the sea. Both kinds of crinoids still exist today.

THE SILURIAN PERIOD

DURING THE SILURIAN PERIOD, AS THE EARTH'S CLIMATE BECAME WARMER AND MORE STABLE, ANIMAL LIFE RECOVERED IN THE SEAS. AT THE SAME TIME, ANIMALS MANAGED TO STRENGTHEN THEIR HOLD ON LAND.

When the Silurian Period started, 438 million years ago, animal life was emerging from the worst catastrophe so far. During the Silurian conditions improved: the climate warmed, and sea levels rose, creating shallow seas that triggered a surge in animal evolution. On land important changes were also underway. The first true plants appeared, creating ankle-high jungles that grew on marshy ground. By the time the Silurian ended, after only 30 million years, land-based animals were widespread, although few were more than an inch long.

▷ *Crawling over the seabed, a giant eurypterid—sea scorpion—catches a meal. These huge arthropods probably lived by hunting and scavenging. Like most modern arthropods, their eyes were compound—consisting of many compartments. Eurypterids would probably have been poor at registering detail, but very good at spotting movement.*

ARMORED PREDATORS

In Silurian times the largest sea animals were giant eurypterids, or sea scorpions— relatives of horseshoe crabs (page 38). One species, called *Pterygotus rhenanius*, was nearly 10 ft. (3m) long, making it a deadly threat to other animals as it roamed the seabed. Like other eurypterids, it had an armor-plated body that could bend at flexible joints. Four pairs of its legs were used for walking; the fifth pair—at the rear —was flattened and worked like oars. Slung underneath its head was a pair of powerful pincers; the head itself was equipped with a pair of saucer-sized eyes. As the sea scorpion lumbered over the seabed, animals would have panicked, but their escape would have been cut short by a lunge of its claws.

Eurypterids lived in brackish water as well as the sea. The Silurian Period marked the heyday of eurypterids as the top predators in water. But fish were also increasing in size. Eventually fish would become a threat to the eurypterids, but during the Silurian things were the other way around.

WEIGHTY MATTERS

While sea scorpions hunted in the shallows other arthropods were evolving on land. These included primitive centipedes and arachnids, the ancestors of spiders and their relatives. These land-based arthropods went on to become extremely successful, but none of them ever rivaled eurypterids in size. Without water to buoy it up, a giant armor-plated body is so heavy that it is almost impossible to move. This factor explains why today's land-based arthropods, such as insects and spiders, are still relatively small, but aquatic species, such as lobsters, can grow to a much larger size.

LIFE AFLOAT

At the other extreme in size, the Silurian seas teemed with planktonic animals, ones that were small and light enough to drift in open water. These included the developing young, or larvae, of mollusks and trilobites and also a group of remarkable invertebrates called graptolites. Graptolites appeared in the Cambrian and flourished for 200 million years. Then the entire group became extinct.

Individual graptolites were rarely more than a few millimeters long, but they lived in colonies or groups that could be 8 in. (20cm) or more in length. Each member of the colony produced a hard, protective cup, built out of a material similar to the one found in mammals' hooves and claws, and the cups were joined together to form a colony. The shape of the colonies varied enormously. Some looked like leaves or small bunches of twigs; others resembled tuning forks, wheels, or even spiders' webs.

Fossil graptolites are extremely common, but scientists once had difficulty deciding what they were. Some were thought to be fossilized plants or even naturally occurring crystals that had grown through sedimentary rock. It is now thought that graptolites were hemichordates—distant relatives of obscure wormlike animals that still exist today.

THE AGE OF ANCIENT LIFE

SILURIAN ANIMALS

Despite the lead taken by small arthropods, the vast majority of Silurian animals lived in freshwater or in the sea. Underwater life was still dominated by animals without backbones, but among vertebrates, some momentous changes were under way. One of these was the evolution of the first fish with true jaws. In time jaws turned out to be a decisive trait, allowing vertebrates to become the most widespread large animals on Earth. But during the Silurian that still lay in the future, as jawed and jawless fishes experimented with different ways of life.

▷ Jamoytius *belonged to a group of fish called anaspids, which had over a dozen gill openings arranged like portholes in the side of a ship. It was about 1 ft. (30cm) long and had three long fins—one on its back and two on its sides as well as a fin on its tail.*

▽ *For early fish, sea scorpions like this* Pterygotus *were a major hazard. But as fish evolved many of them became faster and more maneuverable, moving away from the seabed and the dangers that it held.*

JAWED FISH
When the Silurian Period opened, the only fish in existence were ones that did not have jaws. To us a jawless mouth may sound like a contradiction in terms, but the numerous fossils of jawless fish suggest that it worked adequately. However, jawless fish had limited options when it came to taking in food. One feeding method was to use the mouth like a scoop to dig up sediment—a technique that was probably used by *Jamoytius*, a common species of the time. Alternatively, the mouth could be used like a sucker, attaching the fish to its food. This feeding method is used by lampreys—parasitic animals that are among the few jawless fish that still survive today.

In the early Silurian a group of fish called acanthodians, or spiny sharks, developed a radical alternative to both these ways of feeding. A part of their skeleton—the struts that supported its first pair of gills—gradually turned into a set of jaws. Unlike fish with jawless mouths, these fish could use their jaws as weapons to attack their prey. They could also bite off pieces of food, instead of having to swallow prey whole.

THE ACANTHODIANS
Despite their name, spiny sharks were not true sharks, because these did not evolve until Devonian times. However, they did have bony spines that supported their fins. One common late Silurian, called *Climatius*, was about the size of a typical goldfish, but some later forms grew to over 6.6 ft. (2m) long. Their skeletons were made of cartilage rather than bone, and they had strongly upturned tails. Unlike true sharks, acanthodians had large eyes and short snouts, suggesting that smell played little part in finding prey. Their teeth were small, and although they were constantly replaced, they often grew only in the lower jaw. But they did have another first—a flap, called an operculum, that covered their gills. This could be used like a pump, allowing these fish to breathe without having to swim. For a while spiny sharks were the world's only vertebrates that had jaws, but this unique status was not to last. Once the Silurian came to an end, new groups of jawed fish appeared, and by the early stages of the Permian Period these original trailblazers became extinct.

CORAL REEFS
Until Silurian times algae and sponges had been common inhabitants of reefs, but corals were rarer animals. During the Silurian things changed: corals became widespread, and the first coral reefs began to form. The corals that we know today had not evolved yet, but Silurian corals were like them in many ways. Some species were solitary, meaning that individuals lived on their own, but the reef-building species formed large colonies, with hard cases or cups firmly cemented together. As young coral colonies developed, the older ones beneath them

1
2
3
4
5
6
7
8
9

△ *This view of a Silurian reef is based on fossils that are about 430 million years old. Found in England, it contains tabulate and rugose corals—two groups that became extinct at the end of the Paleozoic Era. Silurian reefs gave safe anchorage for other invertebrates, such as brachiopods, bryozoans, and crinoids.*

1. **TABULATE CORAL**
2. **TABULATE CORAL**
3. **TABULATE CORAL**
4. **SOLITARY RUGOSE CORAL**
5. **BRYOZOAN**
6. **BRACHIOPOD**
7. **TRILOBITE**
8. **CRINOID**
9. **NAUTILOID**

died, forming layers of hard remains. These became glued together by dissolved minerals, turning them into deposits of solid rock.

The way that colonies grew gave each kind a distinctive shape. Some had branches that divided repeatedly, making them look like a set of antlers. These branching colonies often grew quickly but, because they were brittle, could only survive where there was no danger of being broken up by the waves. Others grew more slowly and had rounded or flattened shapes. These types were much better at surviving in rough water, and they often grew on the outer edges of reefs, where breakers rolled in from the open sea.

Modern reef-building corals generally need light to thrive, because they contain microscopic algae that live as onboard partners, using sunlight to make food. Early corals, on the other hand, survived entirely by catching tiny animals, which they trapped with tentacles that carried stinging cells. It was a highly effective system and can still be seen in corals and jellyfish today.

△ *Crinoids became increasingly successful during the Paleozoic. Their chalky stalks usually fell apart after they died, but the main part of the body, with its feeding arms, was often preserved in fossils (above).*

43

THE DEVONIAN PERIOD

OFTEN KNOWN AS THE AGE OF FISHES, THE DEVONIAN PERIOD WAS A TIME WHEN ANIMALS WITH BACKBONES BEGAN THEIR DOMINANCE OF LIFE IN THE SEA AND MADE THEIR FIRST MOVES ONTO LAND.

The Devonian Period began about 408 million years ago, at a time when major changes were taking place in the way the world looked. The giant continent of Gondwana still lay near the South Pole, but it was moving northward; and parts of Europe and North America, together with Greenland, were joined to form a single continent that straddled the equator. The climate was warm, and on land the simple, low-growing plants of Silurian times gradually gave way to ones that were much better at surviving out of water. By the time the Devonian ended the first forests had formed.

▷ The giant placoderm Dunkleosteus *closes in on a young* Cladoselache, *a species of primitive shark.* Dunkleosteus *had a set of tooth plates that lasted for life, while* Cladoselache, *like today's sharks, had dozens of triangular teeth that grew from the inside edge of its jaw, on a nonstop production line. Both of these early fish swam by waving their tails; their other fins were stiff and acted as stabilizers to keep them on course.*

JAWS REVISITED

Evolution has often invented the same adaptation in animal life several times. This is what seems to have happened during the Devonian Period with a group of fish called the placoderms. Placoderms had powerful jaws—bladelike plates that made effective teeth. But since placoderms were not direct descendants of the first jawed fish (page 42), most experts think that they must have evolved jaws themselves. As well as jaws these fish had two hard shields—one that covered the head and one on the front part of the trunk. The shields were connected by a pair of hinges, allowing the front of the head to lift when the fish bit into its prey.

Some placoderms lived on the seabed, where they fed on mollusks and other hard-bodied animals, but toward the Late Devonian others became hunters that lived in open water. Here they became some of the largest predators in the history of animal life so far. One of them, called *Dunkleosteus*, was nearly 13 ft. (4m) long, with mouth plates that could slice other fish in two.

FISH BRANCH OUT

During the Devonian placoderms shared the seas with several other groups of fish. They included jawless species with bizarrely shaped armored bodies (page 46), as well as nonarmored fish, which looked much more like the fish we know today. These nonarmored species were of two kinds: some had skeletons made of cartilage; others had ones made of bone.

The cartilaginous fish were the ancestors of today's sharks and rays. Their bodies were covered in small, rough scales known as denticles, and in their mouths specially enlarged denticles formed a never-ending supply of sharp teeth. Even from their early days many of these fish had the familiar sharklike shape, and by the Late Devonian one species, called *Cladoselache*, was already 6.6 ft. (2m) long. The bony fish were generally small and were covered in scales that became thinner and lighter as time passed. These fish developed gas-filled swim bladders that controlled their buoyancy and mobile fins that made them highly maneuverable.

One group of bony fish, called the lobe-fins, had fins with a fleshy base containing muscle and bone. These interest scientists greatly because they were the animals from which four-legged vertebrates evolved. Not all lobe-fins left the water: several species, including the lungfishes and the coelacanths, still live in freshwater or the sea to this day.

LIFE ON LAND

Despite many years of research, experts do not yet know which of the lobe-finned fish gave rise to primitive amphibians—the first vertebrates to live partly on land. But by the time the Devonian ended, the transition had been made. When the first amphibians appeared they would have seemed slow and awkward compared to other land creatures, but it was a move that would change the whole course of animal life.

DEVONIAN ANIMALS

During the Devonian invertebrate life continued to evolve, although not at the hectic pace that marked the Silurian. Spiral-shelled ammonoids developed from nautiloids, creating a group of mollusks often well preserved as fossils. Trilobites and sea scorpions were on the wane, although when the Devonian ended, both groups still managed to survive for a further 100 million years. But for animal life as a whole the key developments during the Silurian occurred among vertebrates—particularly those that pioneered the difficult move onto land.

▽ *This trio of jawless fish from Devonian times shows different forms of armor protection.* Drepanaspis *(top) and* Cephalaspis *(left) were both bottom-dwellers, with flattened undersides and tails that were triangular in cross section.* Pteraspis *(right) was more streamlined and was built for life in open water.*

FISH THAT WALKED
One of the striking features of the Devonian Period is the number of fish that had heavily armored heads. Armored fish are rare today, but during the Devonian a wide variety of them lived on the seabed and in rivers and lakes. Most of them were bottom-dwellers because their armor—while useful against predators—made swimming in open water hard work.

Among the placoderms (page 44) species that are common as fossils include *Bothriolepis*, which had a semicircular head shield and narrow pectoral (front) fins.

It may have used the fins for balancing on the bottom or perhaps for walking along riverbeds. Another species, called *Pterichthyodes*, looked like a fish that had swum into a bony box, leaving only its tail outside. It, too, had elongated pectoral fins, which may have allowed it to crawl across the mud in lakes. *Groenlandaspis*, a finger-sized species that lived in freshwater, was extremely widespread. Fossils of this little fish have been found not only in Greenland, but also as far away as Australia and Antarctica.

THE END OF ARMOR
Jawless fish also specialized in armor protection in Devonian times. One group, known as the osteostracans, are known for their flattened and horseshoe-shaped heads, which can be well preserved in fossils. One typical species, a freshwater fish called *Cephalaspis*, had a head shield that ended in two backward-pointing horns. The head shield was made of a single piece of bone, which meant that it probably could not grow once it had been fully formed. As a result the shield probably developed when the fish reached adult size. Like its relatives, *Cephalaspis* had another unusual feature—patches of sensory nerves on the sides and top of the shield. These probably helped it navigate or find food, perhaps by sensing vibrations or weak electrical fields.

Armored jawless fish also included species such as *Drepanaspis*, with a shield that was almost round, and *Pteraspis*, an open-water species that had a sharply pointed snout. For tens of millions of years these armored animals were very successful, but as other fish began to evolve alongside them, speed and maneuverability eventually proved to be more useful in the struggle for survival.

LUNGS AND LIMBS
In Early Devonian times tropical lakes and rivers became the home of the world's first lungfish—fish that had gills,

THE FIRST AMPHIBIANS

While Devonian fish left many fossils, Devonian amphibians are extremely rare. Fossils of the two best-known examples— *Ichthyostega* and *Acanthostega*—were both found in Greenland. They had long, fishlike bodies and four legs, but webbed, fishlike tails. Despite their fishy origins, these animals had many adaptations for life on land. They breathed partly through lungs and partly through their skin, and their skeletons were strengthened to support the extra weight they had to bear out of water.

Reconstructions of *Ichthyostega* and *Acanthostega* often show these two animals hunting on land, with their bodies half-crawling and half-slithering across marshy Devonian landscapes. But recent studies of their fossils show that their legs may have had difficulty supporting their weight, making some scientists doubt if they were as agile on land as was once assumed. Instead of being land animals that sometimes took to the water, the real situation may have been the other way around. For *Ichthyostega* and *Acanthostega* water would have been a place to feed and breed, and land would have made a useful refuge from the predatory fish that shared their freshwater home.

△ With a body up to 2 ft. (60cm) long, including its webbed tail, Acanthostega *had webbed feet with eight fingers and toes. Apart from this, it looked much like a giant version of today's salamanders. However, it had many fishlike features, including a streamlined head and a system of sensors called a lateral line, which today's fish use to detect waterborne vibrations.*

▽ Grasping a centipede firmly between its jaws, Icthyostega *prepares to swallow its prey. In theory, at 3.3 ft. (1m) long it would have been able to tackle many land animals of its time. However, whether it could actually hunt like this is a matter of debate—some experts think it made slow progress out of water.*

but could also breathe air when the water's oxygen supply was low. This was particularly useful in warm, stagnant water, where other fish ran the risk of suffocation. One of the earliest of lungfish, called *Dipterus*, is known from fossils discovered in Europe and North America. It was about 19.7 in. (50cm) long, with a cylindrical body and sharply upturned tail.

FINS AND LIMBS

Lungfish belonged to the group known as the lobe-fins (page 44), which had bone and muscle in their fins, making them similar to limbs. This combination of lungs and limblike fins made some biologists believe that they were the ancestors of amphibians, and therefore of all four-legged vertebrates. But a closer look at lungfish shows that they probably did not make the move onto land. Today a different group of lobe-fins are thought to be the most likely candidates for this position in the vertebrate family tree. Known as rhipidistians, they included species such as *Eusthenopteron*, a blunt-headed fish 4 ft. (1.2m) long, with fin bones arranged like those in an amphibian's legs. *Eusthenopteron* also had a braincase like the ones found in early amphibians, providing further evidence that it, or one of its relatives, produced animals that made the move onto land.

THE CARBONIFEROUS PERIOD

A TIME OF IMPORTANT DEVELOPMENTS FOR LIFE ON LAND, THE CARBONIFEROUS SAW THE GROWTH OF VAST LOWLAND FORESTS AND THE EVOLUTION OF THE FIRST REPTILES AND OF THE FIRST ANIMALS THAT COULD FLY.

The Carboniferous Period began 360 million years ago, after a mass extinction (thought to have been triggered by a cooling climate) that killed up to 70 percent of marine animals. In the Western Hemisphere land stretched almost from pole to pole, while in the east most of the world was covered by a Pacific-sized ocean. During the Carboniferous rising sea levels, together with a generally warm and humid climate, created perfect conditions for forests of giant club mosses and ferns, growing on swampy, low-lying ground. The remains of these forests eventually turned into seams of coal, giving the Carboniferous its name.

▷ Hylonomus, one of the world's earliest known reptiles, was about 8 in. (20cm) long. It was fully at home on land. Its remains were discovered inside fossilized tree stumps, together with those of other Carboniferous animals. It seems likely that Hylonomus fell into the tree stumps while hunting and was unable to get out.

ADAPTING TO LIFE ON LAND
At the beginning of the Carboniferous early amphibians were still tied to a water-based way of life. Like today's frogs and toads, they laid their eggs in ponds and streams, and their young went through an aquatic tadpole stage, initially breathing through feathery gills. Even as adults they had to stay close to water, because their skins were thin and they had to stay moist.

In the Carboniferous extensive swamps meant that animals like these were rarely short of somewhere to breed. But water-based life had its dangers. Fish ate a large proportion of amphibian tadpoles, as well as the adults themselves. Amphibians also faced great competition for food—not only from fish and water scorpions, but also from each other. These were just some of the reasons why nature favored amphibians that were better at coping with life on dry land.

BECOMING WATERPROOF
For water-based animals with thin skins the greatest danger on land was drying out. The problem began to diminish when some amphibians developed thicker skin that was protected by scales. This kind of skin acted like a waterproof jacket, keeping most of the body's moisture inside. More importantly, they evolved a new kind of egg—one that was surrounded by a tough membrane called an amnion, which was itself enclosed in a porous shell. The membrane and shell let oxygen in so that the developing embryo could breathe, but they let very little water escape into the air outside. This amniotic egg was an immense leap forward, because it allowed vertebrates to breed away from water. Instead of hatching into swimming tadpoles, their young hatched out as miniature versions of their parents, fully equipped for life on land.

FROM AMPHIBIAN TO REPTILE
In the hunt for the first reptiles, scientists have examined a wide range of fossils to find the earliest ones that fall on the reptile side of the amphibian-reptile divide. Skin and eggs are often missing from the fossil record, but another sign of reptile status is a rib cage that can expand. Unlike amphibians, which gulp air when they breathe, reptiles use their rib cage to suck air into their lungs.

At present the earliest animals that seem to meet all these criteria are *Palaeothyris* and *Hylonomus*, two lizardlike creatures that have been found in present-day Nova Scotia. They were slim and agile and had well-developed legs without any webbing on their feet and a cylindrical, rather than a flattened, tail. *Palaeothyris* and *Hylonomus* lived in the swampy surroundings of Carboniferous forests, but as reptiles evolved they moved farther and farther away from damp surroundings. Eventually—well before the age of the dinosaurs—they would spread to the driest places on Earth.

THE AGE OF ANCIENT LIFE

CARBONIFEROUS ANIMALS

O n land invertebrates still made up the vast majority of animal species during the Carboniferous, but their place was no longer secure. Four-legged vertebrates, or tetrapods, were evolving fast, and by the Late Carboniferous they became the largest predators of their day. Meanwhile, in the freshwater and the seas there was growing success for the cartilaginous and bony fish, mirrored by a steady decline in fish without jaws. During this period in the earth's history crinoids, or sea lilies, continued to thrive, and in some places they formed great underwater forests that carpeted the ocean floor.

△ *With its webbed tail and small, widely spaced legs, Eogyrinus was well equipped for hunting in shallow water, but not suited to life on land. Other amphibians of the Carboniferous— particularly the smaller species—spent much of their adult life out of water, just as most amphibians do today.*

EARLY TETRAPODS
In the Carboniferous many of the largest hunters lived like today's crocodiles and alligators, attacking their prey in lakes and shallows, but sometimes dragging themselves up on dry land. One of the largest was *Eogyrinus*, over 13 ft. (4m) from the end of its snout to the tip of its webbed tail. *Eogyrinus* was an amphibian, and it belonged to a group called the anthracosaurs—a name that means "coal lizards"—which survived until the Permian Period and then became extinct. Anthracosaurs are thought to be the group from which the reptiles evolved.

Another anthracosaur, *Seymouria*, was better adapted to life on land, with stronger legs than *Eogyrinus* and no webbing on its tail. Although it looked like a reptile as an adult, fossils of its young show signs of a lateral line—the sensory system used during their life in water. Because it grew up in the water, *Seymouria* fails the reptile test.

AMPHIBIAN ARRAY
Several different groups, all now extinct, shared the Carboniferous lakes and swamps with their anthracosaur relatives. Among them were amphibians called temnospondyls, a group of species that are the probable ancestors of frogs and toads. One of the largest was an animal called *Eryops*, which looked like a small, frog-eyed crocodile supported by stubby legs. *Eryops* was about 6.6 ft. (2m) long and, like all amphibians, had thin, scaleless skin. It also had bony plates along its back, which may have protected it when it hauled itself out of the shallows. Although *Eryops* was large, it was not the biggest of its group. One species, called *Mastodonsaurus*, had a skull over 3.3 ft. (1m) long—large enough to make it a threat to many of the other amphibians around it.

Over the years paleontologists have found many fossilized tadpoles of *Eryops* and its relatives. Today they are recognized for what they are, but earlier they were thought to be separate species.

REPTILES AND THEIR SKULLS
The earliest reptiles evolved in the Late Carboniferous, and included *Palaeothyris* and *Hylonomus* (page 48). Despite their place at the foot of the reptile family tree, these two animals look like lizards and could be mistaken for them if they lived today. However, internally they had several features that made them distinct. One of the most important was that their skulls had no openings apart from the ones that housed their nostrils and eyes. Reptiles that are built in this way are called anapsids, which literally means "without arches." Anapsids inherited this kind of skull from their amphibian ancestors, and only turtles and tortoises have this kind of skull today. Other reptiles went on to develop extra openings; these reduced weight and provided anchorage for their jaw muscles. Synapsids evolved one pair of extra openings, positioned behind the eyes,

▽ *Meganeuropsis was a giant dragonfly that flew over swamps. Like modern dragonflies, its two pairs of wings could beat in opposite directions, allowing it to hover like a helicopter as it watched for prey.*

while diapsids evolved two. These fossae, or hollows, are of interest because they help in piecing together the path of evolution. Synapsids include animals that went on to produce mammals; diapsids include the ruling reptiles or archosaurs—the group to which all dinosaurs belonged.

TAKING TO THE AIR

For anyone averse to bugs and insects, the Carboniferous landscape would have been a nightmare. Scorpions up to 29.5 in (75cm) long crawled over the ground in search of prey, and giant cockroaches and millipedes vied for rotting plant remains. Centipedes preyed with poison fangs on other land animals after dark. Primitive dragonflies swooped on airborne insects over pools and among trees, flying on wings that could be over 2 ft. (60cm) from tip to tip. Insects were the first animals to fly, and in Carboniferous times they had the air to themselves. However, scientists have found few clues to how and

when the first winged species evolved. According to one theory insect wings may have developed from the flattened pads that some fossil species have attached to their body segments. Initially these pads may have been used for temperature regulation or perhaps in courtship displays, but if they became large enough, they could have been used for gliding. To become true wings they would have then had to develop hinges at the point where they meet the body. Their owners would have had to develop flight muscles by modifying existing muscles inside the middle part of the body, or thorax. As this happened they would have changed from gliders to the first true aviators.

Because winged insects were well developed by the Carboniferous Period, it is likely that they first appeared in the Devonian, but fossils have yet to be discovered that date this far back in time.

▽ *Terrestrial scorpions evolved from ancestors that lived in water. Aquatic scorpions breathed through gills, but land-dwelling forms developed book lungs inside their bodies. In a book lung air flows past thin flaps that are stacked like pages of a book.*

THE PERMIAN PERIOD

THE PERMIAN PERIOD WAS THE FINAL STAGE IN THE PALEOZOIC ERA. IT IS KNOWN CHIEFLY FOR THE DRAMATIC WAY THAT IT ENDED—WITH THE LARGEST MASS EXTINCTION IN THE HISTORY OF LIFE ON EARTH.

By the beginning of the Permian, 286 million years ago, the earth's land masses had converged to form a single supercontinent called Pangaea. Because Pangaea was so vast, climatic conditions on land varied enormously. Over the South Pole an ice cap remained from Carboniferous times, but across the tropics and much of the north, Pangaea was a place of baking heat and little rain. In these arid conditions the moisture-loving trees of Carboniferous times went into retreat, to be replaced by conifers and other seed-forming plants that were better at coping with drought.

▷ Basking in the early morning sunshine, pelycosaurs soak up warmth through their vertical sails. Both the species shown here—Dimetrodon (foreground) and Edaphosaurus (background)—lived in the early Permian, and grew to a length of about 10 ft. (3m). Dimetrodon was a predator, armed with stabbing teeth. Edaphosaurus was a herbivore. Their sails were kept permanently upright by struts of bone.

WATER AND WARMTH
Evolution cannot plan ahead, so it could not prepare animals for the changed conditions of Permian times. But reptiles turned out to be ideally suited to the drier climate that developed when the Permian began. They spread across the supercontinent, to habitats where amphibians could not survive. As they evolved they became better at economizing with water until they could live in desert conditions, like many reptiles do today.

Reptiles also had to deal with the large temperature changes that often occur on land. In water and wetlands, where the first four-legged vertebrates evolved, temperature changes were gradual, and the highest were rarely very high. But in Pangaea's interior it could be close to freezing at dawn and over 104°F (40°C) by the middle of the day. Because reptiles were (and still are) ectothermic, or cold-blooded, their body temperatures rose and fell with the temperature of their surroundings. They would be almost immobilized by the cold at dawn, but by noon, they could be at risk of overheating.

AN INSIDE SOLUTION
Early reptiles would have dealt with this problem in the same way that reptiles do now: by basking in the sunshine when they were cold or by hiding in the shade when they were too hot. In time some reptiles—most notably the pelycosaurs—developed tall sails that probably acted as heat exchangers, helping them warm up and make an earlier start to the day. But later in the Permian descendants of the pelycosaurs called therapsids evolved a very different answer to the problem of temperature control. Instead of depending on the sun's warmth, they started to conserve the heat that their own bodies generated by breaking down food. In other words, they became endothermic, or warm-blooded. To keep in heat, they used something quite new—fur.

WARM-BLOODED VERTEBRATES
Fur rarely shows up in fossils, and there is no direct evidence that furred therapsids actually existed during the Permian Period, or at any later time. However, several pieces of evidence suggest that it is highly likely. One is that therapsids evolved adaptations that improved their breathing rate and oxygen supply—something that is essential in animals that burn lots of food. Another is that some therapsids lived in the south of Pangaea, where winter conditions would have been severe. This is an unlikely habitat for a cold-blooded reptile. But for one that could keep itself warm by burning food, life would have been much easier.

Therapsids were the animals that went on to give rise to the mammals, but they were not mammals themselves. Even though Permian forms probably had fur, they were unlike mammals as we know them today. But being warm-blooded was a key innovation—one that would eventually allow four-legged vertebrates to conquer every habitat of Earth, including high mountains and polar ice.

◁ *Cacops was an armored Permian amphibian. About 15.7 in. (40cm) long, it was well adapted to life on land, but probably laid its eggs in water.*

PERMIAN ANIMALS

D uring the Permian therapsids—or mammallike reptiles—became an increasingly important part of life on land. Although they never reached the gigantic sizes of reptiles in the Mesozoic Era, they were the dinosaurs of their day. Soon after they first appeared, they evolved into a variety of hunters and plant eaters, reaching sizes of up to 16.4 ft. (5m) long and weights of over 1 ton. In the Permian four-legged vertebrates also included a wide variety of amphibians, pelycosaurs, and the archosaurs, the group of animals to which the dinosaurs belonged.

▽ Anteosaurus *launches an attack on* Moschops *in a region of Gondwana that is now South Africa's Karoo Basin.*

THERAPSIDS OF THE KAROO

Much of our knowledge of Permian therapsids comes from fossils found in central and European Russia and in the Karoo, a region of South

Africa. The Karoo fossils often consist of complete skeletons, allowing animals to be reconstructed down to the smallest details.

One of the largest plant eaters from the Karoo was *Moschops*, an animal that grew to about 13 ft. (4m) in length. It had a much shorter tail than most of the earliest reptiles, and the typical barrel-shaped body of a large plant eater, supported by sturdy legs. *Moschops* also had a remarkably thick skull. Some paleontologists think that this would have been used in head-butting contests, although others have suggested that this bony growth might have been the result of disease. Despite its size, *Moschops* did not lead an entirely tranquil life, because the Karoo was home to some formidable flesh-eating therapsids, including *Anteosaurus*, which rivaled *Moschops* for size. In general build the two animals were similar, but *Moschops* had chisellike teeth, and *Anteosaurus* had extra-long stabbing teeth near the front of its jaws—the sign of an animal with a carnivorous way of life.

RUSSIAN THERAPSIDS

Russian therapsids included some decidedly strange-looking animals. One of the oddest was *Estemmenosuchus*, a name that means

◁ *While a herd of* Estemmenosuchus *wanders down to a lake to drink, a solitary* Eotitanosuchus *watches them from the opposite shore, sizing up the possibility of making a kill. In the generally dry conditions of Permian times oases like these would have made good hunting grounds.*

▽ *Watched by* Varanosaurus, *two* Caseas *lie on a sandy bank, soaking up the sunshine. Casea's sprawling gait meant that it rested with its body on the ground—unlike many plant eaters of later times, which spent most of their time on all fours.*

"crowned crocodile." With its bulky body and short tail, *Estemmenosuchus* bore very little resemblance to a crocodile, but it did have a crown of four hornlike outgrowths—two projecting from the sides of its face and two from the top of its head. These outgrowths could have been used for defense, but since they were short and blunt, a more likely explanation is that they were used to show an animal's status during courtship displays. The horns would have been largest in adult animals, particularly mature males.

Scientist disagree as to whether *Estemmenosuchus* was carnivorous, but another large therapsid from Late Permian Russia, called *Eotitanosuchus*, certainly was. It had saberlike canine teeth, set in a skull that had narrow and powerful jaws.

PERMIAN PELYCOSAURS
Although pelycosaurs gave rise to the therapsids, they continued to flourish alongside them during Permian times. The best-known examples are the sail-backed species (page 53), but the pelycosaur group also included animals that looked much more like some reptiles that exist today. One carnivorous species, called *Varanosaurus*, has been given its name because of its resemblance to today's monitor lizards and like them could be over 5 ft. (1.5m) long. Another species, called *Casea*, was a plant eater and a member of the last family of

pelycosaurs to appear. It had a fat, sprawling body like that of a modern iguana, with a small head and a slender tail. Its dentition was highly unusual, with peglike teeth in the upper jaw, but no teeth in its lower jaw—exactly the reverse of the arrangement in many large plant eaters today. This curious feature must have been an asset rather than a handicap, because *Casea's* descendants became abundant and survived almost to the time when the Permian Period came to its calamitous close.

55

THE AGE OF ANCIENT LIFE

END OF AN ERA

About 245 million years ago the Permian Period came to an end in the greatest mass extinction since animal life began. Its effects were the worst in the oceans, where about 96 percent of all marine species died out; on land the figure was around 75 percent. The victims of this great calamity included trilobites, Paleozoic corals, and a number of other invertebrates, as well as the pelycosaurs, which in Permian times had been some of the most successful reptiles on land. By clearing away so many living species, this immense upheaval had a profound effect on the future course of animal evolution.

▷ *Some scientists believe that the existence of a single supercontinent, Pangaea, triggered environmental changes that devastated life at the end of the Permian.*

▷ *After existing for over 260 million years and surviving two mass extinctions, trilobites finally became extinct.*

▽ *Volcanic gases from eruptions may have trapped incoming heat and made temperatures spiral upward.*

MISSING EVIDENCE

Many theories have been put forward to explain the Permian mass extinction, but there are three or four primary explanations, or several of them acting together. The first of these—and the most quick-acting—is an impact by an asteroid or some other object from space. If this were large enough, it would have created a devastating shock wave that spread around the world, mirroring the event believed to have wiped out the dinosaurs (page 204). Chemical evidence has recently given weight to this idea, but scientists still think that the extinction was caused by natural changes on Earth.

A HOMEGROWN DISASTER

One leading Earth-centered theory is that a massive wave of volcanic eruptions blasted billions of tons of ash into the sky. If the eruptions continued over a long period, the ash clouds would have cut off much of the sunlight on which plant life depends. Without plants on land and microscopic algae in the sea, most animals would soon have perished. Signs of immense eruption have been found in Siberia.

Another possiblity is that falling sea levels in the Late Permian obliterated the shallow inshore waters on which much of marine life depended. As Pangaea had a relatively short coastline, this would have left corals and other invertebrates with a rapidly shrinking habitat. However, the decimation of land life is harder to explain, which is why falling sea levels may have been an additional factor in the mass extinction, rather than its main cause.

Many scientists think that the fourth explanation—climate change—may have dealt a deadly blow. There is evidence that the climate warmed and then suddenly cooled as the Permian drew to a close, which would have made life difficult for animals on land and in the sea. With falling sea levels and volcanic eruptions thrown into the equation, the result may have been the cataclysm that the fossil record shows.

THE AGE OF REPTILES

The Mesozoic Era—between 245 and 66 million years ago—was the time when reptiles became the unchallenged rulers of life on Earth. The dinosaurs became the largest plant eaters and predators to exist on land, and other groups of reptiles successfully conquered the seas and took to the skies. Divided into three periods—the Triassic, Jurassic, and Cretaceous—the Mesozoic saw immense changes on the face of the earth. Sea levels rose and fell, and Pangaea, the giant supercontinent, slowly broke up. The Mesozoic Era ended with the most famous of all mass extinctions.

THE TRIASSIC PERIOD

AT THE BEGINNING OF THE TRIASSIC PERIOD ANIMAL LIFE WAS EMERGING FROM THE AFTERMATH OF THE PERMIAN MASS EXTINCTION. BY THE TIME THE TRIASSIC ENDED, THE FIRST DINOSAURS HAD APPEARED.

The Triassic Period gets its name from the Latin word for "three," because it was first identified from three layers of rock found in Germany. At the start of the Triassic, about 245 million years ago, most of the world's land was still locked together in the supercontinent Pangaea, but as the Triassic came to an end Pangaea began to break apart. Until this happened, land filled much of the Western Hemisphere, and sea levels were at record lows. Across most of Pangaea the climate was warm and dry, but it cooled as the northern and southern continents began to move apart.

▷ In the heart of Pangaea moisture-loving plants create a splash of greenery in an arid landscape. In Triassic times these plants included tree ferns and horsetails, and also conifers, which often grew on drier ground. These ribbons of green were vital for plant-eating reptiles—and for the meat-eating animals that stalked them.

THERAPSIDS IN DECLINE

The Triassic world was not unlike the earth in Permian times. Instead of being kept separate by the sea, land animals could roam all over, and fossils of the same species are found in places far apart. The therapsids, which had evolved during the Permian, made full use of this freedom to spread. Fossils of one plant-eating species—a barrel-shaped animal called *Lystrosaurus* (page 61) —have been found in places as far apart as Europe and Antarctica, providing evidence that these continents were once joined.

However, for therapsids as a whole the Triassic period brought difficult times. Although they dominated life on land during the Permian, they failed to maintain their position after the great extinction that brought the Permian to a close. A group of reptiles, the archosaurs, went through a rapid burst of evolution, consigning the therapsids to a dwindling share of the stage. During their decline the therapsids gave rise to the earliest mammals, but these remained small and unobtrusive. They stayed that way for millions of years, until the Age of Reptiles came to its violent end.

THE RULING REPTILES

The first archosaurs—or ruling reptiles— appeared just before the beginning of the Triassic from long-bodied animals that looked like crocodiles, but which were often adapted for life on land. Unlike earlier reptiles, their hind legs were usually longer than their front legs, and they evolved specialized ankles that allowed them to walk with a more upright posture, instead of sprawling with their legs out to the side.

Early offshoots of the archosaur line included *Tanystropheus* (page 60), a fish eater with a bizarrely long neck, and *Scaphonyx* (page 63), a beaked lizard, or rhynchosaur. By the Late Triassic archosaurs themselves went on to become a much more diverse collection of animals. Among them were a host of new reptile groups, including the pterosaurs, or flying reptiles, the dinosaurs, and the crocodilians—the only one of these groups that has survived to the present day.

In Triassic times most archosaurs were predators, and they included some fearsome animals such as *Saurosuchus* (page 63). Although *Saurosuchus* was not a dinosaur, its impressive size provided a hint of what the future held. By comparison, the earliest dinosaurs themselves were sometimes surprisingly small—*Eoraptor* (pages 86–87), for example, which dates back to the Late Triassic, was just 3.3 ft. (1m) long.

MARINE GIANTS

In Triassic times reptiles included nothosaurs—lizardlike animals that probably spent much of their time on the shore— and pistosaurs, which had paddles rather than claws. One group of reptiles, the ichthyosaurs, had become as well-adapted for ocean life as whales and dolphins are today. *Shonisaurus* (page 193), a Late Triassic species, was the largest reptile afloat, weighing perhaps as much as 20 tons.

◁ Sharovipteryx *was one of the first vertebrates to take to the air, gliding from tree to tree. It had large rear wings, and possibly a smaller front pair to steer.*

This bizarre reptile may have fished from rocks. It belonged to a group of reptiles called prolacertiforms, which died out when the Triassic came to an end.

MAXIMUM LENGTH	9.8 ft. (3m)
TIME	Mid Triassic
FOSSIL FINDS	Europe (Germany), Asia (Israel)

PROTEROSUCHUS

This animal is the earliest archosaur for which complete fossilized skeletons have been found. Like today's crocodiles, it had sprawling legs, and it probably spent much of its time in water, catching fish and other animals with its powerful jaws. It had sharp, conical teeth, and there were secondary teeth in the roof of its mouth—a feature shared by other early archosaurs, but lost as they evolved.

MAXIMUM LENGTH	6.6 ft. (2m)
TIME	Early Triassic
FOSSIL FINDS	Africa (South Africa), Asia (China)

TRIASSIC ANIMALS

D uring the Triassic Period reptiles strengthened their hold of life on land. Dinosaurs appeared in the Late Triassic, but until then an array of different reptiles competed for supremacy. Many were carnivores, hunting other reptiles, fish, or smaller forms of life; others had teeth or sharp-edged jaws that had evolved for cropping plants. With the rise of the archosaurs, these forerunners of today's mammals found themselves increasingly threatened.

▷ *Like other early archosaurs,* Proterosuchus *probably lowered its underside onto the ground when resting, raising it to move.*

▽ Tanystropheus *may have used its extraordinary neck to catch fish without having to enter the water.*

TANYSTROPHEUS

Tanystropheus was one of the most remarkable vertebrates of all time. Its head was small, but its slender neck was longer than the rest of its body. The front and rear of its body look so dissimilar that when the first fragmentary fossils were found, they were thought to belong to two entirely different animals. *Tanystropheus'* neck had only 13 vertebrae in some species and as few as 9 in others, which would have limited its ability to bend.

SHAROVIPTERYX

Discovered in the early 1970s, this extraordinary animal is one of the earliest known gliding reptiles and also one of the strangest. Attached to its hind legs, and perhaps its front legs as well, were flaps of elastic skin, which could be stretched out to form wings. Its main wings were positioned at the rear of its body, so its tail would have been crucial for staying balanced in midair.

MAXIMUM LENGTH	49 ft. (15m)
TIME	Late Triassic
FOSSIL FINDS	Russia

ERYTHROSUCHUS

Meaning "red crocodile," *Erythrosuchus* was a close relative of *Proterosuchus,* but better adapted to hunting prey on land. One of the

TRIASSIC ANIMALS

largest land-based predators of the Early Triassic, it it weighed half a ton and had a head of about 3.3 ft. (1m) long. *Erythrosuchus* would have fed mainly on plant eaters, including therapsids such as *Lystrosaurus*, grasping and killing them with its large, backward-curving teeth.

MAXIMUM LENGTH 6.6 ft. (2m)

TIME Early Triassic

FOSSIL FINDS Africa (South Africa)

TICINOSUCHUS

Fossils of this archosaur show an animal that was well equipped for running after fast-moving prey. Although its body was crocodile-like, it had legs that were upright instead of sprawling and feet with fully developed ankles and heels. This foot anatomy was important because by lifting its heels, it could push down its feet, giving the leverage needed to run.

MAXIMUM LENGTH 9.8 ft. (3m)

TIME Mid Triassic

FOSSIL FINDS Europe (Switzerland)

LYSTROSAURUS

Unlike the other animals on these two pages, *Lystrosaurus* belonged to a group of plant-eating therapsids called dicynodonts, which evolved in the Late Permian period, becoming extinct at the end of the Triassic. It had only two teeth, which grew in its upper jaw. It cut through its food with a sharp-edged beak in much the same way that tortoises do today.

MAXIMUM LENGTH 3.3 ft. (1m)

TIME Early Triassic

FOSSIL FINDS Africa (South Africa), Asia (India, China, Russia), Antarctica

◁ *Ticinosuchus' upright stance was similar to that of later dinosaurs.*

▽ *As well as moving its lower jaw up and down, Lystrosaurus could slide it backward to slice through giant horsetails.*

61

THE AGE OF REPTILES

◁ Longisquama *may have used its scales to glide through forests, folding them back when it had landed. Only one fossil of this animal has been found.*

LONGISQUAMA

Ever since its fossilized remains were found in 1969, debate has raged over this small and enigmatic reptile. *Longisquama* had a lizardlike body, with two rows of what look like feathers fastened to its back. If they are true feathers, as some experts believe, it suggests that this animal is a direct ancestor of birds (page 132) and may have been able to fly. However, most paleontologists are not convinced. They believe that the feathers are actually long scales, which may have been used by the animal to regulate its temperature or to disply during courtship. *Longisquama's* mouth was lined with small, sharp teeth, suggesting that it might have fed on insects.

MAXIMUM LENGTH 6 in. (15cm)
TIME Late Triassic
FOSSIL FINDS Asia (Turkestan)

▽ *Lightly built, fast on its feet, and armed with sharp, backward-curving teeth,* Euparkeria *was well equipped for hunting and killing. The bony plates running down its back protected it from larger predators, although its first defense would have been to run away on its back legs.*

STAGONOLEPIS

With its short legs and long, scaly body, *Stagonolepis* looked like an early crocodile, as did many other early archosaurs. But instead of having long jaws that match a predatory life, it had short ones shaped for feeding on plants. Its teeth were peglike and were positioned at the back of its mouth. The end of its snout was shaped like a trowel, which suggests that it may have rooted for food on or beneath the ground. *Stagonolepis* was slow moving but had armored scales that would have helped protect it from attack.

MAXIMUM LENGTH 9.8 ft. (3m)
TIME Late Triassic
FOSSIL FINDS Europe (Scotland)

EUPARKERIA

Like *Stagonolepis*, this slender-bodied archosaur also bore some resemblance to a small-scale crocodile, with viciously toothed jaws, a series of bony scales along its back, and a long, powerful tail. But its legs were unlike a crocodile's, partly because they were more upright, but also because the hind legs were significantly larger than

the front pair. This difference makes it very likely that *Euparkeria* could run on two legs, either to escape danger or to catch its prey. This way of moving was rare in early reptiles but became widespread when dinosaurs evolved.

MAXIMUM LENGTH 2 ft. (60cm)
TIME Late Triassic
FOSSIL FINDS Africa (South Africa)

TRIASSIC ANIMALS

LAGOSUCHUS

The remains of four skeletons, missing only parts of the skull, show that *Lagosuchus* was a slender, long-legged, and long-tailed archosaur, which could probably raise itself up on its back legs to run. Its elongated shinbones, combined with its light build, mean that it would have been an effective sprinter, allowing it to catch insects and small reptiles. Its feet were also shaped for speed. They had long metatarsals (bones that form part of the sole in human feet), and these were carried off the ground, helping increase the length of the stride.

MAXIMUM LENGTH 17.7 in. (45cm)

TIME Mid Triassic

FOSSIL FINDS South America (Argentina)

SCAPHONYX

Scaphonyx was a typical rhynchosaur, a plant-eating relative of the archosaurs, with a barrel-shaped body, a narrow beak equipped with tusks, and highly unusual teeth. The teeth on each side of the upper jaws formed a flat plate with a central groove, and the teeth in the lower jaw were pointed and pressed into the groove when the mouth was closed. Most paleontologists think that rhynchosaurs used these strange teeth to eat plants, chopping them up with a scissorlike action and perhaps digging up roots with their tusks. Rhynchosaur fossils have been found on every continent except Australia, and their numbers suggest they were as common as grazing mammals today.

MAXIMUM LENGTH 6.6 ft. (2m)

TIME Mid Triassic

FOSSIL FINDS South America (Brazil)

△ Lagosuchus *had elongated feet, with only its toes touching the ground. This anatomy was common in carnivorous dinosaurs, as well as many mammals.*

SAUROSUCHUS

Weighing up to 2 tons, this archosaur was one of the largest land-based predators in Late Triassic times. Its head alone was up to 3.3 ft. (1m) long and armed with teeth like a crocodile's to tear chunks of flesh from its prey. Although not a dinosaur, *Saurosuchus* showed some striking similarities to tyrannosaurs and other hunters, particularly in the shape of its jaws and teeth and in the way its legs were arranged almost vertically beneath its body. Unlike a tyrannosaur, it moved mainly on all fours, but it is likely that it could run on its back legs alone to launch an attack. *Saurosuchus* belonged to a group of archosaurs called rauisuchids, which also included *Ticinosuchus* (page 61). These animals were an early example of the

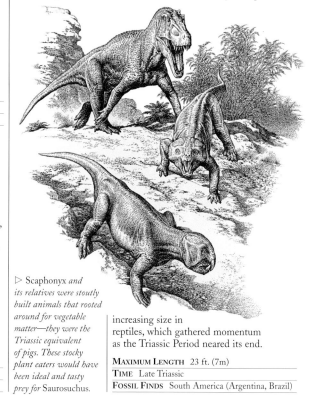

▷ Scaphonyx *and its relatives were stoutly built animals that rooted around for vegetable matter—they were the Triassic equivalent of pigs. These stocky plant eaters would have been ideal and tasty prey for* Saurosuchus.

increasing size in reptiles, which gathered momentum as the Triassic Period neared its end.

MAXIMUM LENGTH 23 ft. (7m)

TIME Late Triassic

FOSSIL FINDS South America (Argentina, Brazil)

EARLY DINOSAURS

THE FIRST DINOSAURS EVOLVED IN THE LATE TRIASSIC—OVER 15 MILLION YEARS AFTER THE AGE OF REPTILES BEGAN. RARE AT FIRST, THEY BECAME THE LEADING LAND ANIMALS BY THE TIME THE JURASSIC PERIOD BEGAN.

Studies of dinosaur anatomy show that they all share several key features, which means that they must have evolved from a single ancestor. That ancestor was almost certainly a thecodont, or primitive archosaur, which gave rise to a new line of reptiles that could walk on two legs. How and when this line split into the ornithischians and saurischians is not yet known, but the result was a range of reptiles that developed major differences in body shape and ways of life.

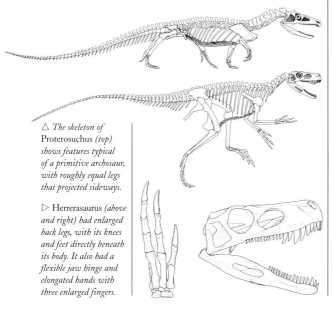

△ *The skeleton of* Proterosuchus *(top) shows features typical of a primitive archosaur, with roughly equal legs that projected sideways.*

▷ Herrerasaurus *(above and right) had enlarged back legs, with its knees and feet directly beneath its body. It also had a flexible jaw hinge and elongated hands with three enlarged fingers.*

FOSSIL EVIDENCE

Early dinosaurs walked with just three of their toes in contact with the ground, rather than four or five. As a result, three-toed footprints are strong evidence of dinosaurs on the move. One or two specimens have been dated back to the Early Triassic, but most paleontologists are unconvinced. The earliest reliable dinosaur footprints date to the Late Triassic—the time Herrerasaurus *and* Eoraptor *were alive.*

EARLY DAYS

Proterosuchus (page 60) looked much more like a crocodile than a dinosaur—but in fact, both crocodiles and dinosaurs evolved from animals like this. While crocodiles kept *Proterosuchus'* sprawling four-legged gait, the dinosaurs developed differently. Their back legs became larger than their front legs, and the femur, or thighbone, evolved a sharp bend near the point where it joined the rest of the body. Also, the head of the femur developed a ball-like shape, fitting into a socket in the hip. These changes added up to one thing: a new group of carnivorous reptiles that could stand upright on their back legs, instead of moving on legs that sprawled out toward their sides.

Dinosaurs had several features that help to separate them from other reptiles. Among these were a reduced number of bones in the fourth finger (if present) and hip sockets that had a central hole, or window. By contrast, typical hip sockets—including human ones—are closed, like a cup.

WORLDWIDE HUNT

Where these animals first appeared is still not clear, partly because most of the world's land was joined together in Triassic times. But Argentina's so-called Wild West has produced a clutch of fossils that include some of the earliest dinosaurs on record. Fragments of one *Herrerasaurus* were found in the 1950s, followed by a partial skeleton in 1988 that showed that *Herrerasaurus* was a bipedal carnivore up to 19.7 ft. (6m) long, with long jaws and backward-curving teeth. It resembled a theropod (page 113), with long-fingered hands for grasping prey.

In 1991 the same part of the world produced fossils of *Eoraptor*, or "dawn thief," a bipedal hunter just 3.3 ft. (1m) long. *Eoraptor* lived about 228 million years ago and was less specialized than *Herrerasaurus*, thus even closer to the original protodinosaur. But in 1999 paleontologists working in Madagascar found jawbones of two even earlier dinosaurs, provisionally dated at more than 230 million years old. The bones showed that these dinosaurs were not carnivores, but plant eaters called prosauropods, which some thought had evolved from meat-eating ancestors.

CHANGING TIMES

The existence of plant-eating dinosaurs so long ago shows that dinosaurs were already diversifying as the Mid Triassic ended and the Late Triassic began. Many existing animal groups, such as the mammallike reptiles, or therapsids, either declined or disappeared. Dinosaurs may have triggered this change by outcompeting existing animals. Another possibility is that the world's climate might have abruptly altered, triggering a wave of extinctions and clearing the way for dinosaurs to expand.

◁ *Herrerasaurus* may have been an early theropod—a group that included all the predatory dinosaurs. The bipedal posture was effective for hunting, and in Cretaceous times theropods included the largest carnivores that have ever lived.

▽ Known from many well-preserved fossils, *Plateosaurus* was a plant-eating prosauropod that lived in the Late Triassic. Compared to the small prosauropods recently found in Madagascar, it was a large animal, about 23 ft. (7m) long. Prosauropods looked similar to sauropods (page 71), but had feet with long toes.

THE JURASSIC PERIOD

FAMOUS FOR ITS DINOSAURS, THE
JURASSIC PERIOD WAS AN EVENTFUL TIME
FOR REPTILIAN LIFE AS A WHOLE. FOR THE
FIRST TIME REPTILES DOMINATED LIFE ON
LAND, IN THE SEA, AND IN THE AIR.

Named after a chain of mountains in Europe, the Jurassic started about 208 million years ago. Compared to the Triassic Period, it was a time of great change in the earth's crust, as the giant supercontinent of Pangaea began to break up. The climate became wetter and warmer, and sea levels rose, flooding large areas of low-lying land. For animal life these changes created new opportunities. On land a moister climate meant that plant food was easier to find; in the sea warm shallows created perfect conditions for coral reefs.

▷ *Average temperatures were warm in the Jurassic, with little or no ice at the poles. This scene shows a typical Jurassic landscape, dominated by forests of conifers, with scattered cycads and tree ferns. Dinosaurs probably scattered cycad seeds, just as mammals today scatter the seeds of some plants.*

A PARTING OF WAYS
With the breakup of Pangaea the continents began their long journey into the positions they occupy today. The Atlantic Ocean started to form, and North and South America split apart. These changes had an important effect on land animals, because it meant that they could no longer mix freely. Instead, each continent began to develop its own characteristic wildlife—a feature that became more pronounced the longer they remained apart. The separation can often be seen through fossil evidence. For example, giant sauropods lived in both North and South America during the Jurassic, but each continent had its own particular kinds—neither is found in both.

DINOSAURS IN THE ASCENDANT
When the Jurassic Period began dinosaurs had established themselves as the prominent animals on land. They had already split into several lines, and most of these were set to continue for nearly 150 million years, until the Age of Reptiles abruptly came to an end. However, there were some casualties along the way. Among the sauropods, for example, the cetiosaur family died out at the end of the Jurassic, and several other dinosaur families disappeared.

The warm and humid conditions that lasted for most of the Jurassic were ideal for large plant eaters to evolve, because there was a vast supply of food. And as plant eaters increased in size, so did the animals that preyed upon them. From relatively modest beginnings predatory dinosaurs evolved into giants such as *Megalosaurus*, which was up to 29.5 ft. (9m) long. Outwardly *Megalosaurus* was similar to the better known tyrannosaurs, but it evolved millions of years before they appeared.

These huge predators had no natural enemies, but not all dinosaurs were built on a giant scale. *Compsognathus*, which lived in the Late Jurassic, was also a hunter, but it weighed only about 6.6 lb. (3kg).

LIFE IN THE SEA AND AIR
During the Jurassic several new families of marine reptiles appeared. Among them were the long-necked plesiosaurs and elasmosaurs and also the pliosaurs, which included some of the largest predators to live in the seas. Marine life was particularly rich in the Jurassic, because sea levels were generally higher than they are today. Sunlit shallows rich in sediment teemed with mollusks and other small animals.

In the air even greater changes were underway. The first flying reptiles, or pterosaurs, had evolved in the Late Triassic, and during the Jurassic they took command of the skies on their leathery wings. But from a branch of the dinosaur world—the theropods—a completely new group of flying animals came into being. Instead of flying on wings of skin, they used feathers (page 133), and they rapidly diversified as the Jurassic came to its end. We know them as birds—the only dinosaurs still in existence today.

THE CRETACEOUS PERIOD

A TIME OF DRAMATIC SHIFTS IN THE WORLD'S CONTINENTS, TOGETHER WITH RECORD SEA LEVELS, THE CRETACEOUS PERIOD SAW AN EXPLOSIVE GROWTH IN LIFE—ONE THAT CAME TO A CATACLYSMIC END.

The Cretaceous Period began 144 million years ago when the supercontinent of Pangaea had broken up. Two major fragments—Laurasia in the north and Gondwana in the south—began cracking up as well, to form the continents that exist today. These continental movements produced major changes in the earth's climate and sea levels up to 660 ft. (200m) higher than they are now. Microscopic life abounded in the seas, and tiny shells built up in vast banks on the ocean floor, eventually turning into chalk. Known in Latin as *creta*, chalk gave the Cretaceous its name.

LIFE ON LAND

Unlike the Triassic or Jurassic Periods, the Cretaceous was similar in some ways to the world we know today. Flowering plants probably evolved in the Late Jurassic or Early Cretaceous, but it was during the Cretaceous that they really began to make their mark. These plants included the first broad-leaved trees, which slowly ousted conifers in many parts of the world. As flowering plants evolved, so did pollinating insects such as bees. It was the start of a phenomenally successful partnership, which continues to the present day.

The Cretaceous landscape was also home to mammals, which had clung on to life throughout Jurassic times. Like their Jurassic forebears they were still small, and they avoided direct competition with reptiles by foraging for food at night. They included primitive marsupials, which raised their young in a pouch, as well as some

▷ With volcanoes erupting in the distance, Late Cretaceous plants bloom to attract pollinating insects. Volcanic activity was a feature of the Cretaceous Period, and average temperatures were much higher than they are today. Subtropical landscapes—like the one shown here—extended as far north as present-day New York City.

pocket-size placentals—species that grew their young inside their bodies, as most mammals do today. There were birds, but much more evident were pterosaurs—a sign that the reign of reptiles was still at its height. The Cretaceous also produced the largest, fastest, and most intelligent dinosaurs that the world had yet seen.

LATE ARRIVALS

By the beginning of the Cretaceous dinosaurs had a history dating back over 80 million years. During this long finale of the reptile age several new groups of dinosaurs came into being, and others rapidly expanded. They included the armored dinosaurs, the duck-billed dinosaurs, or hadrosaurs, and the titanosaurs—a group of southern sauropods that may have included the heaviest dinosaurs. Apart from these plant eaters, the Late Cretaceous also saw the arrival of the tyrannosaurs, a meat-eating family that included the largest land predators ever to have stalked the earth.

In the seas reptiles still held sway. They included plesiosaurs and ichthyosaurs, which had existed throughout the Jurassic, and a new group—the mosasaurs, giant marine lizards that became the dominant oceangoing reptiles as the Cretaceous neared its end. Turtles were common, having changed little in over 200 million years. They all shared the seas with fish known as teleosts. These fish had thinner and lighter scales than earlier fish, making them faster and more maneuverable.

END OF THE CRETACEOUS

If the Cretaceous world had continued, reptiles might still be the earth's dominant animals, and mammals might have died out. But 66 million years ago something happened that devastated life on land and in the sea, sweeping aside all of the dinosaurs and many other reptiles as well. Most experts now believe that this catastrophe was caused by an impact from outer space (page 204), but other factors—such as volcanic eruptions—may have already set the process in motion. In any event, with this multiple catastrophe the Mesozoic Era ended, and the great Age of Reptiles was over.

THE TERTIARY PERIOD

DINOSAUR GROUPS

Early in their evolution dinosaurs split into two groups: the ornithischians, or bird-hipped dinosaurs, and the saurischians, or lizard-hipped dinosaurs. As well as a different hip anatomy, these two groups developed other distinctive features and different ways of life. The ornithischians were plant eaters and walked either on four legs or on two. The saurischians included the plant-eating sauropods, which walked on all fours, and all the predatory dinosaurs, or theropods, which were almost entirely bipedal. Birds are actually descended from lizard-hipped dinosaurs, and they are the only members of the two troups alive today.

Bird-hipped dinosaur (ornithischian)

Lizard-hipped dinosaur (saurischian)

△ *In bird-hipped dinosaurs two hipbones—the ischium and pubis—pointed backward and were close together. In lizard-hipped dinosaurs the two bones pointed in different directions.*

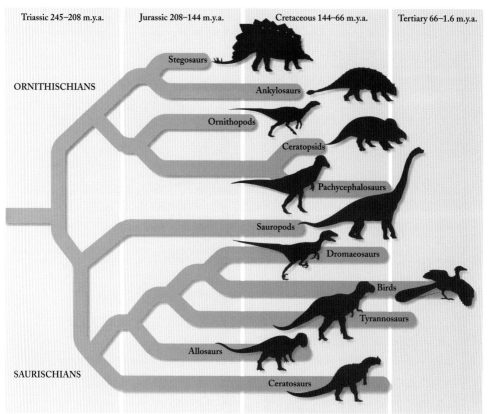

Triassic 245–208 m.y.a.   Jurassic 208–144 m.y.a.   Cretaceous 144–66 m.y.a.   Tertiary 66–1.6 m.y.a.

ORNITHISCHIANS

Stegosaurs
Ankylosaurs
Ornithopods
Ceratopsids
Pachycephalosaurs
Sauropods
Dromaeosaurs
Birds
Tyrannosaurs
Allosaurs
Ceratosaurs

SAURISCHIANS

PLANT-EATING GIANTS

With their gigantic necks and barrel-shaped bodies, the sauropods were the unrivaled giants of the dinosaur world. These slow-moving plant eaters evolved during the Jurassic Period, and over the next 50 million years they developed into the largest land animals the world has ever seen. Some of them tipped the scales at over 80 tons—close to the limit for any animal that moves on legs. There were several families of sauropods, including cetiosaurs, brachiosaurs, diplodocids, and titanosaurs, and they processed almost unbelievable amounts of plant food.

GIANTS AMONG GIANTS
A carnosaur, Ceratosaurus *(page 117), lurks menacingly on a hillside overlooking a herd of* Apatosaurus *(pages 80–81) as the gentle diplodocids munch their way through a forest. Diplodocids probably used their long, whiplike tails and their massive forelimbs to defend themselves against attack from such predatory carnosaurs.*

PLANT-EATING GIANTS

CETIOSAURS

Cetiosaurs were among the first sauropods, dating back to the Early Jurassic, and they were also the first to be discovered. Their huge bodies were supported by four pillarlike legs, and they had very small heads, but extremely long necks and tails. They grazed on trees and low-growing plants, swallowing their food whole, because like most plant-eating dinosaurs, they were not able to chew. The cetiosaur family shared a key characteristic—vertebrae that were almost solid. This feature is a primitive one, and as sauropods evolved their backbones became increasingly hollowed out as a way of saving weight.

OMEISAURUS

Identified in 1939, this Chinese cetiosaur was named after the mountain where its fossils were found. Fragments of most parts of its skeleton have been discovered, giving us a very good picture of what it looked like. *Omeisaurus* had a long neck, a small, wedge-shaped head, and a slightly forward-sloping gait, with its hips higher than its shoulders. Its tail was relatively short, although still huge by today's standards, and it may have had a clubbed tip, though this may not have been a feature of all species. Like all sauropods, *Omeisaurus* did not simply trail its tail on the ground. Instead, it probably held its tail almost horizontal when on the move, using it as a counterbalance or even as a weapon.

MAXIMUM LENGTH	50 ft. (15m)
TIME	Late Jurassic
FOSSIL FINDS	Asia (China)

CETIOSAURUS

The first fossils of *Cetiosaurus* were found in the early 1800s, several decades before the existence of dinosaurs became known. Its name, which means "whale lizard," was given to it in 1841—one of many examples of dinosaur remains being confused with those of other animals. It was originally thought to be some kind of giant marine reptile, until it was finally recognized as a dinosaur in 1869. *Cetiosaurus* was a massive animal, weighing up to 27 tons. It had a relatively short neck and tail, but its legs were impressive—its thighbones were nearly 6.5 ft. (2m) long. Its front and back legs appear to have been roughly the same length, which means that its back would have been almost level. This sets it apart from many later sauropods, which had front and back legs of distinctly different lengths. No traces of a skull have been found, so scientists do not know how it ate, but its teeth probably worked like a rake, allowing it to strip leaves off of trees and other plants.

MAXIMUM LENGTH	60 ft. (18m)
TIME	Mid to Late Jurassic
FOSSIL FINDS	Europe (England), Africa (Morocco)

◁ Omeisaurus *was almost certainly a herd-forming animal. Despite its size, it was vulnerable to predators and needed the protection that came from living in groups.*

CETIOSAURS

◁ *For many years* Cetiosaurus *was the largest land animal known to science. Since then many other sauropod fossils have been discovered. They show that, despite its great size,* Cetiosaurus *was actually a middleweight member of the sauropod group.*

BARAPASAURUS

This animal is the oldest sauropod discovered so far. Its exact classification is uncertain, but it was a massively built animal, equal to *Cetiosaurus* in size and weight or possibly even heavier. Six partial skeletons of *Barapasaurus* have been uncovered, as well as a number of less complete remains, but so far none includes skulls or feet. However, paleontologists have found fossilized teeth—spoon-shaped with serrated edges and ideal for tearing off leaves. *Barapasaurus* shows that sauropods were already very large animals near the beginning of the Jurassic. Some scientists classify this animal in a separate family of very primitive sauropods, called the vulcanodontids. The founding member of this family, called *Vulcanodon*, was found in Africa.

MAXIMUM LENGTH	60 ft. (18m)
TIME	Early Jurassic
FOSSIL FINDS	Asia (India)

SHUNOSAURUS

Compared to some cetiosaurs, this Chinese dinosaur is a recent discovery—the first fossil find dating back to 1977. Measuring just 33 ft. (10m) long, it was almost petite by sauropod standards and probably weighed no more than a fully grown female elephant. Another interesting feature is the tip of its tail. This ended in a bony club, which would have made a very effective weapon. A similar defense system appeared later in a different group of plant eaters—the ankylosaurs (page 164). Over 20 discoveries of almost complete *Shunosaurus* skeletons have been found, giving an unusually good picture of what this animal looked like. Compared to most sauropods, the nostrils were positioned low down on its muzzle, and it had relatively small teeth with elongated crowns.

MAXIMUM LENGTH	33 ft. (10m)
TIME	Mid Jurassic
FOSSIL FINDS	Asia (China)

HAPLOCANTHOSAURUS

Haplocanthosaurus is the most primitive sauropod that has been discovered in North America, with the first known fossils being unearthed about a century ago. It had a long neck and tail and showed similarities to the brachiosaurs (page 76) and the diplodocids (page 80). Establishing its exact place in classification is not easy, because as with many other cetiosaurs, no skull remains have been found. In evolutionary terms *Haplocanthosaurus* seems to have been something of a throwback. It lived toward the end of the Jurassic Period, a time when most other cetiosaurs had died out, and has been described as a living fossil of its time.

MAXIMUM LENGTH	73 ft. (22m)
TIME	Late Jurassic
FOSSIL FINDS	North America

▽ Barapasaurus *is the earliest known sauropod. Its weight may have been as much as 30 tons.*

△ *By flicking its tail like a whip,* Shunosaurus *would have been able to inflict a deadly blow with its tail club. The spikes in the club were extensions of the bones inside the tail.*

75

PLANT-EATING GIANTS

BRACHIOSAURS AND CAMARASAURS

◁ Brachiosaurus *was the dinosaur equivalent of the giraffe, but on a much larger scale. Its blood pressure was exceptionally high; this made sure oxygen reached its brain.*

The brachiosaurs were spectacularly long-necked sauropods, the camarasaurs were smaller, with shorter necks and tails. Although both groups were plant eaters, differences in their body shape and in the design of their teeth mean that they were unlikely to have eaten the same food. Brachiosaurs had remarkably long front legs, and their teeth were shaped like chisels. Camarasaurs looked more like other sauropods, but they had forward-pointing teeth set in an unusual bulldoglike snout.

▽ Brachiosaurus' *neck had a framework of 14 hollow but extremely strong vertebrae. Like the jib of a crane, it raised its head high into the treetops.*

BRACHIOSAURUS

As well as being one of the heaviest dinosaurs, with a weight of up to 80 tons, *Brachiosaurus* is the largest species to have had its skeleton assembled in a museum (page 161). Its front legs were much longer than its hind legs, and this, together with its long neck, allowed it to reach up to 53 ft. (16m), which is more than two and a half times as high as a giraffe. Its head was relatively small, with large, upward-facing nostrils that opened in a dome on top of its head. At one time, paleontologists thought that *Brachiosaurus'* nostrils showed that it fed in lakes. However, this is unlikely to be true, because its lungs would have collapsed if they were more than about 10 ft. underwater. Despite its huge size, *Brachiosaurus* may not have been the largest member of its family. In 1994 an American team unearthed fossils of a bigger animal, *Sauroposeidon*, which stood over 60 ft. (18m) tall.

MAXIMUM LENGTH	85 ft. (26m)
TIME	Mid to Late Jurassic
FOSSIL FINDS	North America, Africa, Europe (Portugal)

CAMARASAURUS

Weighing about 20 tons, *Camarasaurus* was much more compact than *Brachiosaurus*. Many fossils of this dinosaur have been found, including several complete skeletons, which, for a sauropod, makes this species almost unique. *Camarasaurus* would probably have lived in herds for protection, although like *Brachiosaurus*, it could have lashed out at its enemies with extra-long claws on its thumbs. *Camarasaurus* had large nostrils and may have had a keen sense of smell. Its boxlike head and the size of its nostrils have led some scientists to suggest that it had an elephantlike trunk. However, trunks are made entirely from soft tissue, which very rarely shows up in fossils. As a result this intriguing idea, which has been suggested for other sauropods, is very difficult to prove.

MAXIMUM LENGTH	60 ft. (18m)
TIME	Late Jurassic
FOSSIL FINDS	North America (U.S.A.), Europe (Portugal)

OPISTHOCOELICAUDIA

The only known skeleton of this sauropod, minus its head and neck, was found in 1965. As a result its exact appearance is still a matter of guesswork, and so is its place in the sauropod world. It had one highly distinctive feature: tail vertebrae that were hollowed out behind, rather than in front, which is the more normal pattern for sauropods. This arrangement would have made its tail unusually strong, allowing *Opisthocoelicaudia* to rear up on its hind legs, using its tail as a prop.

MAXIMUM LENGTH	16.5 ft. (5m)
TIME	Late Cretaceous
FOSSIL FINDS	Central Asia

EUHELOPUS

Smaller than *Camarasaurus* but similar in overall shape, *Euhelopus* would never have crossed paths with its American relative, because it lived in the Far East. Its neck was much longer, and its head was also longer and more pointed, although still with a steeply sloping front. *Euhelopus* had up to 19 neck vertebrae, unlike *Camarasaurus*, which had 12—one reason why it is sometimes classified in a separate family.

MAXIMUM LENGTH	50 ft. (15m)
TIME	Late Jurassic
FOSSIL FINDS	Asia (China)

▽ Camarasaurus *(top)* means "chambered lizard." It gets its name from the hollow chambers in its vertebrae, which kept it light for its size. Its neck was relatively short.

▽ Opisthocoelicaudia *(middle) may have been a camarasaur, but some paleontologists think it is more likely to have been a titanosaur (page 88).*

▽ Euhelopus *(bottom) probably weighed 15-20 tons. It had teeth all around its jaws. Many other sauropods had them only in the front.*

FEEDING ON PLANTS

ALTHOUGH THE EARLIEST DINOSAURS WERE HUNTERS, PLANT-EATING SPECIES STEADILY OUTNUMBERED THEM AS THE AGE OF REPTILES WORE ON. MANY COULD NOT CHEW—THEY SWALLOWED THEIR FOOD WHOLE.

These fossilized stones are gastroliths, or stomach stones, from a plant-eating dinosaur find. Dinosaurs swallowed these to help them grind their food—an important digestive aid for animals often lacking chewing teeth. The food would travel through the digestive system, but the stones, being heavier, stayed behind. Crocodiles, ostriches, and some other birds do the same thing today.

When the first plant-eating dinosaurs evolved, in the Late Triassic, there were no flowering plants, so there was no grass. Instead of grazing, like many of today's hooved mammals, early plant-eating dinosaurs fed on coniferous trees and other plants with tough foliage and tall trunks or stems. The same was true for most of the Jurassic Period, but during the Cretaceous flowering plants became widespread. They created a carpet of succulent, low-growing foliage, which made it easier to feed at or near ground level.

▷ *Ferns, cycads, and horsetails (left to right) were important foods for dinosaurs in the Jurassic.*

▽ *Magnolias were among the first flowering plants. Compared to other prehistoric plants, their leaves were juicy and nutritious.*

A CHANGING MENU

Plant-eating dinosaurs evolved in step with the vegetation around them. During the Triassic and Jurassic most had long necks to allow them to browse high off the ground. They may also have used their necks like horizontal booms so that they could crop wide areas of shorter plants, but many paleontologists doubt that this was common. There was probably not enough of this vegetation to make low-level feeding worthwhile. With the evolution of flowering plants, this began to change. For the first time there was plenty of plant food close to the ground, and because flowering plants tended to be faster-growing, they recovered quickly after being eaten. This new food supply was quite different from the plant cover of the past, and it probably explains why smaller ornithopods (pages 91–112) and armored dinosaurs (pages 151–168) became so widespread in Cretaceous times.

HOW SAUROPODS FED

Plant-eating mammals have two main types of teeth. The incisors, at the front of the jaw, bite off the food, and the molars, near the back, grind it. By comparison, sauropods— by far the largest plant-eating dinosaurs— had a much simpler arrangement. Their teeth formed a matching set, usually in the front of the jaw, and they could collect food, but could not chew it. A sauropod would swallow food whole, which was ground up in its stomach. The plant pulp was then broken down by microbes living in the animal's

▷ Apatosaurus' muscular stomach worked like a cement mixer. It churned up leaves, branches, and tough cones and broke them into small, easily digested pieces with the help of gastroliths.

stomach. Once the microbes had done their work, the dinosaur could absorb the nutrients released.

1   2   3   4   5

CHEWING TEETH

Ornithopods had a more mammalian way of eating. Many gathered their food using a toothless beak that formed the front of the jaw. They would then move the food to the back of their mouth, where it was sliced or ground up by a battery of specialized teeth. By the time the food arrived in the stomach, it was ready for microbes to break it down. Some bird-hipped dinosaurs had just a handful of teeth, but hadrosaurs (pages 104–107) often had hundreds.

△ Plant eaters' teeth were usually peglike, although some were flat. They all had an endless supply of teeth throughout their lives. From left to right, these teeth belonged to Heterodontosaurus (1), Plateosaurus (2), Diplodocus (3), Apatosaurus (4), and Stegosaurus (5).

▽ A fully grown Apatosaurus probably ate under half a ton of food a day—less than one-fiftieth of its body weight. It could survive on this meager diet because it was cold-blooded. Today's warm-blooded plant eaters need a much higher food intake.

79

PLANT-EATING DINOSAURS

DIPLODOCIDS

The diplodocids include the longest dinosaurs that are known from complete skeletons. *Diplodocus*, the best-known species, was up to 89 ft. (27m) long, but the partial remains of *Seismosaurus* (page 83) suggest that some diplodocids were even longer than this. If so, they may well have been the longest vertebrates ever to have existed on Earth. Diplodocids were built like living suspension bridges, with pillarlike legs, extraordinarily long necks, and even longer, narrow-tipped tails. Despite their great length, they were not as heavy as many other sauropods, because their skeletons were shaped to save weight. They had elongated heads, large nostrils located on top near their eyes, and unusually small, rodlike teeth.

DIPLODOCUS
Diplodocus means "double beam"—a name that describes this dinosaur's tail. Beneath each of its tail vertebra was a length of bone that ran the length of the tail, stengthening it and protecting the blood vessels inside it. It could lash out with the tip of its tail if it came under attack. *Diplodocus'* remarkable length has led to many questions about how it moved and ate. Some scientists believe that it would have moved with its head held almost horizontal in front and its tail in a similar position at the rear. It is also likely that it could raise itself on its hind legs and lift its head high up into the trees to eat. Like its relatives, *Diplodocus* had teeth only in the front of its mouth.

Apatosaurus

Diplodocus

▷ *The first fossil of* Apatosaurus—*without the skull—was found in 1877, but the first complete skeleton of this dinosaur was not assembled until 1975.*

▷ Diplodocus *had slender teeth that worked like a comb, gathering in the soft parts of plants. It may have fed on low-growing vegetation as well as trees.*

MAXIMUM LENGTH	88.6 ft. (27m)
TIME	Late Jurassic
FOSSIL FINDS	North America (western U.S.A.)

Dicraeosaurus

▷ Dicraeosaurus *was smaller than most diplodocids and probably fed on low-growing plants. Unlike its later relatives, it did not have a whiplike tip to its tail.*

DIPLODOCIDS

▽ Mamenchisaurus' *neck accounted for half the entire length of its body. It had 19 neck vertebrae. When stretched, they made the neck extra-long.*

Mamenchisaurus

▷ Barosaurus' *thighbone measured up to 8 ft. (2.5m)— taller than an adult man. Its back legs and tail may have acted like a tripod, allowing it to reach high into the trees.*

Barosaurus

APATOSAURUS

Once also known as *Brontosaurus*, *Apatosaurus* was slightly smaller than *Diplodocus* but at 30 tons much more heavily built. As with *Diplodocus* uncertainty surrounds exactly how it lived. For many years scientists have assumed that it could rear up on its hind legs to eat, using its tail as a prop. But some recent research suggests that its neck might have been surprisingly inflexible, so that when it was on all fours, it could raise its head no more than 16.4 ft. (5m) above the ground. *Apatosaurus* probably defended itself by using its tail and the sharp toe claw on each of its front feet. *Apatosaurus* bones have been found with *Allosaurus* teeth marks, but it is not possible to tell whether these giant plant eaters had been attacked while alive or scavenged when already dead.

| MAXIMUM LENGTH 82 ft. (25m) |
| TIME Late Jurassic |
| FOSSIL FINDS North America (western U.S.A.) |

DICRAEOSAURUS

Dicraeosaurus was a relatively compact diplodocid, and one of the earliest members of the family. Compared to later forms, it had a short neck and tail and a comparatively large head. Its vertebrae also show some peculiarities, with unusual Y-shaped spikes running along the length of the backbone and into the neck. These may have channeled supporting ligaments and would have formed a clearly visible ridge along its spine.

| MAXIMUM LENGTH 46 ft. (14m) |
| TIME Late Jurassic |
| FOSSIL FINDS Africa (Tanzania) |

MAMENCHISAURUS

Until the discovery of *Sauroposeidon* in 1994 (page 82), *Mamenchisaurus* held the record for neck length of a dinosaur— an astounding 46 ft. (14m). This cranelike neck may have been used horizontally as much as vertically, allowing *Mamenchisaurus* to reach for plants growing on marshy ground or in dense thickets, while the rest of its body was safely distanced. When this dinosaur was on the move, it probably held its head directly in front of its body, so that its neck was roughly level. Its neck vertebrae were unusually light and thin, with interconnecting rodlike ribs for strength. Its neck was not very flexible and bent mainly at the head and shoulders, rather than in between. Some paleontologists think that *Mamenchisaurus* is so unusual that it should be classified in a family of its own.

| MAXIMUM LENGTH 82 ft. (25m) |
| TIME Late Jurassic |
| FOSSIL FINDS Asia (China) |

BAROSAURUS

Barosaurus, which means "heavy lizard," was a huge diplodocid, weighing perhaps as much as 40 tons. Similar in form and structure to *Diplodocus*, but with particularly elongated neck vertebrae, it would have used size as its main defense. Like some of its relatives, *Barosaurus'* center of gravity was far back down its body, a feature that would have helped it if it reared up on its back legs to feed from trees. Judging from fossil finds in Africa and North America, this dinosaur was one of the most widespread members of the diplodocid family.

| MAXIMUM LENGTH 88.6 ft. (27m) |
| TIME Late Jurassic |
| FOSSIL FINDS North America (U.S.A.), Africa (Tanzania) |

PLANT-EATING GIANTS

▷ Giant sauropods like
Supersaurus *(on the*
left) had very similar
body structures, even
though on a gigantic
scale. The exact size and
weight of these enormous
plant eaters is uncertain
because no complete
fossils have been found
yet. Other contenders
for the title of largest
dinosaur ever include
Argentinosaurus
(page 88) and a colossal
brachiosaur called
Sauroposeidon, *whose*
remains were found in
the grounds of a prison
in Oklahoma in 1994.

AMARGASAURUS

An almost complete skeleton of
Amargasaurus was discovered in Argentinian
Patagonia in 1984. It revealed that this
diplodocid had a highly unusual row of
vertebral spines, up to 25.6 in. (65cm) long,
running along the back of its neck. These
may have formed a spiky mane, or they
may have been covered in skin, creating
a structure like a double sail. Whichever
form they took, they were a remarkable
feature and may have played a part in the
animal's social life, or they may have been
used in defense—a valuable plus for an
animal that was under half the length of
many of its larger cousins. *Amargasaurus*
also had a slender, whiplike tail and blunt
teeth shaped for stripping foliage from
branches. Like other sauropods, it
probably swallowed stones or gastroliths
(page 78) to help it break down its food.
With its spiky vertebrae, *Amargasaurus*
is similar to *Dicraeosaurus* (page 81), and
some paleontologists classify these two
dinosaurs in a family of their own.

MAXIMUM LENGTH 39.4 ft. (12m)

TIME Early Cretaceous

FOSSIL FINDS South America (Argentina)

SUPERSAURUS

A giant among giants, *Supersaurus* has
the distinction of being one of the largest
land animals ever to have walked the earth.
The first fossils were discovered in 1972 in
Dry Mesa Quarry, Colorado—a site that
has produced some of the most spectacular
sauropod finds in the world. The *Supersaurus*
remains were far from complete, but they
included shoulder blades 7.9 ft. (2.4m) long
and nearly 3.3 ft. (1m) wide—enough room
for two people to lie on, with plenty of
legroom to spare. From remains like these
paleontologists estimate that *Supersaurus*
might have weighed as much as 50 tons.
With its head held high, it would have
towered 50 ft. (15m) above the ground—
higher than the average house. *Supersaurus'*
tremendous weight was supported
by four pillar-shaped legs, the
hind legs being longer
than the front ones.

DIPLODOCIDS

Like other diplodocids, it had elephant-like feet with five toes and a large claw on each front thumb. The claws may have been used as defensive weapons, although its huge tail would have been a more substantial deterrent. Analysis of its fossilized tracks show that it moved slowly—as would be expected for an animal of such size.

MAXIMUM LENGTH	125 ft. (42m)
TIME	Late Jurassic
FOSSIL FINDS	North America (Colorado)

ULTRASAUROS

There are doubts about whether *Ultrasauros* is truly a separate species of dinosaur or whether its remains are actually a mixture from two other dinosaurs—*Supersaurus* and *Brachiosaurus*. The first of these remains, which were found in 1979, came from the same quarry that produced *Supersaurus*, and they include bones that show *Ultrasauros* would have stood about 26.2 ft. (8m) tall at the shoulder, over two times the height of an average man.

Ultrasauros gets its unusual spelling because scientific names can never be used twice for different animals. It was originally called *Ultrasaurus*, but had to be renamed because the name *Ultrasaurus* had already been used two years earlier for a smaller sauropod found in South Korea.

MAXIMUM LENGTH	100 ft. (30m)
TIME	Late Jurassic
FOSSIL FINDS	North America (Colorado)

SEISMOSAURUS

Known from remains discovered in 1979, *Seismosaurus*, meaning "earthquake lizard," was built on a massive scale. Some estimates put its total length at up to 165 ft. (50m), although 131 ft. (40m) is probably more likely. However, with a weight of perhaps 30 tons, or more than double that according to some calculations, it would have more than lived up to its name. Like other diplodocids, it had extra bones beneath its spine to help support its neck and tail. Its tail had the standard diplodocid whiplike tip, but it also seems to have had a kink—a feature that has not yet been explained. In comparison with the rest of its body its head was tiny—a characteristic feature of sauropods as a whole. Stomach stones, or gastroliths, have been found among *Seismosaurus'* fossilized remains, indicating that it lived on a diet of tough plants that needed to be ground down before they could be digested. The only known fossil of this dinosaur has still not been fully excavated because it lies deeply buried in sandstone. The latest technology—including ground-penetrating radar—has been used to pinpoint the fossilized bones that still remain hidden beneath the surface.

MAXIMUM LENGTH	Up to 165 ft. (50m)
TIME	Late Jurassic
FOSSIL FINDS	North America (New Mexico)

◁ *This reconstruction of* Ultrasauros *(center) is very much an artist's impression because only partial remains of this animal have been found, and they may not even belong to the same animal. If* Ultrasauros *really did exist, its weight might have been well over 50 tons.*

◁ *The only known remains of* Seismosaurus *(on the right) were found when two hikers literally stumbled on the tip of its fossilized tail. When paleontologists began to excavate, the remains they found turned out to be among the largest discovered so far. The fossils show that* Seismosaurus *was a typical diplodocid, but one built on an extra-large scale.*

A QUESTION OF SIZE

HOW HEAVY WERE THE LARGEST DINOSAURS?
WHY DID THEY GROW TO SUCH ENORMOUS
SIZES? QUESTIONS LIKE THESE ARE EASY
TO ASK, BUT AS PALEONTOLOGISTS HAVE
DISCOVERED, NOT SO EASY TO ANSWER.

Sauropod dinosaurs were without doubt the largest land animals that have ever lived on Earth, weighing perhaps 15 times as much as any four-legged animal alive today. For biologists and for engineers, these giant plant eaters exert a powerful fascination, because they probably reached the physical proportions that limit animal size. Enormous dimensions must have brought advantages, or these giants would not have evolved, but they would also have created a range of practical problems—ones that evolution had to overcome.

WHY BE LARGE?

There are several reasons why gigantism may have evolved in plant-eating dinosaurs. One is that plant digestion works best on a large scale. Like today's plant eaters, sauropods relied on microbes to break down their food, and the microbes released heat as they worked. This heat helped speed up the process of digestion, and the larger the dinosaur's stomach, the more heat it would have generated. In relative terms giant dinosaurs needed less food for each ton of body weight, as they used proportionately less in moving around and staying alive.

Being gigantic is also a useful defense against predators once an animal has safely come through its early years and reached adult size. This explains why a number of

△ *American scientist Robert Bakker stands behind an* Apatosaurus *femur. Sauropod femurs are the largest single dinosaur bones.*

These sauropod bones are part of an immense collection at Dinosaur National Monument, on the border of Colorado and Utah. Giant leg bones, like the ones shown in the foreground, have been used to estimate the weight of the heaviest dinosaurs, including plant eaters and their predators. These estimates are made by measuring the bones' cross-sectional area at their narrowest point.

plant eaters, from horses to elephants, have grown larger during their evolutionary history. Unfortunately (from a plant eater's point of view), predators can also increase in size. During the dinosaur age the trend toward increasing size in plant eaters was mirrored by a similar trend in carnivores. This meant natural selection favored even larger plant eaters, and the process went on.

REACHING THE TOP

The bigger-is-better trend could not continue indefinitely, because the problems of being gigantic eventually started to outweigh the benefits. One of these problems was the difficulty of pumping blood to a head that towered many feet above the ground. *Brachiosaurus* and other long-necked sauropods would have needed powerful hearts, even if they did have tiny brains. Animals like these would also have faced increasing difficulties mating and laying eggs—a major consideration because producing plenty of young is the key to evolutionary success. But from an engineering standpoint a more fundamental problem concerned their weight: as they evolved larger and larger bodies, this climbed at a prodigious rate.

To visualize how this happened, imagine three dinosaurs shaped like cubes with sides 3 ft. (1m), 15 ft. (5m), and 30 ft. (10m) long. The second dinosaur is only five times as long as the first, but its weight is 125 times as great (the result of multiplying 5x5x5). The third dinosaur is 10 times as long, which means that it weighs a thousand times as much as the first. Once sauropods reached lengths of about 60 ft. (20m), each additional three feet meant a jump in weight of over a ton—a tremendous burden that still had to be supported by just four legs.

The strength of a leg depends on its cross-sectional area, rather than its volume. This means that if an animal gets larger but keeps the same overall shape, its weight outstrips its strength, so its legs are put under greater and greater stress. Sauropods coped with this by modifying their leg bones and by keeping bending to a minimum, but in the end it would have been weight, rather than anything else, that brought their growth to a halt.

WEIGHING A DINOSAUR

Leg dimensions are a useful way of weighing sauropods, even though these animals have been dead for millions of years. By measuring the cross-sectional area of a major leg bone, paleontologists can calculate the total weight of the living animal. Another method consists of making scale models: the model's volume is measured by putting it in water, and this figure is scaled up to calculate the final weight. But neither of these methods is 100 percent reliable. As a result the true weight of the world's heaviest dinosaurs will probably never be known.

▷ *Seen next to a* Brachiosaurus, Troodon *looks in danger of being squashed.* Brachiosaurus *may have weighed up to 80 tons—about 2,500 times as much as* Troodon *and about 80,000 times as much as* Saltopus, *the smallest dinosaur known.*

FOSSIL HUNTING IN SOUTH AMERICA

SOUTH AMERICA HAS PRODUCED SOME OF THE EARLIEST FOSSIL DINOSAURS, AND ALSO THE LARGEST, AS WELL AS SOME REMARKABLE EXTINCT MAMMALS AND BIRDS FROM MORE RECENT TIMES.

The geological history of South America makes it a fascinating place. Until the middle of the Mesozoic Era it was part of the great southern continent, Gondwana, which means that it shared many of the dinosaur families found in today's Africa and India. After the dinosaurs died out South America became an island, before joining with North America in much more recent times.

IN PATAGONIA

▽ *Rodolfo Coria—the scientist who unearthed* Argentiosaurus—*rests on one of the dinosaur's enormous spinal vertebrae.*

Over 160 years ago the renowned English naturalist Charles Darwin visited South America during his historic voyage on HMS *Beagle*. On this around-the-world expedition, he found fossils of extinct mammals such as the giant ground sloth *Megatherium*—an animal almost as large as an elephant—which was buried in gravel near the shore. The first fossil *Megatherium* had been seen by European scientists 50 years before, but for Darwin the process of uncovering its remains was momentous. It helped him appreciate the fact that extinction was a natural process—something that contributed to his theory of evolution.

Paleontologists still comb the

FOSSIL EVIDENCE

This fossilized skull, found in Ischigualasto National Park, Argentina, belonged to one of the earliest known dinosaurs, Eoraptor, *a bipedal hunter just 3.3 ft. (1m) long. Although it lived over 200 million years ago, several almost complete skeletons have been found. In outward appearance, this small reptile was remarkably similar to some predatory dinosaurs that lived 100 million years later.*

bleak Patagonian coastline, collecting fossils from the crumbling sedimentary rocks. But some of the most important discoveries have been found much farther inland, along the foothills that separate Argentina from neighboring Chile. This is South America's dinosaur country—a dry and dramatic part of the world where much older rocks bring a wealth of remains to the surface.

THE HUNT FOR EARLY DINOSAURS

From the late 1950s onward the moonlike surroundings of Argentina's Ischigualasto National Park have been the scene of some major dinosaur discoveries. In 1958 a local farmer found the first fragments of a small, meat-eating animal that lived during the Late Triassic, making it the earliest dinosaur then known. Named *Herrerasaurus*, it shed new light on how dinosaurs might have originated from carnivorous reptiles (page 64). In 1988 American paleontologist Paul Sereno found further remains—a complete *Herrerasaurus* skull and several partial skeletons. In 1991 he identified the remains of an even older animal, called *Eoraptor*, which provided clues to how dinosaurs might have evolved.

Since South America was part of Gondwana when these animals were alive, it is unlikely that they lived only in this part of the world. But bare ground makes fossil hunting easier, which is why Ischigualasto is one of South America's foremost fossil hunting sites.

SOUTHERN GIANTS

South America is well known as a source of fossil sauropods—particularly titanosaurs, which were widespread in the southern continents. The list of species discovered in Argentina reads almost like a road map, because many of them, such as *Saltasaurus* and *Neuquensaurus*, take their names from the provinces where their fossil remains were found. But pride of place among these giants goes to *Argentinosaurus*, an animal named by two leading paleontologists, José F. Bonaparte and Rodolfo Coria, in 1993. *Argentinosaurus* may prove to be the world's largest dinosaur, although in North America there are several other contenders.

Rodolfo Coria also identified a giant predator, *Giganotosaurus*, whose remains were spotted in 1994 by an amateur fossil hunter in the foothills of the Andes. Weighing up to 8 tons, this tyrannosaur look-alike might have been the world's largest carnivorous dinosaur. Like *Argentinosaurus*, it lived throughout the Late Cretaceous, until the Age of Reptiles came to an end. So the world's largest plant eater and meat eater may have lived at the same time, and also in the same place—a double first!

FLYING GIANTS

In Argentina paleontologists have also found the remains of some enormous birds. Several of these were flightless, but one, *Argentavis magnificens*, may well have been the largest ever to have existed. Discovered in 1979 in the dusty pampas west of Buenos Aires, this animal had a wingspan of about 24.6 ft. (7.5m), which is more than twice the size of the largest flying

△ *A team of excavators including Rodolfo Coria (center) works at the Plaza Huincul site in Argentina, uncovering the enormous fossil bones of* Argentinosaurus huinculensis.

birds today. *Argentavis* lived about 6 million years ago, and it belonged to a group of vulturelike birds called the teratorns, which later became extinct. It probably hunted living prey, using its large, hooked beak to make its kills. So did the phorusrhacoids, or terror birds—a line of flightless South American predators that stood up to 10 ft. (3m) high. Fossils suggest that these fearsome animals ran down their prey before using their beaks to rip it apart. Remains of over two dozen species have been found, but as with the teratorns, the entire group eventually disappeared.

◁ *In the far west of Argentina the stark landscape of Ischigualasto National Park, with its strangely sculpted cliffs and plateaus, is a magnet for paleontologists. Conditions can be tough: in the summer the heat is stifling, and the layers of pale claylike rock give off an intense glare in the bright sunshine.*

◁ *Unlike earlier reptiles,* Eoraptor *had fused vertebrae in its hip region. This gave it the extra structural strength needed to maintain an upright posture, with just two legs in contact with the ground.*

PLANT-EATING GIANTS

TITANOSAURS

Titanosaurs were the last sauropods to evolve, appearing in the Late Jurassic and surviving some 80 million years until the end of the Cretaceous. They were found across most of the world, but they were most widespread in the ancient southern continent of Gondwana. South America—which formed part of Gondwana—is where most of their remains have been discovered. They bore some resemblance to diplodocids, but were unique among sauropods in having bony armor, which consisted of hard plates scattered over their backs. Their other claim to fame is that a few grew to a truly incredible size. Remains of one as yet unclassified sauropod were found in southern Patagonia in 1999. The fossils included two vertebrae measuring 4 ft. (1.2m) in height and a thighbone 6 ft. (1.8m) long!

▽ *A titan among titans,* Argentinosaurus *may have been the largest dinosaur ever to have walked the earth—even if at a slow pace. As an adult this gigantic animal probably would have been immune from attack by most predators, but its young would still have been vulnerable. Here an adult is shown without armor-plating—whether it had plates is not known.*

ARGENTINOSAURUS
Argentina has produced some exciting fossil finds in recent years, and many paleontologists believe that this species—named in 1993—may turn out to be the largest dinosaur ever, although not the longest. So far only a few vertebrae and limb bones have been found, but they are built on an awe-inspiring scale. The biggest of the vertebrae measures 5 ft. (1.5m) in height, with a load-bearing center the size of a small tree. Scaling up from remains like these, experts estimate that the complete animal may have weighed in the range of 80 to 100 tons. Like other titanosaurs, *Argentinosaurus* had some unusual anatomical features not found in other sauropods. It had an extra vertebra in its sacrum—the part of the backbone that joins to the pelvic girdle. If it was like its relatives, its tail vertebrae would have been linked together with ball-and-socket joints. No traces of armor plating have actually been found, but as these plates are often scattered after death, it is still possible that *Argentinosaurus* shared this common family feature. With so little fossil evidence it is hard to say how this immense animal lived, although given its size, it would probably have needed to eat several tons of food a day.

MAXIMUM LENGTH 100 ft. (30m)
TIME Late Cretaceous
FOSSIL FINDS South America (Argentina)

ANTARCTOSAURUS
Despite its name, remains of this dinosaur have not been found in the Antarctic, but they have been discovered in South America and India, which once formed part of the great southern continent of Gondwana. None of these fossils is complete, but—unusually for a titanosaur—they include parts of the skull. From these finds *Antarctosaurus* seems to have been one of the largest and most widespread dinosaurs in the Southern Hemisphere. It had a square-ended lower jaw and small teeth, but so far no traces of armor-plating have been unearthed. In South America fossilized eggs have been found that are likely to have belonged either to this species, or to other members of the titanosaur family. About the size of small melons, some of them contain the fossilized embryos complete with impressions of skin.

MAXIMUM LENGTH 59 ft. (18m)
TIME Late Cretaceous
FOSSIL FINDS South America (Argentina, Brazil, Chile, Uruguay), Asia (India)

△ *An adult,* Antarctosaurus *probably weighed more than 35 tons. Like several of its relatives, it is believed to have had a covering of bony plates, or osteoderms.*

SALTASAURUS

Saltasaurus was officially named in 1980 after the province in Argentina where it was found. Compared to *Argentinosaurus*, it was a relatively small animal, with a back not much higher than an elephant's, although with a much longer and heavier body overall. Several fossilized skeletons have been found with thousands of small, bony plates lying around them, leading paleontologists to conclude that these plates would have covered the skin like armor. Some of the plates are no larger than peas and are attached to small relics of skin.

Others are about the size of a human hand and may have had a defensive spike. This discovery solved a long-running puzzle, because scattered plates have been uncovered before *Saltasaurus* fossils were found. Some scientists thought they belonged to nodosaurs (page 164), a group of unrelated dinosaurs that used armor for protection. *Saltasaurus* had robust limbs and a flexible tail, which may have helped it sit upright to feed. Remains of *Antarctosaurus* and *Argyrosaurus* have been found close to *Saltasaurus* fossils, raising the possibility that they, too, would have had armor-plated skin.

△ Saltasaurus *(center right), with its bony body armor, which would have protected it from predators, was a compact and stocky titanosaur with a small head and blunt teeth.*

MAXIMUM LENGTH 40 ft. (12m)

TIME Late Cretaceous

FOSSIL FINDS South America (Argentina, Uruguay)

NEUQUENSAURUS

Named after a town in Patagonia, this dinosaur closely resembled *Saltasaurus*, with a relatively small body covered in bony plates. The evidence for this comes from several fossil finds, including vertebrae, limb bones, and plates that were found in 1997. The similarities between the two dinosaurs seem to be very strong, and it is possible that future finds may show that they were actually the same dinosaur.

MAXIMUM LENGTH 50 ft. (15m)

TIME Late Cretaceous

FOSSIL FINDS South America (Argentina)

ARGYROSAURUS

The first remains of *Argyrosaurus* were discovered in the late 1800s. Its name means "silver lizard"—a reference to Argentina, or the "land of silver," which is where its fossils have been found. A massive animal, weighing as much as 80 tons, *Argyrosaurus* is known from only a few body parts, including the legs and some vertebrae. Paleontologists do not agree about where this animal fits into the titanosaur family— some think that the fossils may actually belong to *Antarctosaurus*.

MAXIMUM LENGTH 59 ft. (18m)

TIME Late Cretaceous

FOSSIL FINDS South America (Argentina)

HYPSELOSAURUS

Hypselosaurus was a relatively compact European titanosaur first identified from fossils in southern France nearly 150 years ago. The fossils were missing their skulls, but alongside them were several dozen basketball-sized eggs. These eggs were almost certainly laid by a *Hypselosaurus* and, at about 1 ft. (30cm) long, they are some of the largest dinosaur eggs currently known. Sauropods probably squatted down when they were ready to lay their eggs, but they may also have had an egg-laying tube that allowed the eggs to slide gently down to the ground.

MAXIMUM LENGTH 40 ft. (12m)

TIME Late Cretaceous

FOSSIL FINDS Europe (France, Spain)

PLANT-EATING GIANTS

MALAWISAURUS

Originally known as *Gigantosaurus*—
a name easily confused with *Giganotosaurus*
(page 143), a meat-eating allosaur—
Malawisaurus, is the oldest-known titanosaur
from Africa, dating back over 100 million
years. Relatively small by titanosaur standards,
it may have been armor-plated, but fossilized
plates have yet to be found. However, some
Malawisaurus fossils do include parts of the
animal's skull—rare for a titanosaur and for
sauropods as a whole. Titanosaur remains
have been found recently in nearby
Madagascar. Fortunately, these fossilized
remains also include parts of the skull.

MAXIMUM LENGTH   33 ft. **(**10m)

TIME   Early Cretaceous

FOSSIL FINDS   Africa (Malawi)

TITANOSAURUS

The most widespread member of its family,
Titanosaurus was first discovered in 1877
in India. The original fossil consisted of a
broken thighbone and some tail vertebrae,
but since then further finds have been
made in many places around the world,
including Madagascar. The Indian find
was particularly important, because it was
the first major dinosaur discovery in what
was once part of Gondwana, although
continental drift was not known about at
the time. Some paleontologists think that
Titanosaurus had armor-plating, but there
is not strong enough evidence of this.

MAXIMUM LENGTH   65.6 ft. (20m)

TIME   Late Cretaceous

FOSSIL FINDS   South America (Argentina),
Europe (France), Asia (India),
Africa (Madagascar)

ALAMOSAURUS

Alamosaurus is the only titanosaur found
in North America. It was also one of the
last sauropods, surviving until the end of
the Cretaceous Period when it—and all
other dinosaurs—died out. Found in the
western United States, its remains are more
complete than those of most of its relatives,
although they are missing the skull.

Alamosaurus weighed about 30 tons,
and had a long, whip-ended tail. Unlike
many other titanosaurs, it seems to have
had no body armor. Even when it was
alive, *Alamosaurus* would have looked like
a relic from the past, because by the Late
Cretaceous Period sauropods were no longer
the dominant plant eaters and had dwindled
to a fraction of the importance they had
had in Jurassic times. *Alamosaurus'* status as
North America's sole titanosaur is probably
explained by geological changes. For
millions of years North and South America
were separated by sea, but during the Late
Cretaceous temporary land bridges linked
the two continents. *Alamosaurus*—or its
ancestors—took this opportunity to head
north, but its history was cut short when
the Age of Dinosaurs came to an end.

MAXIMUM LENGTH   69 ft. (21m)

TIME   Late Cretaceous

FOSSIL FINDS   North America (Montana,
New Mexico, Texas, Utah)

▽ Alamosaurus *lived
in North America in
the dying days of the
dinosaurs. It was named
after the Ojo Alamo
trading post in New
Mexico, where a set
of its remains
was found.*

ORNITHOPODS

The ornithopods were a group of ornithischian, or bird-hipped, plant eaters that first appeared early in the Jurassic, about 200 million years ago. They included the iguanodonts—some of the first dinosaurs to be discovered—as well as the hadrosaurs, a remarkable family of reptiles often adorned with bizarre crests. Together with the fabrosaurs, heterodontosaurs, and hypsilophodonts, these animals included some of the most successful and numerous plant eaters during the Cretaceous. Ornithopods never equaled sauropods in size, but they were abundant when sauropods themselves were in decline.

DANGER ON THE HORIZON

Making their daily visit to a sandy riverbed, a mixed group of hadrosaurs—including mothers with their young—pause to drink and rest in the morning sunshine. But this tranquil scene is not destined to last. A tyrannosaur has appeared on a distant sandbank, and some of the adult hadrosaurs are getting ready to run. The hadrosaurs could call to each other using their hollow crests, to warn of the impending danger. (See key on page 94.)

DANGER ON THE HORIZON

1. **CORYTHOSAURUS (MALE)**
2. **LAMBEOSAURUS (MALE)**
3. **CORYTHOSAURUS (FEMALE)**
4. **CORYTHOSAURUS (JUVENILE)**
5. **TYRANNOSAURUS**
6. **PARASAUROLOPHUS**
   (FEMALE WITH YOUNG)
7. **PARASAUROLOPHUS (MALE)**

LIFE IN A GROUP

FOR PLANT-EATING DINOSAURS, LIVING IN
HERDS WAS A VITAL SURVIVAL TECHNIQUE IN
A WORLD FULL OF DANGEROUS PREDATORS.

Millions of years after the dinosaurs died out, there is still plenty of evidence showing that some of them lived in herds. This includes fossilized mass graves, where entire herds were overtaken by disasters such as sandstorms, as well as communal nesting sites and sets of tracks left by herds on the move.

HERD SIZES

How large were dinosaur herds? Fossilized bones and tracks provide the best clues, but they have to be interpreted with care. Animals can be at the same place at the same time without forming a herd. This often happens at waterholes, when animals that normally live on their own gather to drink. Collections of bones can also be misleading, because they may belong to animals that died weeks or even years apart. This can happen when they are the victims of the same hazard—a slippery slope— or when hunters use a favorite spot for attacking their prey.

   Paleontologists have examined many sets of fossils and come up with a variety of figures for different species. There are records of iguanodonts traveling in groups of four or five; hadrosaurs such as *Maiasaura* seem to have lived in herds of several hundred, scattered over a wide area.

DINOSAUR SOCIAL LIFE

Herd-forming species almost certainly showed complex forms of behavior. As with today's herding mammals, animals of different ages and sexes would have had different statuses, and often a different position in the herd. Some fossilized tracks back up this idea, because the smallest prints —belonging to young animals—are often found in the center, and those left by the largest adults are at the front and around the sides. This would have protected the young

and allowed the adults to form
a barrier if a predator did try to attack.

JOINING AND LEAVING
Animals grow up and die, so the makeup
of a herd changes all the time. But herds
can change in other ways. In many of today's
herding animals, such as elephants, males
leave the herd once they can look after
themselves and live in bachelor herds for
several years. The strongest adult males then
head herds of their own, which include several
females and young. It is likely that some
dinosaurs had similar social systems. During
their time in bachelor herds the males would
have engaged in mock fights with their rivals.
This kind of fighting is unlikely to have
caused permanent injuries, but it would have

separated out the strongest and fittest males,
allowing them to father the most young.

INDIVIDUAL RECOGNITION
Dinosaur fossils often show variations
between members of the same species. The
most obvious differences are between males
and females, but there are also differences
between one individual and another. These
small variations may have worked like
identity badges, helping herd members
identify each other. Because dinosaurs were
often long-lived, older animals could have
decades of experience in recognizing the
other members of their herd. Each animal
would have known where it fit in the herd's
pecking order and where its place was
if the herd came under attack.

▽ *Threatened by a pair
of tyrannosaurs, adult*
Centrosaurus *form a
defensive ring around
their young. In this kind
of emergency the young
animals would have
instinctively rushed for the
middle of the ring, while
the adults turned their
horns on the aggressors.
The disadvantage of
the ring defense was
that the entire herd
was effectively trapped—
until the predators either
abandoned their attack
or made a kill.*

ORNITHOPODS

HYPSILOPHODONTS

The hypsilophodonts were the dinosaur world's equivalent of horses and antelopes, living in large herds, and feeding on low growing plants. Like other ornithopods, they had a short, beaklike muzzle, muscular cheeks, and well-developed chewing teeth. Their cheeks were an important step forward, because they helped them hold their food in place to chew. Hypsilophodonts were fairly small animals, but during their 100-million-year history they became widespread and were eventually found on almost every continent, including Australia.

▽ Hypsilophodon
(left) gets its name from its tall, ridged cheek teeth. The upper and lower sets met to form a perfect grinding surface, and they were self-sharpening—features that were shared by all members of the family. Dryosaurus (right) used its beak to tear up mouthfuls of vegetation. While it was chewing it would probably have raised its head so that it could watch for danger—a kind of behavior seen in most of today's plant eaters that live in open habitats.

DRYOSAURUS
Dryosaurus was a medium-sized member of the family and one of the earliest to evolve. Its body was supported by a pair of sturdy legs, with a stiff, heavy tail that acted as a counterbalance for its head and neck and its large plant eater's stomach. Its muzzle ended in a hard-edged beak, which could tear off plants close to the ground. Like other ornithopods, it had few defenses, and it is likely to have been an effective middle-distance runner. Unusually for a hypsilophodont, its feet had only three toes.

MAXIMUM LENGTH 13 ft. (4m)

TIME Late Jurassic

FOSSIL FINDS Africa (Tanzania), North America (Colorado, Wyoming)

HYPSILOPHODON
Less than 3.3 ft. (1m) tall and with a head no larger than a human hand, *Hypsilophodon* is known from some superbly preserved fossils. They include a group of about two dozen animals discovered on England's Isle of Wight, which may have been members of

a small herd trapped by a rising tide. These fossils show that it had five-fingered hands and four-toed feet, and perhaps a double row of bony plates running down its back. During the 1800s, when *Hypsilophodon* was first discovered, British zoologist Thomas Huxley suggested it was shaped for climbing and might have lived in trees like today's tree kangaroo. Paleontologists now think that it is likely to have lived on the ground.

MAXIMUM LENGTH 7.5 ft. (2.3m)

TIME Early Cretaceous

FOSSIL FINDS Europe (Portugal, Spain, U.K.), North America (South Dakota)

HYPSILOPHODONTS

LEAELLYNASAURA

Studies of this Australian hypsilophodont have provided support for the idea that some dinosaurs were warm-blooded (page 148). Its fossilized remains were found at a site on the Southern coast of Australia, known as Dinosaur Cove, well within the Antarctic Circle when *Leaellynasaura* was alive. Although the climate was significantly

FULGUROTHERIUM

This dinosaur was named after Lightning Ridge in New South Wales, Australia, a well-known opal mining area and dinosaur fossil site where incomplete remains—a skull, a thighbone, and teeth—were found in 1932.

MAXIMUM LENGTH 6.6 ft. (2m)

TIME Early Cretaceous

FOSSIL FINDS Australia (New South Wales)

△ *Weighing as little as 22 lbs. (10kg), Leaellynasaura (left) was about the size of an ostrich. If it was warm-blooded, it may have had featherlike insulation. It lived in herds, feeding on cycads, ferns, and conifers. Fulgurotherium (right) also lived during the Cretaceous, when Australia was one of the coldest parts of the southern continent Gondwana.*

warmer then, life this far south would still have been a challenge—particularly in the winter, when daylight and food were in short supply. If *Leaellynasaura* was warm-blooded rather than cold-blooded, it could have remained active all year round. There is no physical evidence for this, but *Leaellynasaura* did have enlarged eye sockets and a large brain, which means that it would have been good at finding its way in the dim winter light. *Leaellynasaura* was discovered in 1989, and named after the daughters of the two paleontologists who found it.

MAXIMUM LENGTH 9.8 ft. (3m)

TIME Mid Cretaceous

FOSSIL FINDS Australia (Victoria)

TENONTOSAURUS

Tenontosaurus was exceptionally large for a hypsilophodont, and this, with details of its skull anatomy, make some paleontologists think that it may have been an iguanodont. Its teeth, however, are of the typical hypsilophodont type—an important point, because it is rare for identical tooth types to evolve twice. Like other ornithopods, *Tenontosaurus* probably dropped onto all fours when feeding, and, because it weighed over a ton, it may have rested like this as well.

MAXIMUM LENGTH 23 ft. (7m)

TIME Early Cretaceous

FOSSIL FINDS North America (Arizona, Montana, Oklahoma, Texas)

ORNITHOPODS

FABROSAURS

▽ *Although not tough enough to deter large predators,* Scutellosaurus' *body armor would have made it a tricky target for a hunter nearer its own size. Body armor was an unusual feature in dinosaurs this small.*

S mall and lightly built, the fabrosaurs were the reptilian equivalent of hare or small deer, using their narrow mouths to pick out nutritious vegetation on or close to the ground. They walked and ran only on their back legs, using their long tails for balance. Most of them were less than 6.6 ft. (2m) long, and unlike many other plant eaters, they may have foraged alone. Fabrosaurs were among the earliest ornithopods to evolve. Some paleontologists actually consider them to be a parallel group, because they did not have the features shared by ornithopods as a whole.

▽ *From the neck down* Lesothosaurus *looked similar to some of the smaller theropods, but its shorter jaws showed that it was a plant eater, not a hunter.*

LESOTHOSAURUS

Only a handful of *Lesothosaurus* fossils are known. But one set is very interesting, because it shows a pair of animals huddled together, possibly in a burrow underground. *Lesothosaurus* lived in a hot, dry habitat, and the likeliest explanation for this huddle is that the two animals were estivating—a summer equivalent of hibernation. By becoming dormant, they would have saved energy at a time of year when plant food was difficult to find. Physically *Lesothosaurus* looked like some small predatory dinosaurs, but its pointed teeth were shaped for dealing with plants. It had long leg bones, and its defense against predators would have been to run away.

▷ *Echindon is sometimes classified as a heterodontosaur, because it shared their pattern of varied teeth. As a small plant eater it could not process large quantities of food, and it probably survived by being selective about what it ate. Its narrow snout was ideal for this way of life.*

MAXIMUM LENGTH 3.3 ft. (1m)

TIME Early Jurassic

FOSSIL FINDS Africa (Lesotho)

SCUTELLOSAURUS

This fabrosaur's name means "little shield lizard." It is the only fabrosaur known to have had body armor, consisting of small bony plates down its neck and back. This coat of armor brought practical problems—mainly extra weight. *Scutellosaurus* may have spent some of its time on all fours, to spread the load. However, even with its armor, it probably weighed only about 22 lb. (10kg).

MAXIMUM LENGTH 4 ft. (1.2m)

TIME Early Jurassic

FOSSIL FINDS North America (Arizona)

ECHINDON

Echindon was a tiny plant eater, weighing not much more than a large domestic cat. It had a small head and narrow snout, with two types of teeth. It probably nipped off nutritious new plant growth, leaving tougher leaves for other animals.

MAXIMUM LENGTH 2 ft. (60cm)

TIME Late Jurassic

FOSSIL FINDS Europe (England)

HETERODONTOSAURS

Dinosaurs sometimes had a lot of teeth, but as a rule, each kind of dinosaur had only a single type. Heterodontosaurs were different because they had teeth that were specifically shaped for carrying out different tasks. This kind of specialized dentition is common in mammals, including humans, but in reptiles it was—and still is— highly unusual. Heterodontosaurs walked on their hind legs, and they relied on speed to escape from their enemies.

HETERODONTOSAURUS

When *Heterodontosaurus* was discovered in the 1960s, it quickly became clear that it was an early ornithopod with some remarkable features. It had three types of teeth. These included sharp cutting teeth at the front of its upper jaw, which bit down onto a toothless lower beak; and cheek teeth, which ground up its food. It also had two pairs of extra-long teeth, or tusks, that resembled a mammal's stabbing canines—strange for an animal that clearly fed on plants. The most widely accepted explanation is that *Heterodontosaurus* used the tusks for fighting rivals. A very similar animal called *Abrictosaurus* did not have tusks, and many experts think this is actually a female *Heterodontosaurus* that has been classified by mistake. An adult, *Heterodontosaurus* stood about 19.7 in. (50cm) high and probably weighed less than 44 lb. (20kg).

MAXIMUM LENGTH 4 ft. (1.2m)

TIME Early Jurassic

FOSSIL FINDS Africa (South Africa)

LYCORHINUS

Like *Heterodontosaurus*, this small plant eater also lived in southern Africa, but so far only its lower jaw has been discovered. It was thought to belong to a mammal, because it had specialized teeth, including two tusks. However, a closer look showed that the animal's lower jaw was made of several bones rather than one— a sign that it was actually a reptile. Judging from its jaw, *Lycorhinus* was similar in size to *Heterodontosaurus* and would also have been a grazer, feeding on low-growing plants.

MAXIMUM LENGTH 4 ft. (1.2m)

TIME Early Jurassic

FOSSIL FINDS Africa (South Africa)

PISANOSAURUS

Uncertainty surrounds this small South American plant eater which was discovered in the 1960s. From its fragmentary remains, some paleontologists have concluded that it was an ornithopod, perhaps belonging to the heterodontosaur line. If true, this would make it one of the earliest ornithischians, or bird-hipped, dinosaurs (page 70). If they were heterodontosaurs, this family provides evidence that Africa and South America were joined together in Triassic times.

MAXIMUM LENGTH 3.3 ft. (1m)

TIME Late Triassic

FOSSIL FINDS South America (Argentina)

△ *The name* Heterodontosaurus *means "different teeth." The animal in this reconstruction has large canines, which may have been a feature found only in males. The front of the lower jaw was toothless, and the upper jaw had teeth— an interesting reversal of the jaw structure found in today's grazing mammals.*

◁ Pisanosaurus *was discovered in the same rock formation as* Herrerasaurus *and* Eoraptor, *two other very early dinosaurs from South America. However, unlike these animals, it was a plant eater, although it still retained the primitive feature of walking on two legs.*

ORNITHOPODS

IGUANODONTS

Iguanodonts were among the first dinosaurs to be discovered and identified, nearly 200 years ago. They were probably descended from the hypsilophodonts, but they got their name because their teeth resembled those of present-day iguanas. Iguanodonts were large, relatively slow-moving plant eaters. Their back legs were larger than their front legs, and they could probably move on either four legs or two. Most species had sharply pointed thumbs.

▷ *Iguanodonts may have used their spikelike thumbs as defensive weapons. Here an* Iguanodon *fends off a predatory theropod.*

▽ *Many iguanodonts had dextrous front feet, with four fingers as well as a sharp thumb. The three middle fingers were hooflike. The fourth was much smaller and could fold across the palm. It allowed them to pick up food.*

IGUANODON
Easily the largest member of its family, *Iguanodon* stood three times the height of a man and weighed 4.5 tons. It is one of the most famous dinosaurs, because it was discovered by Mary Mantell in 1822, when dinosaurs were still unknown to science. The English geologist who described it—Mary's husband, Gideon Mantell—realized that it was a giant reptile, but mistakenly thought that its thumb spikes were horns. *Iguanodon* was a highly successful plant eater with a long skull, beaklike jaws, and rows of grinding cheek teeth that help to distinguish ornithopods from other herbivorous dinosaurs. It lived on all the continents except for Antarctica. In some fossil sites—for example, in Belgium—the remains of many iguanodons have been found side by side, suggesting that they lived in herds.

MAXIMUM LENGTH 30 ft. (9m)
TIME Early Cretaceous
FOSSIL FINDS Europe, North Africa, Asia (Mongolia), North America

CALLOVOSAURUS
Little is known about *Callovosaurus*, because the only fossil remains are of a single thighbone, which was discovered in England. However, the rocks surrounding this fossil show that this is the earliest iguanodont that has been found so far.
It was probably similar in general appearance to *Camptosaurus*, although little more than half its length.

MAXIMUM LENGTH 11.5 ft (3.5m)
TIME Mid Jurassic
FOSSIL FINDS Europe (England)

CAMPTOSAURUS
Another early iguanodont, *Camptosaurus* was common in North America and Europe about 150 million years ago, where it most likely lived in herds. It was a heavy-boned creature, weighing over one ton, with much shorter arms than legs, and a long skull that ended in a toothless beak. Its teeth were at the rear of its mouth—the ideal place for producing the force needed to crush plant food. While earlier plant eaters had to pause to breathe *Camptosaurus* had a long bony palate attached to the roof of its mouth, allowing it to breathe and eat simultaneously. Unlike *Iguanodon*, its wrists were not well developed, which suggests that it walked on its back legs, rather than on all fours.

MAXIMUM LENGTH 23 ft. (7m)
TIME Late Jurassic
FOSSIL FINDS Western North America, Europe (England, Portugal)

VECTISAURUS
Vectisaurus—named after the Latin for the Isle of Wight in England—was a close relative of *Iguanodon* and lived at the same time. It differed only in its smaller size and

IGUANODONTS

in having a spiny ridge running along its backbone. Paleontologists are unsure what part this ridge played in the animal's daily life. It may have been used to regulate body temperature, but its small size makes that doubtful.

MAXIMUM LENGTH 13 ft. (4m)
TIME Early Cretaceous
FOSSIL FINDS Europe (England)

OURANOSAURUS

Like *Vectisaurus*, this animal also had a spiny ridge along its back, but it was much more pronounced, forming a fan-shaped structure up to 20 in. (50cm) high. The ridge ran from the shoulders and extended halfway down the tail. *Ouranosaurus* also had an unusual head for an iguanodont, with a flat top, a raised bony brow above the eyes, and a snout leading to a wide, beaklike mouth.

MAXIMUM LENGTH 23 ft. (7m)
TIME Early Cretaceous
FOSSIL FINDS West Africa

MUTTABURRASAURUS Named after a small town in Queensland, Australia, *Muttaburrasaurus* is believed to have been another close relative of *Iguanodon*. It was similar, although smaller, with some telltale differences in the structure of its head. One of these was a characteristic bony lump on its nose, which may have been used in courtship displays. Another was a pair of unusually large nostrils, suggesting that it had a good sense of smell to find food. *Muttaburrasaurus* also had teeth shaped for cutting rather than grinding, which may mean that it was at least partly carnivorous. Like most other iguanodonts, it had large spikelike thumbs.

MAXIMUM LENGTH 7m (23 ft.)
TIME Early Cretaceous
FOSSIL FINDS Australia

◁ *The first remains of* Muttaburrasaurus *were discovered in 1963. This iguanodont lived at a time when Australia was slowly separating from the southern continents, carrying dinosaurs and other animals with it. Even today little is known about Australia's dinosaurs.*

▽ Ouranosaurus *herds once roamed what is now West Africa, eating plants in the hot and sometimes swampy landscape. The fan-shaped skin on their backs may have helped with heat regulation. By turning the fan to face the sun, they could have absorbed heat.*

101

COLORS AND CAMOUFLAGE

AT ONE TIME DINOSAURS WERE THOUGHT TO BE UNIFORMLY DRAB AND GRAY. HOWEVER, TODAY'S EXPERTS BELIEVE THAT THE DINOSAUR WORLD MAY HAVE BEEN A SURPRISINGLY COLORFUL PLACE.

Fossils reveal a great deal about the internal structure of dinosaurs, but they very rarely include any sign of their skin. This is because, like most other soft parts of the body, skin usually breaks down before fossils are formed. Occasionally some traces of the skin texture are left, and these show that dinosaurs were often covered with pebblelike nodules or sometimes lizardlike scales. But so far no clear evidence of skin pigmentation has been found. Without this, paleontologists have to rely on studies of living animals to picture what dinosaurs may have looked like.

HIDING AWAY
The colors and patterns of dinosaurs almost certainly depended on how they lived. Giant plant eaters, such as the brachiosaurs and titanosaurs, had relatively few enemies when they were fully grown, so they had very little need to hide away. Added to this, their huge size meant that they would have been almost impossible to conceal. As a result they probably had plain but muted colors— the kind of color schemes that all dinosaurs were once thought to have had and the ones that elephants and rhinos have today.

But with smaller planteaters, such as hadrosaurs, the situation was very different. These animals had many enemies, and one of their best defenses, apart from running away, was to avoid being seen. Over a long period of time evolution may well have given them camouflage as a form of self-protection. To see what they may have looked like, biologists turn to reptiles that live today. Plant-eating reptiles are now very rare, and most of them, such as iguanas, are brown or green.

CHANGING COLOR
Some of today's reptiles, most famously the chameleons, can change their color to mimic their background. It is very likely that some dinosaurs were also able to do this, because the few fossils that have been found show that their skin seems to have the same structure. But chameleons do not switch color only to hide, they also do it to show their mood. Unlike camouflage colors, these mood-indicating colors are often vivid, with contrasting streaks and stripes. As a form of communication they are difficult to miss.

FLUSHES AND BLUSHES

The variations in skin colors would have been produced by pigment-containing cells close to the surface of the skin. By altering the distribution of pigment in each cell, different color schemes could be produced. But there is another way that dinosaurs might have changed color—by altering the flow of blood. Many experts believe this could have happened in stegosaurs (pages 158–159), which had rows of bony plates extending down their backs. There are signs that these plates had a rich blood supply flowing through them and through a surface layer of skin. Stegosaurs may have used the plates to warm up or cool down, blushing as they increased their supply of blood.

These blushes might have served a double function, by also acting as a form of communication between the dinosaurs. It is not hard to imagine one blushing male *Stegosaurus* squaring up to another as the two prepare to fight.

SEX DIFFERENCES

In living reptiles males and females often look similar, but the same is not true of many birds. Because dinosaurs were the ancestors of birds, it is possible that they, too, showed marked color differences between the sexes. In some species, for example the bone-headed dinosaurs (pages 166–167), males and females differed in size, so they may have differed in color as well.

FOSSIL EVIDENCE

This remarkable fossil from Wyoming shows the knobbly skin of Edmontosaurus, *a duck-billed dinosaur. The fossil was formed from a mummified corpse. The process of mummification hardens the skin, so it fossilizes along with the animal's bones. Traces of skin texture are sometimes preserved in dinosaurs that died on damp mud. The mud makes a mold of the skin, and this is preserved when the mud is fossilized.*

▽ *These three reconstructions show imaginary color schemes for* Parasaurolophus, *a duck-billed dinosaur. Even though it grew to 33 ft. (10m) long,* Parasaurolophus *would have made a tempting target for tyrannosaurs, and camouflage would have been a useful first step toward avoiding attack. The green and brown pigments shown here are typical of those found in today's reptiles.*

HADROSAURS

Hadrosaurs are often known as duck-billed dinosaurs, because they had flattened, beaklike snouts. Some also sported hollow crests, which had a variety of eccentric shapes. These crests contained nasal tubes, and it is possible that they allowed hadrosaurs to make loud calls (see page 112). Hadrosaurs were herd-forming vegetarians, generally feeding on four legs, but able to run away on two. They were one of the last and most successful of the dinosaur families, originating in Asia and spreading to North America and Europe.

MAIASAURA

Many of the dinosaurs left few traces to show how they lived and bred, but with *Maiasaura* the evidence is astounding. Paleontologists have discovered this hadrosaur's nests and eggs and animals at almost every age, from hatchlings to adults. The females built nest mounds out of mud, and they may have covered their eggs with soil to keep them warm and hidden from hungry eyes. After the young hatched it is likely that the females cared for them until they were capable of fending for themselves. Fossils also show that *Maiasaura* lived in herds—possibly thousands strong. *Maiasaura* had only a modest crest, but when fully grown it weighed up to four tons. Fossilized droppings indicate that it fed on tough, woody plants.

MAXIMUM LENGTH	30 ft. (9m)
TIME	Late Cretaceous
FOSSIL FINDS	North America

BACTROSAURUS

Bactrosaurus was probably one of the earliest hadrosaurs to evolve, and it had fewer teeth in its cheeks than later species. It was also one of the smallest, although still a substantial animal. It had a flat, uncrested head, and high spikes on its vertebrae produced a ridge down its back. Unlike larger hadrosaurs, it always walked on its hind legs.

MAXIMUM LENGTH	20 ft. (6m)
TIME	Late Cretaceous
FOSSIL FINDS	Asia (Mongolia, China)

HADROSAURUS

Hadrosaurus, which means "big lizard," was the first dinosaur to be discovered in the U.S.A., in 1858. The partial remains— which were missing the skull—were enough to show that this massive plant eater could stand on two legs. Since then many more fossils have been found, revealing that *Hadrosaurus* had a duck-billed head with a raised lump on its snout, but not a crest like some other members of its family. It also had a battery of grinding teeth at the back of its jaws. These were continuously replaced as they wore down, unlike the teeth of today's plant-eating mammals, which have to last for life. *Hadrosaurus* fed on a tough diet of leaves, branches, and seeds.

MAXIMUM LENGTH	33 ft. (10m)
TIME	Late Cretaceous
FOSSIL FINDS	North America (Alberta, Montana, New Jersey, New Mexico)

◁ *Standing by her nest mound, a female* Maiasaura *tends her newly hatched young.* Maiasaura *nests were up to 6.5 ft. (2m) across and held up to two dozen grapefruit-sized eggs.*

TSINTAOSAURUS

This Chinese hadrosaur has a particularly bizarre crest, consisting of a single horn nearly 3.3 ft. (1m) long, emerging from a point between the eyes. When the first fossilized skull was found the crest was thought to be an accidental result of preservation. However, further finds showing the same feature proved that this was not the case. The crest is usually shown as jutting forward, but no one knows exactly how it was really positioned. It may have been an isolated structure—making *Tsintaosaurus* look like the dinosaur equivalent of a unicorn—but it is also possible that it was connected to flaps of skin. Otherwise *Tsintaosaurus* seems to have had a typical hadrosaur build, with relatively small front legs but much larger hind ones.

MAXIMUM LENGTH   33 ft. (10m)

TIME   Late Cretaceous

FOSSIL FINDS   Asia (China)

CORYTHOSAURUS

Corythosaurus, meaning "helmet lizard," was a large hadrosaur with a dome-shaped crest. The crest was hollow, and it contained spaces that were connected to its nasal passages. The crest's size varied from one animal to another and was probably largest in mature males. This size difference makes it likely that the crest was used in courtship displays, but it may also have played a part in helping *Corythosaurus* keep cool. Fossilized impressions of this animal's skin show that it had a pebbly texture.

MAXIMUM LENGTH   30 ft. (9m)

TIME   Late Cretaceous

FOSSIL FINDS   North America (Alberta, Montana)

EDMONTOSAURUS

Hadrosaurs were the only dinosaurs that could chew their food because of their unusual teeth, which were arranged in several interlocking rows at the back of their jaws. *Edmontosaurus* —one of the largest of the family—had up to 1,000 teeth, which were brought together by powerful cheek muscles. Fossils of mummified animals show that *Edmontosaurus* had raised nodules on the surface of its skin, and many scientists think that it had loose skin around its nose. It may have been able to inflate this like a balloon, either as a mating ritual or as a warning to rivals. Like other hadrosaurs, its only real defense was to run away from danger on its back legs, although it may have been able to swim. Its size meant that it was not a sprinter, leaving it vulnerable to tyrannosaurs and other giant predators.

MAXIMUM LENGTH   43 ft. (13m)

TIME   Late Cretaceous

FOSSIL FINDS   North America (Alberta, Montana)

KRITOSAURUS

Very similar in size and appearance to *Hadrosaurus*, this crestless hadrosaur may have been one of its closest relatives. Like *Hadrosaurus*, it had a bony lump on its snout, making it look as if it had a broken nose. It probably weighed between two and three tons. Its remains were found in 1910 by Barnum Brown, a great collector from the American Museum of Natural History, in New York City.

MAXIMUM LENGTH   43 ft. (13m)

TIME   Late Cretaceous

FOSSIL FINDS   North America (Texas, New Mexico)

▽ *The hadrosaur family divided into two groups.* Tstintaosaurus *and* Corythosaurus *belonged to the lambeosaurine group, containing species with flamboyant crests.* Edmontosaurus *and* Kritosaurus *belonged to the hadrosaurine group— their crests were either small or nonexistent.*

Corythosaurus

Tsintaosaurus

Edmontosaurus

Kritosaurus

ORNITHOPODS

▷ Fossils of
Lambeosaurus
magnicristatus *have
been found in Alberta,
and in Montana.
The animal's helmet-
shaped crest had a small,
backward-pointing spike,
but this was probably
covered by a flap of skin
that merged with the
neck. This illustration
shows an adult male.*

▷ Saurolophus *had
a long, flattened head
ending in a hornlike
crest. Unusually, it
also had a ring of
bones around its eyes—
a feature common in
reptiles but absent from
many other members of
the hadrosaur family.
Its long "beak" was
toothless, but hundreds
of teeth were packed
together toward the rear
of the animal's jaws.*

▷ Parasaurolophus'
*crest was the longest
of all the hadrosaurs'
creasts. Males had larger
crests than females, giving
strength to the theory
that their elongated crests
were primarily used in
courtship, either through
their appearance or by
making sounds.*

LAMBEOSAURUS

Lambeosaurus is the largest duck-billed dinosaur discovered so far. One species, *Lambeosaurus lambei*, had a bizarre two-part crest (page 92) consisting of a backward-pointing spike and a forward-pointing part that looked like the blade of a hatchet emerging from between its eyes. Another species, *Lambeosaurus magnicristatus*, looked more like *Corythosaurus* (page 105), with a dome-shaped crest. At one time it was thought that *Lambeosaurus* and its relatives fed in water, using their tails as paddles, but most paleontologists are now convinced that they lived on land.

MAXIMUM LENGTH	50 ft. (15m)
TIME	Late Cretaceous
FOSSIL FINDS	North America

SAUROLOPHUS

Found in North America and Asia, *Saurolophus* had a solid bony crest, about 6 in. (15cm) long, on top of its head. Some paleontologists think that the crest may have been connected to a flap of skin that could be inflated with air. If this is true, *Saurolophus* could have used it to produce honking sounds, which would have carried a long distance to attract mates or warn the rest of the herd of danger. Many fossils have been found—the largest specimens come from Asia.

MAXIMUM LENGTH	40 ft. (12m)
TIME	Late Cretaceous
FOSSIL FINDS	North America, Asia (Mongolia)

PARASAUROLOPHUS

With its extraordinary crest, this dinosaur was one of the most remarkable products of the dinosaur age. The crest was up to 6 ft. (1.8m) long, and it swept backward from the animal's head, ending in a bony knob. The nostrils were connected to the crest by hollow tubes, which ran all the way along the crest and then back down. At first sight this bizarre structure looks like a type of snorkel, but because it was not open-ended, it could not have worked in this way. Instead, it may have been used during courtship displays and could have produced calls as deep as a foghorn, which would have been audible many miles away. *Parasaurolophus* had well-developed front legs, suggesting that it spent most of its time on all fours.

MAXIMUM LENGTH	33 ft. (10m)
TIME	Late Cretaceous
FOSSIL FINDS	North America

ANATOSAURUS

A lot is known about *Anatosaurus* because some exceptionally well-preserved fossils have been found, as well as some mummified specimens that reveal details of skin and internal organs. Weighing over 3 tons, it was a classic duck-billed dinosaur, with a wide head ending in a beaklike mouth. (*Anatosaurus* means "duck lizard.") As in other hadrosaurs, its beak had no teeth. These were located farther back in its jaws. Stomach remains show that it ate pine needles, twigs, seeds, and fruit. It was once thought to be semiaquatic because some foot remains seem to show webbing between the toes. Experts have since concluded that these flaps of skin were the remains of pads that bore the animal's weight on land.

MAXIMUM LENGTH	43 ft. (13m)
TIME	Late Cretaceous
FOSSIL FINDS	North America

SHANTUNGOSAURUS

Shantungosaurus was one of the largest of the hadrosaurs and one of the largest plant-eating dinosaurs capable of walking on two legs. It weighed about 7 tons and when standing on its back legs would have been about 23 ft. (7m) tall. Half its length consisted of its huge tail, which would have acted as a counterbalance when it walked upright. This dinosaur did not have a crest, but it did have the beaklike mouth that is typical of its family, with teeth positioned at the back of the jaws. Even though it was a bird-hipped dinosaur, rather than a lizard-hipped sauropod, *Shantungosaurus* would have had almost as much effect on plant life as they did, because of its immense size. *Shantungosaurus* gets its name from Shandong province, in eastern China, where an almost complete skeleton was found in 1973.

MAXIMUM LENGTH 50 ft. (15m)

TIME Late Cretaceous

FOSSIL FINDS North America, Central Asia

▽ Hypacrosaurus *had a prominent, hollow crest, like some ground-dwelling birds have today. It would have been useful for pushing through vegetation, but its true function will probably never be known.*

HYPACROSAURUS

Like *Corythosaurus* (page 105), this dinosaur had a hollow, helmetlike crest, with an almost identical internal structure. It also had a ridged back and lived in herds, feeding on all fours. An insight into this dinosaur's family life has come from a nest of eight large fossilized eggs discovered in Alberta. The eggs were the size of melons and contained fossilized embryos. Arranged in rows, they were probably buried until they were ready to hatch. The eggs may have been covered with soil and vegetation—a mixture that would have produced heat as the plants rotted, helping the young dinosaurs develop. Like *Maiasaura*, the parents probably guarded their nests.

MAXIMUM LENGTH 30 ft. (9m)

TIME Late Cretaceous

FOSSIL FINDS North America (Alberta, Montana)

FOSSIL HUNTING IN ASIA

STRETCHING ALMOST HALFWAY AROUND THE GLOBE, ASIA CONTAINS SOME OF THE BEST FOSSIL-HUNTING SITES IN THE WORLD. PALEONTOLOGISTS HAVE UNEARTHED A WEALTH OF SPECTACULAR FINDS.

Southern Asia has seen a number of important dinosaur discoveries, but perhaps the most interesting finds have been farther north, in Russia, Mongolia, and China. During the 1900s political problems meant access for western experts was limited, but this did not stop research. Russian scientists have built up the largest museum collections of fossils in the world, and in China recent discoveries have thrown new light on the evolution of birds.

FOSSIL EVIDENCE

With its giant jaws gaping wide, this fully assembled fossil of Tarbosaurus gives a spine-chilling impression of Asia's largest land predator. The first remains of Tarbosaurus were found in the Gobi region in 1955, and since then about a dozen skeletons have been found. Some are almost complete and show the huge difference in size between the animal's back legs and its tiny arms.

DESERT RICHES

The Gobi Desert, in the heart of Central Asia, is a harsh but spectacular region that attracts many fossil hunters. It contains huge deposits of rock dating back to the time of the dinosaurs, and because it lies so far from the sea, rainfall is very low, and much of the rock is bare. This is the kind of landscape where fossilized remains literally stick out of the ground. However, finding them needs sharp eyesight and dedication— particularly when the hot summer wind hurls stinging sand through the air.

During the 1920s the American Museum of Natural History mounted several large-scale

△ The Bayn Dzag, or Flaming Cliffs, of southern Mongolia were laid down during the Cretaceous. The cliffs are being slowly eaten away by wind and sporadic desert storms.

▷ Using a pocket knife, a Mongolian paleontologist carefully chips away at the bedrock surrounding a fossilized Protoceratops skull revealed beneath the surface of the cliffs.

expeditions to this isolated region, using trucks and camels to carry their supplies. Initially the aim was to unearth fossils of early humans, but none were found. However, other fossils were there in abundance. At a site known as the Bayn Dzak, or Flaming Cliffs, in southern Mongolia, one team discovered large numbers of fossilized eggs, and the remains of over 100 *Protoceratops*—animals that probably died after they and their eggs were buried by sand. These expeditions also uncovered remains of *Velociraptor* and *Oviraptor*, small predatory theropods.

During the Soviet Era the Gobi was closed to western scientists, but since Mongolia became independent in the early 1990s, entry to the area has become easier, and expeditions have been undertaken by experts from all over the world.

DEATH ON DUTY

Over the years dozens of species of dinosaur have been found in the Gobi, including heavyweight plant eaters such as *Saurolophus* and fearsome predators such as *Tarbosaurus*—a close relative of *Tyrannosaurus*, which rivaled it in size. Researchers have also found the fragmentary remains of several species of segnosaurs—mysterious dinosaurs unique to central Asia that may have been predators, plant eaters, or perhaps even a mixture of the two. As well as unearthing fossils that paint portraits of these extinct animals, paleontologists have also made some finds that show how they behaved.

One of the most famous of these fossils was found in 1923—an *Oviraptor* apparently smothered by sand while in the process of stealing another dinosaur's eggs. For several decades the egg thief's guilt seemed to be beyond doubt. But the accusation has turned out to be based on false evidence, because further fossils have been found. In one of

them the remains of a smashed egg include tiny *Oviraptor* bones. These show that the adult *Oviraptors* were actually incubating eggs of their own.

Together with fossils from other parts of the world, these finds have helped undermine the long-held idea that dinosaurs played little or no part in raising their young. Instead, *Oviraptor* seems to have been a devoted parent, doggedly remaining with its eggs, even when sandstorms threatened its life.

FOSSILS FROM THE FAR NORTH

Nineteen hundred miles (3,000km) north of the Gobi, the forests of Siberia flank the Arctic Circle. During the height of the last Ice Age, about 20,000 years ago, this area lay under a continental ice cap, but as the ice retreated the ground turned to tundra— a treeless landscape of low-growing plants that provided food for mammoths, woolly rhinos, and the so-called Irish elk. It was an icy version of today's African plains, with large herds of plant-eating mammals and predators such as wolves migrating with the seasons.

Compared to dinosaurs, these animals became extinct in the recent past: the last woolly mammoth, for example, may have been alive on Wrangel Island, off the northest coast of Siberia, just 6,000 years ago. As a result the fossilized remains of these creatures sometimes include traces of skin and hair, and in the case of deep-frozen animals (page 17), even flesh.

△ *In 1971 one expedition to the Gobi region unearthed something unique—a fossil of two dinosaurs that had both died while locked together in combat. The attacker was* Velociraptor, *and its intended victim was* Protoceratops. *In Mongolia this extraordinary relic from the dinosaur age has been designated a national treasure.*

◁ *Discovered in 1994, this* Oviraptor *was probably smothered by sand while sitting on its eggs. If the parent was cold-blooded, sitting on the eggs would have protected them against marauders, but if it was warm-blooded—as seems likely—incubation would have helped the eggs develop. From the fossil it is not possible to say whether the adult was male or female.*

FOSSILS FROM THE EAST

During the 1920s paleontologists working at Zhoukoudian, in northeast China, discovered the remains of Peking Man, a human ancestor who lived over 400,000 years ago. As well as fossil bones and tools, the excavators also found deposits of ash deep inside caves—one of the earliest known examples of the deliberate use of fire. Peking Man was very similar to a modern human, but it belonged to a species called *Homo erectus* (page 216), which disappeared about 200,000 years ago.

Northern China is still an important area for fossil hunting today, but for many scientists the focus is not so much on the ancestors of our own species as on dinosaurs —and in particular, the ancestors of birds.

MILLION-YEAR-OLD EGGS

Some historians believe that dinosaur fossils, or "dragon bones," were known about in China over 2,000 years ago. But scientific fossil hunting did not begin in earnest until the

The history of fossil hunting is peppered with finds that later turn out to be fakes. People make fake fossils for several reasons: some enjoy fooling the experts, but others do it to make money. The fossil shown here is a particularly skillful one which was "unearthed" in China in 1997. Named Archaeoraptor liaoningensis, it looks like a link between feathered dinosaurs and flying birds. It convinced several leading paleontologists, and also National Geographic magazine, but on closer inspection, it turned out to be mixture of two different animals— a bird and a small theropod dinosaur.

1900s, when western paleontologists embarked on lengthy expeditions in search of animal remains. However, the people who worked on the fossils were not always from abroad. China had its own experts, foremost among them being Yang Zhong-jian (also known as C. C. Young). He studied fossils in Europe and North America before returning to China in the late 1920s.

Most of the early fossil hunting in China concentrated on the northwest of the country—the area that borders Mongolia and includes part of the Gobi Desert. Finds here have included a wide range of armored dinosaurs, which lived during Cretaceous times, and also a number of other large plant eaters. Among them were *Shantungosaurus* and *Tsintaosaurus*— two of the largest duck-billed dinosaurs,

▽ *Two Chinese paleontologists examine a fossilized dinosaur egg in Hubei Province, in central China. Matching an egg to a particular dinosaur is very difficult. Instead, eggs—just like dinosaur tracks— are often given their own scientific names. Dinosaur eggs fetch high prices, and every year hundreds of Chinese eggs are smuggled abroad.*

▷ *Watched by a large crowd, scientists work on an unusual find—a collection of fossilized eggs, together with dinosaur bones. If the bones and eggs are of the same age, this suggests that some disaster overtook the adult animal while it was at the nest.*

or hadrosaurs—as well as *Tuojiangosaurus* and *Huayangosaurus*, two stegosaurs, both from the Jurassic, which were very different in size. The fossil-hunting expeditions also unearthed remains of *Mamenchisaurus*, a sauropod that was Asia's largest dinosaur and had a spectacularly long neck.

China has also proven to be a treasure trove for dinosaur nests and eggs. The nests include one find nearly 10 ft. (3m) across—a world record. There are some containing the remains of embryos, and others with more than 2 pints (1l) of rock-hard, fossilized yolk.

FEATHERED DINOSAURS

The first fossil to link dinosaurs and birds was *Archaeopteryx*, discovered in southern Germany in 1861. Although it was a bird, it clearly had some reptilian features, such as wing claws and a long, bony tail. But before birds like *Archaeopteryx* evolved, there must have been earlier forms that looked more like typical dinosaurs. In the last decade paleontologists sifting through layers of soft rock in Liaoning Province, northeast China, have helped fill in the missing links.

Sinosauropteryx, discovered in 1996, was one of these. A small theropod, or bipedal carnivore, it had strong back legs, but short arms ending in small clawed hands. It is certain that it could not fly, because it did not have even the beginnings of wings, but even so, its body was covered in downy plumage, which helped it keep warm (page 148).

Liaoning has produced several other fossils. Among them are *Protarchaeopteryx* and *Caudipteryx*, both found roughly a year after *Sinosauropteryx*, and also feathered, but flightless, theropods. These discoveries make it likely that, far from being unusual, feathers were common in small theropods and maybe other dinosaurs too, although unlike birds, these animals used them for insulation rather than for flight.

But why has this one part of China yielded

so many fossils of these feathered theropods? One reason is that, like southern Germany, this region was covered with shallow lakes and lagoons at the time when the ancestors of birds were alive. In southern Germany, *Archaeopteryx* probably crashed into the water and drowned, sinking to the bottom and becoming covered in fine silt. In Liaoning small feathered theropods probably fell in after a natural disaster, such as a volcanic eruption. As with *Archaeopteryx*, lake silt created superbly detailed fossils, which allow the outline of feathers to be seen today.

EARLY VERTEBRATES

Compared to feathered dinosaurs, tiny fish do not sound like the most exciting of fossil finds. But in 1999 Chinese researchers announced that they had found the fossils of two species over 500 million years old (page 30). This is an exciting breakthrough, because it pushes back the date when animals with backbones first appeared.

The finger-size fossils were found in Yunnan Province, in the far south of China. One of the animals, *Myllokunmingia*, had gill pouches and a saillike fin along its back; the other, *Haikouichthys*, was more slender and may have had slime-producing glands, like a modern hagfish. The search is now on for further finds of these ancient, but important animals.

△ Sinosauropteryx *was a feathered, but flightless, dinosaur that lived about 140 million years ago. It was unlikely to have been a direct ancestor of modern birds, but it shows some of the features that would have been present during the early stages of bird evolution.*

▽ *At 23 ft. (7m) long,* Tuojiangosaurus *was a stegosaur that lived in eastern Asia. China has produced a greater range of stegosaur fossil finds than anywhere else in the world.*

Sounds

TODAY'S REPTILES ARE LARGELY SILENT, BUT DINOSAURS MAY HAVE COMMUNICATED WITH GRUNTS AND ROARS THAT COULD BE HEARD FROM MANY MILES AWAY. THE EVIDENCE FOR THIS COMES LARGELY FROM THEIR SKULLS.

Animals use sound mainly to keep in touch and to ward off their rivals and enemies. For dinosaurs, particularly herd-forming plant eaters, this kind of communication could have been a valuable aid to survival. Periodic contact calls made by animals as they fed would have helped the herd stay together. Much louder alarm calls produced when a predator was spotted would let other herd members know that they were in imminent danger of attack. And for dinosaurs as a whole, far-reaching courtship calls would have allowed males to attract mates.

ECHOES FROM THE PAST
Animals make sounds in two different ways: by rubbing body parts together or by using their vocal cords to make air vibrate when they breathe. Most dinosaurs probably had vocal cords, but none have survived in fossils.

Other soft parts, such as cheeks and lips, modify the sound that is made, but few signs of these survive. Fossil skeletons do show the air spaces in the skull and the length of the trachea, or windpipe. As with wind instruments, the larger these are the deeper the sound that would be made.

If they did make sounds, the smallest dinosaurs, such as *Saltopus*, would probably have produced a high-pitched piping like birdsong. Giant sauropods would have made deep sounds too low for the human ear to hear. Each species would have had its own calls, and within each species individuals would have had their own distinctive voice.

COMPUTING A CALL
For sound specialists, hadrosaurs (pages 104–107) are particularly interesting, because their crests look as though they might have evolved partly as a way of producing calls. The crest contained extensions of the nasal tubes, leading from the nose to the lungs. In *Parasaurolophus* the tubes double back on themselves, a feature similar to the coiled airways of cranes.

In 1997 a group of American scientists used a medical scanner on a *Parasaurolophus* skull to identify the exact shape of the air passages which were preserved as solid rock. They were able to generate sounds that the dinosaur might have made. The result was a collection of low-pitched rumblings, the first dinosaur calls to be heard on Earth for over 65 million years.

▷ Parasaurolophus' *crest, with its trombonelike arrangement of airways, was a natural resonating chamber. In this artist's impression a male is calling by inflating his cheeks and blowing air out of his nose. The nostrils may have acted like valves, allowing it to alter the sound.*

THE MEAT EATERS

The theropods—a word that means "beast-footed"— were distant cousins of the sauropods (page 71), but their shape and way of life could hardly have been more different. Instead of walking slowly on all fours, most theropods ran on two, and they ate meat— not plants. This large and varied group of carnivores included some early species that were not much larger than a cat, as well as (later) the largest predators that have ever lived on dry land. Most giant theropods hunted alone, but the smaller species, described in this chapter, were smart killers that worked in packs.

HUNTERS ON THE RUN

Sprinting across a Late Triassic landscape, a pack of Coelophysis approach a cetiosaur feeding in the marshy shallows of a lake. They usually hunt much smaller prey, but the plant eater is at a disadvantage on the soft ground, and the pack may stand a chance of making a kill.

THE MEAT EATERS

CERATOSAURS

The earliest carnivorous dinosaurs evolved in the Late Triassic, about 220 million years ago. Contrary to popular belief, few of these meat eaters were giants, but what they lacked in size they made up for in speed and agility. Sprinting on their back legs and balancing with their long tails, lightweight species called ceratosaurs could snap at animals on the ground or even leap after insects in the air. Many had beaklike jaws armed with small but needlelike teeth, and slender hands with sharp claws—ideal implements for gripping and holding down struggling prey.

△ Procompsognathus *(above left and center) and* Compsognathus *(above right) lived over 50 million years apart, but they had many features in common. Among these were a slim body, a long, stiff tail, and a slender head on a flexible neck. Both dinosaurs would have had good eyesight, essential for catching fast-moving prey.*

PROCOMPSOGNATHUS

One of the oldest theropods discovered so far—and one of the earliest dinosaurs—*Procompsognathus* is known from a single skeleton, which is far from complete. However, judging from the remains of its badly crushed skull, it seems to have had a long, pointed snout and sharp teeth. It probably lived on a diet of insects and small lizards, which it caught either in its jaws or with its large, five-fingered, clawed hands.

MAXIMUM LENGTH 4 ft. (1.2m)

TIME Late Triassic

FOSSIL FINDS Europe (Germany)

COMPSOGNATHUS

Lightly built and highly agile, *Compsognathus* probably weighed up to 6.6 lb. (3kg), about as much as a large chicken. Its name means "elegant jaw"—a flattering description of a narrow mouth that was packed with small but sharp teeth. Like its relatives, it was birdlike in appearance, with long back legs, three-toed feet, and hollow bones. Fossilized stomach remains show that it ate lizards, and it also may have been cannibalistic.

MAXIMUM LENGTH 4.6 ft. (1.4m)

TIME Late Jurassic

FOSSIL FINDS Europe (Germany, France)

SALTOPUS

Saltopus is one of the smallest dinosaurs known, weighing about 2.2 lb. (1kg)—the same as a small domestic cat. Fossil evidence is scant, making an accurate reconstruction impossible, but remains show that this tiny hunter had five-fingered hands—a primitive feature that changed as theropods evolved. Some scientists have suggested that *Saltopus* may have hopped like some rodents and marsupials do today, but this interesting idea cannot be proven. Given its small size, insects were probably an important part of its diet, although it may also have scavenged animals killed by larger dinosaurs.

MAXIMUM LENGTH 2.3 ft. (0.7m)

TIME Late Triassic

FOSSIL FINDS Europe (Scotland)

COELURUS

Another small predatory dinosaur of similar stature and behavior to *Compsognathus*, *Coelurus* lived in the swamps and forests of Jurassic North America. Unlike earlier theropods, it had only three fingers on each hand, each armed with a sharp, curved claw. Its head was relatively small—about the size of a human hand—with a narrow but blunt-ended snout. When fully grown, *Coelurus* probably weighed up to 44 lb. (20kg).

MAXIMUM LENGTH 6.6 ft. (2m)

TIME Late Jurassic

FOSSIL FINDS North America (Wyoming)

COELOPHYSIS

Unlike some of the animals on the opposite page, *Coelophysis* is very well known from fossils. One spectacular find, at Ghost Ranch in Colorado has yielded the remains of about 1,000 specimens, from juveniles to adults, making this one of the best-known Triassic dinosaurs. This mass grave strongly suggests that *Coelophysis* was sociable, although the discovery of fossilized bones inside larger specimens may well mean that they were not averse to eating each other's young. From this wealth of fossils two types—known as robust and gracile forms—have been identified. Paleontologists think that these are males and females, rather than members of two separate species.

MAXIMUM LENGTH 10 ft. (3m)

TIME Late Triassic

FOSSIL FINDS North America (Arizona, Colorado, New Mexico)

CERATOSAURUS

Weighing up to one ton, *Ceratosaurus* was a sizable hunter, although not as large as the true giants of the theropod world. Its most characteristic feature was a horn on the top of its nose, which may have been used in duels between males at mating time. It also had hard brow ridges above its eyes, a narrow line of bony plates running down its back, and four-fingered hands. The first nearly complete remains of *Ceratosaurus* were found alongside those of *Allosaurus* in a quarry in Colorado in 1883. Fossilized footprints discovered since then show that it may have hunted in packs. Unlike packs of smaller theropods, *Ceratosaurus* packs would have been able to attack and kill plant eaters weighing many tons.

MAXIMUM LENGTH 20 ft. (6m)

TIME Late Jurassic

FOSSIL FINDS North America (Colorado), Africa (Tanzania)

◁ Coelophysis *was a medium-sized predator, standing about as high as an adult man. When running quickly, it probably would have stablilized itself by lowering its neck and holding its tail almost horizontal. Its small, serrated teeth were designed mainly for dealing with prey smaller than itself.*

▽ Ceratosaurus *attacks a* Brachiosaurus. *On its own* Ceratosaurus *would have been a serious threat to large sauropods, but it would have been deadly if, as seems likely, it also hunted in packs.*

MOVING ON TWO LEGS

THE WORLD'S LARGEST DINOSAURS WALKED ON FOUR LEGS, BUT THE FASTEST AND MOST AGILE SPECIES—INCLUDING ALMOST ALL OF THE HUNTERS—WALKED OR RAN ON TWO.

Dinosaurs evolved from reptiles that walked and ran on all fours, but many of them moved on their back legs alone (pages 64–65). This way of moving brought three advantages: two-legged reptiles could often run faster, they could see farther, and because their front legs were not needed for moving, they became free to carry out other tasks instead. The disadvantage of this way of moving was that, at high speed, a single misplaced step could send a dinosaur crashing to the ground.

△ *Moving at full speed, tyrannosaurs held their tails high to balance the weight of their heads. When standing still, they kept their bodies upright.*

BIPEDAL DINOSAURS

Two groups of dinosaurs walked partly or wholly on two legs: the theropods (both light- and heavyweight hunters) and the plant-eating ornithopods (pages 91–112). Many of the ornithopods were facultative bipeds. This means that they walked on all fours most of the time, but could switch to two legs to get to food, to defend themselves, or to get away from danger. Their front and back legs differed in size, but their front legs were strong enough to support their body weight.

In theropods the two-legged lifestyle went much further. Most of these dinosaurs always stood on their back legs and were incapable of walking on all fours. Their front legs were much less powerful than their back legs, but they often had long fingers armed with sharp claws, which could be used for unearthing eggs, gripping food, or slashing at their prey.

Tyrannosaurs—the largest of these bipedal hunters—had back legs that could be twice the height of an adult human, but front legs that were not much longer than a human arm. These tiny front legs could have played no part in moving around and would not have been much use for feeding. Some experts think that they may have been used as props when lying down, or perhaps when mating, but they remain a mystery.

SPRINTERS AND PLODDERS

Moving on two legs made small hunters fast and very maneuverable. One of the speediest of them all, the bird mimic *Dromiceiomimus*, had very long bones in the lower part of its back legs—the ideal shape for running. It could reach a speed of over 40 mph (60km/h), fast enough to overtake most land animals today.

But not all two-legged dinosaurs were good long-distance runners. With its massive back legs and seven ton body, *Tyrannosaurus* was probably too heavy to keep up the chase for long, and when it was running, it would have found it almost impossible to twist and turn after its prey. Many paleontologists believe that it was more likely to have been a stand-and-wait predator, lurking among vegetation and bursting out of cover once its prey was within striking range.

right position for staying balanced. In theropods the head and trunk leaned forward in one direction and the tail in another. To keep their center of gravity above their back legs, they had to make sure that these two parts of the body were balanced. For the largest hunters having

△ *On the inside of each hind foot* Deinonychus *had a retractable toe armed with a giant, sickle-shaped claw. The claw swiveled downward when the animal was about to launch an attack.*

STAYING BALANCED

For animals that move on two legs, staying balanced is vital. This would have been true for large hunters like *Tyrannosaurus*, because once it was in motion, it developed an almost unstoppable momentum. If it tripped, it risked a dangerous accident, with only its tiny front legs to break its fall. For lightweight hunters, such as *Deinonychus*, falls were less critical.

The human body is vertical, so our center of gravity is above our legs—the

▷ *At about 13 ft. (4m) long,* Deinonychus *was a middleweight bipedal hunter, but one with well-developed front legs. Like other theropods, it used its tail partly as a counterbalance and partly as a stabilizer to absorb energy—like kangaroos do today.*

a huge head was a problem— it threatened to destabilize them and make them fall over. So they probably leaned forward only when they ran.

BACK TO ALL FOURS

Many paleontologists believe that sauropods—the largest planteaters of the dinosaur world—evolved from bipedal ancestors. But as they evolved and grew in size this two-legged lifestyle was soon abandoned. Some sauropods could probably stand on their hind legs, propped up by their tails, but with their huge and heavy digestive systems, it is highly unlikely that they could have taken a single step on their back legs alone.

STUDYING DINOSAUR TRACKS

BECAUSE DINOSAURS DIED OUT SO LONG AGO, WE HAVE VERY LITTLE IDEA OF HOW THEY BEHAVED. FOSSILIZED TRACKS ARE VALUABLE EVIDENCE IN THIS AREA OF RESEARCH.

Although fossilized dinosaur tracks have been found all over the world, they are rarer than fossilized bones. This is because footprints are preserved only when conditions are exactly right. The ground must be soft, but not so soft that the prints soon fill in, and the prints must be covered by something that protects them—such as sediment or sand—not long after they are made. Most dinosaur tracks belong to single animals, but in some places entire herds have left their imprint on the ground.

▽ *Tracks at Lark Quarry, in Australia, show the world's largest fossilized stampede. About 150 small theropods and ornithopods seem to have been running for their lives from a large carnosaur. The tracks do not show if the predator managed to make a kill.*

IDENTIFYING FOOTPRINTS

With living animals it is often easy to match footprints with the animals that made them. But with dinosaurs it is usually more difficult. From a print's shape experts can generally tell what type of dinosaur left it. For example, the prints left by sauropods and theropods look different because sauropods had rounded or oval feet, and theropods had birdlike feet, with long toes and large claws. However, deciding which kind of sauropod or theropod left a set of prints is much harder. To avoid guesswork, tracks are often given their own scientific names.

▽ *Walking slowly in the heat of the midday sun, a small herd of* Iguanodon *make their way along a beach. Damp sand sometimes produced clear fossil prints, whereas sticky mud would blur the shape.*

GAUGING SPEEDS

As well as showing where a dinosaur went, tracks can often give an idea of its speed. To calculate this, a track expert needs to know two measurements—the length of the dinosaur's leg and the length of its stride. These measurements show that ornithomimids—the fastest dinosaurs—could probably reach about 40 mph (60km/h), and because they were light, they would have been able to accelerate and stop quite quickly. The largest sauropods and carnosaurs were much slower and would have taken longer to build up speed. They probably had a maximum speed of about 20 mph (30km/h)—roughly twice as fast as a human can run. For giant sauropods, such as *Seismosaurus*, true running is likely to have been impossible, because it would have put immense strain on their legs. These animals probably broke into an accelerated walk if threatened, moving one foot at a time, with the other three in contact with the ground.

Like other animals, dinosaurs did not waste energy unnecessarily, so tracks that show running are rare. Lark Quarry, in Queensland, Australia, is one of the few sites where the track makers—a group of small theropods and ornithopods—seem to be moving at top speed. It is believed that the animals were escaping from a predator.

TRACKWAYS

Collections of footprints—called trackways—can reveal a lot about dinosaurs on the move. Some trackways contain prints formed by several animals in a herd, but occasionally trackways contain prints from more than one species. One of the most famous examples, at the Paluxy River in Texas, shows the three-toed footprints of a large predatory theropod apparently stalking its sauropod prey. Trackways also indicate social interactions, such as the large adult dinosaurs walking on the outside of a herd to protect the young in the middle.

Like today's animals, dinosaurs gathered at particular places to feed or to drink. Where this happened, the ground became trampled, leaving a confusing jumble of tracks. Track experts, or ichnologists, call this kind of trampling dinoturbation. Dinoturbation is common in rocks that have formed from ancient lake shores where dinosaurs left their footprints in the mud. In other places, called megatrack sites, dinosaurs have left telltale footprints across huge areas of ground. Some paleontologists think that these were migration routes—prehistoric dinosaur paths that may have been used for thousands of years.

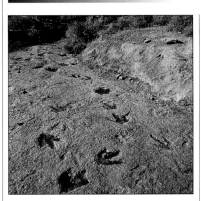

FOSSIL EVIDENCE

This collection of footprints in Utah was left by several dinosaurs walking over the same patch of damp ground. Dinosaurs sometimes stepped in each other's prints, so track experts can often tell the order in which the tracks were made. This provides useful evidence about whether the dinosaurs were interacting with each other at the time. Utah is rich in fossilized tracks. Some prints, left by a hadrosaur, hold the world record at 4.4 ft. (1.35m) long.

△ *Closing in on a slow-moving sauropod, a theropod moves in for the attack. This scene—and events leading up to it—is recorded in tracks discovered in the bed of the Paluxy River in Texas. The predator left the typical three-toed footprints of a theropod; the sauropod's prints were rounded, with small claw marks visible at the front. Shortly after the attack the prints were covered by sediment. Millions of years later they were revealed as fossils.*

121

THE MEAT EATERS

▷ *With its long neck and slender body and back legs,* Dromiceiomimus *bears a startling resemblance to a present-day flightless bird. Birds evolved from close relatives of these animals (page 134).*

BIRD MIMICS

Bird mimics, or ornithomimids, were long-legged, slender-bodied dinosaurs that probably lived and hunted in small packs. They fed on smaller reptiles and insects as well as plants and eggs, and they behaved like today's large flightless birds, running up to 45 mph (70km/h) to escape danger. Bird mimics had beaklike jaws without teeth, and slender arms for picking up food. They were quick-thinking, and had large brains relative to their size.

▽ *Running for their lives, a herd of* Struthiomimus *quickly outpace a lumbering* Tyrannosaurus.

DROMICEIOMIMUS

Studies of *Dromiceiomimus* fossils show that this animal must have been one of the most intelligent dinosaurs of its time. Its large eye sockets make it likely that it hunted at night, and its relatively long lower leg bones show that it would have been exceptionally swift, perhaps reaching speeds of 40 mph (65km/h). Its jaws were weak, and it probably snapped up insects and other small items of food, perhaps digging them out with its three-fingered hands. Its wide pelvis could be a sign that it gave birth to live young or laid very large eggs.

MAXIMUM LENGTH	44.5 ft. (13.5m)
TIME	Late Cretaceous
FOSSIL FINDS	North America (Alberta)

STRUTHIOMIMUS

Struthiomimus means "ostrich mimic"—an appropriate name for a dinosaur with slender legs and large, birdlike eyes. It had long, gangly arms and well-developed claws on its fingers. It also had a remnant fourth toe on its hind feet. Its tail kept it balanced as it ran and as it swerved to avoid attack. *Struthiomimus* was probably carnivorous, but its lack of teeth would have restricted it to small prey. This dinosaur was originally classified as a form of *Ornithomimus*, and some experts think that as more fossils are found it may prove to be the same animal. All bird mimics look very similar—apart from the giant *Deinocheirus*—so classifying them has proven difficult.

MAXIMUM LENGTH	13 ft. (4m)
TIME	Late Cretaceous
FOSSIL FINDS	North America

BIRD MIMICS

ORNITHOMIMUS

Bird mimics were built for speed, and *Ornithomimus* was no exception to this rule. It had light, hollow bones and long, powerful, birdlike legs with clawed feet. With good eyesight and quick reactions, it was

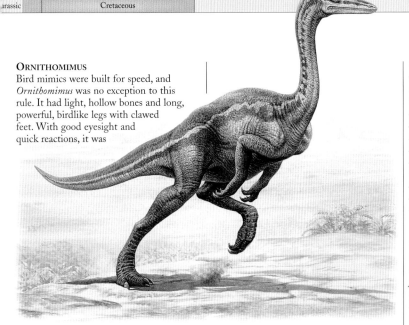

◁ Ornithomimus *was a typically athletic member of the bird mimic family, running quickly whenever food beckoned or danger threatened. It would have run with its head held high, giving it a good view of its surroundings. Its long, stiff tail acted as a counterbalance.*

▽ *Running with its head up,* Gallimimus *was like a mobile lookout post with a far-reaching view of its surroundings. Its eyes were on the sides of its head, like those of ostriches and other flightless birds. This arrangement is not good for judging depth, but it is ideal for spotting possible danger from any direction.*

probably an efficient hunter and a successful scavenger. However, recent studies of this dinosaur's skull suggest that it—and perhaps other bird mimics—were cold-blooded, which means that they would have been able to run only in short bursts. *Ornithomimus* was initially identified from only feet and leg bones—the first complete skeleton was found 30 years later, in 1917.

MAXIMUM LENGTH	13 ft. (4m)
TIME	Late Cretaceous
FOSSIL FINDS	North America (Alberta, Colorado, Montana), Asia (Tibet)

ANSERIMIMUS

All that is known about *Anserimimus*— a name that means "goose mimic"—comes from one fossilized skeleton found in Mongolia. Even though this lacks part of its head, the species seems to have been a typical ornithomimid, although one with particularly strong, short arms and long-fingered claws. This suggests that *Anserimimus* may have relied on digging for finding food.

MAXIMUM LENGTH	10 ft. (3m)
TIME	Late Cretaceous
FOSSIL FINDS	Asia (Mongolia)

GALLIMIMUS

Despite its name, which means "chicken mimic," *Gallimimus* may have been the largest member of the ornithomimid family. It stood about twice as high as an adult man, but even so was relatively light for its size, allowing it to run at fast speeds. Its face and beak were elongated, and its hands were shovellike, indicating that it dug for food.

MAXIMUM LENGTH	20 ft. (6m)
TIME	Late Cretaceous
FOSSIL FINDS	Asia (Mongolia)

DEINOCHEIRUS

Known only from a pair of arms and some shoulder bones, *Deinocheirus* is one of the great mysteries of the dinosaur world. If it was an ornithomimid, it was certainly the giant of the family, because its arms were over 8 ft. (2.5m) in length. They were armed with claws over 10 in. (25cm) long, which could have made formidable weapons.

MAXIMUM LENGTH	33–66 ft. (10–20m)
TIME	Late Cretaceous
FOSSIL FINDS	Asia (Mongolia)

△ Dromaeosaurus *(top)*, Deinonychus *(center), and* Velociraptor *(bottom) were highly efficient predators, all armed with a single retractable claw on each foot. The claw stayed off the ground when the animal was moving, keeping its point needle-sharp.*

DROMAEOSAURS

Fast and ferocious, dromaeosaurs were killers of other dinosaurs. They were perfectly built for speed and slaughter, with light bodies, athletic legs, and sharp, sicklelike claws. Their heads were relatively large, and their long jaws were armed with sharp, curved teeth. They had well-developed brains, and they often worked in packs to hunt down animals several times their own size.

DEINONYCHUS
Although it was far smaller than many other predators that lived during the Cretaceous Period, *Deinonychus*, meaning "terrible claw," was a serious threat even to the largest plant-eating dinosaurs. By operating in packs, like modern wolves, it would harass and exhaust its prey before closing in for the final attack. When the moment came to make the kill the members of the pack would jump at their victim and slash it with their retractable sickle-shaped claws— formidable weapons that were up to 5 in. (12cm) long. As the pack members leaped and ripped into their prey they used their stiff tails as counterbalances to prevent themselves from becoming destabilized. Like other dromaeosaurs, *Deinonychus* had a large brain for its size. This gave it the intelligence and rapid reactions needed in a

hunter that operated in groups. *Deinonychus* was such an active and energetic predator that some experts think it may have been warm-blooded (pages 148–150), a theory that has yet to be proven.

MAXIMUM LENGTH	13 ft. (4m)
TIME	Early Cretaceous
FOSSIL FINDS	North America

DROMAEOSAURUS

Half the size of *Deinonychus*, but built along very similar lines, *Dromaeosaurus* was another fast-footed predator, probably able to reach speeds of around 40 mph (60km/h). It also had a sicklelike claw on the inner toe, which could be retracted when not in use. Fossils of this animal were discovered 50 years before its larger relative, which is how the dromaeosaur family got its name. These early remains were only partial, and paleontologists could not interpret them fully until they had studied *Deinonychus* and seen the similarities.

MAXIMUM LENGTH	6 ft. (1.8m)
TIME	Late Cretaceous
FOSSIL FINDS	North America

VELOCIRAPTOR

Similar in size and body shape to *Dromaeosaurus*, although with a longer and flatter head, *Velociraptor* was first discovered in Mongolia in the 1920s. Its way of life was vividly illustrated when many years later an expedition uncovered the fossilized remains of a *Velociraptor* that had been killed while attacking a *Protoceratops* (page 155). *Velociraptor* means "speedy thief"—a good description of a small, fast-moving, and intelligent hunter that could probably reach speeds of 40 mph (60 km/h). Although it could run at this speed only in short bursts, *Velociraptor* may have been second only to the bird mimics (page 122) in top speed. Like other dromaeosaurs, little is known about its breeding habits and whether it laid eggs.

MAXIMUM LENGTH	6 ft. (1.8m)
TIME	Late Cretaceous
FOSSIL FINDS	Asia (Mongolia, China)

SAURORNITHOLESTES

Uncertainty surrounds *Saurornitholestes*, because knowledge of it is limited to remnants of a skull, some teeth, and arm bones found in Alberta, in 1978. Based on this slender evidence, paleontologists have classified it as a dromaeosaur, but it may have been a "bird lizard," or saurornithoid (page 126). An agile hunter, it had large hands with grasping fingers.

MAXIMUM LENGTH	6 ft. (1.8m)
TIME	Late Cretaceous
FOSSIL FINDS	North America (Alberta)

▽ *Like other predatory dinosaurs,* Deinonychus *could not slice into its prey. Instead, it used its backward-curving teeth to rip away chunks of flesh. It also had large eyes, and it would have relied mainly on its sharp eyesight to spot potential prey when hunting. Its sense of smell was probably less important for finding food.*

THE MEAT EATERS

TROODONTS

The animals on these two pages belonged to several families, but most were lightweight theropods with unusually large brains. The troodonts in particular were highly intelligent by dinosaur standards, with large eyes that suggest they hunted at night. Fast and agile, some of them may have been warm-blooded, retaining their body heat with a layer of insulating feathers. *Baryonyx* was a much larger animal and probably not much brighter than other theropods of its time.

been a dromaeosaur, but it is possible that these swiveling claws evolved more than once. It also had large, serrated teeth, grasping hands, and eyes that faced partly forward—a combination that would have made it a very effective hunter. If *Troodon* did hunt after dark, as the size of its eyes suggests, its main prey might have been mammals, which were almost all nocturnal in the Cretaceous. *Troodon* teeth were first discovered nearly 150 years ago, but nothing was known about the animal itself until the 1980s.

MAXIMUM LENGTH 6 ft. (1.8m)
TIME Late Cretaceous
FOSSIL FINDS North America (Alberta, Montana, Wyoming)

▷ *Oviraptor made up for its lack of teeth by having sharp shearing edges on its beak. Because its beak was short, it would have closed with considerable force— enough to break bones. The size of the crest probably varied according to sex and age.*

OVIRAPTOR
With its birdlike head and short, toothless beak, *Oviraptor*, meaning "egg thief," was an unusual and distinctive animal. Standing about the same height as an adult man, it had thin but well-developed arms, and fingers that were equipped with slender claws. Its beak was hooked and had sharp edges for slicing through food. Recent fossil discoveries show that, although it may have eaten other dinosaurs' eggs, it was careful with its own (page 109).

MAXIMUM LENGTH 8.2 ft. (2.5m)
TIME Late Cretaceous
FOSSIL FINDS Asia (Mongolia)

SINORNITHOIDES
Another member of the troodont family, *Sinornithoides* is the only one known from a complete fossil skeleton. It was a small and very slender animal, weighing perhaps just 6.6 lb. (3kg) when fully grown, and its food is likely to have consisted of insects and other small animals that it may have found by scratching with its front claws.

MAXIMUM LENGTH 8.2 ft. (1.2m)
TIME Early Cretaceous
FOSSIL FINDS Asia (China)

BARYONYX
Discovered in an English clay pit in the early 1980s, *Baryonyx*, meaning "heavy claw," is one of the most intriguing European dinosaurs to surface in recent times. For a theropod its skull had a very unusual shape, ending in a flattened, crocodile-like snout. Its teeth were conical rather than bladelike and packed in dense rows along its jaws. It had at least two very large claws, about 12 in. (30cm) long. No close relatives of this animal have been found yet, and it is classified in a family of its own.

▽ *Lean and energetic,* Troodon *was one of the most intelligent land animals of the Late Cretaceous. This artist's impression shows it with bare skin, but it is possible that it had a covering of downy, heat-retaining plumage.*

TROODON
From a distance, *Troodon* looked like a bird mimic (pages 122–123), but it shared the same kind of weaponry as the dromaeosaurs— a lethal claw on each of its second toes, which could be swiveled upward when it ran. Some paleontologists think it may actually have

MAXIMUM LENGTH 29.5 ft. (9m)
TIME Early Cretaceous
FOSSIL FINDS Europe (England)

TROODONTS

Standing in shallow water, Baryonyx *uses its extra-large front claws to grab unsuspecting fish. Two* Brachiosaurus *in the background know that this specialized predator does not present a threat.*

DINOSAUR BRAINS

DINOSAURS WERE THE PROVERBIAL DIMWITS OF THE PREHISTORIC WORLD. BUT IS IT A REPUTATION THEY REALLY DESERVED, AND IF SO, HOW DID THEY MANAGE TO SURVIVE?

Myths abound about dinosaurs' rumored stupidity: one is that they had two brains; another is that their lack of brainpower helped make them extinct. But as living animals prove, large brains are not essential for biological success. Research shows that brain size and intelligence varied greatly from one group of dinosaurs to another. Some were slow to grasp situations, but others were just as intelligent as many mammals alive today.

NERVOUS SYSTEMS

Because dinosaurs were vertebrates, their nervous systems would have been similar to those of today's vertebrates. In a vertebrate the control center of the system is the brain, which merges with the spinal cord—a multistranded filament of nervous tissue that runs through the hollow core of

△ Stegosaurus *had a brain about the size of a walnut, weighing roughly 2.6 oz. (75g), but some of its nerve cells supplying distant parts of its body were over 10 ft. (3m) long. How fast its nerves worked would have depended on whether or not it was cold-blooded.*

the backbone. Nerves lead away from the spinal cord to all parts of the body, collect information from the sense organs, and send signals to trigger muscles into action.

In all vertebrates the brain plays a key role in initiating movement and making sure the body works in a coordinated way. But some movements, called reflex reactions, are triggered without the brain being directly involved. If you step on something sharp, for example, your leg will immediately pull back, because an automatic response has been triggered by your spinal cord.

Reactions like these are potential lifesavers, and they have to be fast—but the larger an animal is, the farther the signals have to travel. In today's reptiles, signals move along nerves at up to 130 ft. (40m) per second—quick enough to produce an almost

◁ *This diagram (above left) shows the brain cavity of a* Stegosaurus *and other structures close to it. The ear opening is shown in black; the circular objects above it are part of the inner ear, which played a part in controlling balance.*

◁ *Dome-headed dinosaurs, or pachycephalosaurs, looked as though they had large brains, but this was because their small brain cavity was covered by a mound of bone.*

instant response. But in large dinosaurs nerve signals would often have had to travel many feet, creating a significant time lag.

This time-lag effect may help explain what is called the "second brain," which is seen in stegosaurs and some other dinosaurs. Instead of being a true brain, this was actually an enlarged relay center that controlled these automatic reactions.

RELATIVE BRAIN SIZE

Dinosaur skulls often contain the remains of a brain cavity. This allows their brain volume to be measured by computerized imaging or by the more simple technique of filling the cavity with fluid and then measuring the fluid when it is poured out.

Dinosaur brains varied between the size of a walnut and a grapefruit. But the size of the body also has to be taken into account, because the larger an animal, the more nerves were needed to control it.

With living animals researchers have made detailed studies of the ratio between brain weight and total body weight. For humans the figure comes out at about 1:40; for an average dog it is about 1:125. For a stegosaur the figure was about 1:50,000—indicating that these animals were not very

bright. But body size and brain size do not always correlate. In small birds the ratio can be 1:12, which would appear to make them brighter than humans.

In gauging the relative intelligence of related animals, a more useful figure is an encephalization quotient, or EQ, which gives an idea of relative brain development. As the chart below shows, sauropods had the lowest figure among dinosaurs, with values of about 0.2, whereas small theropods did well, with scores above 5.5. Among mammals humans have an EQ of about 7.4, but this does not tell us much about dinosaur brainpower, as figures from very different groups cannot be directly compared.

INSTINCT AND LEARNING

Given their way of life, it is no surprise that plant-eating dinosaurs are on the bottom of the EQ list. Unlike hunting species, these animals did not need to stalk or ambush their food, and their daily life consisted largely of eating and digesting. By contrast, small hunters such as *Dromiceiomimus* survived by learning from experience, which gave them the best chance of making successful kills. For them intelligence was essential for survival.

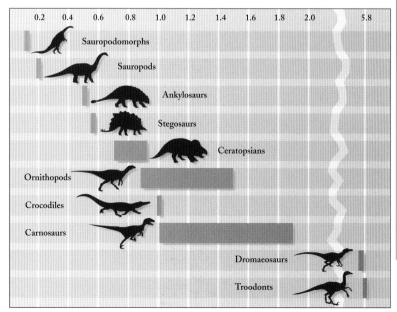

◁ This chart shows typical encephalization quotients, or EQs, for dinosaurs and crocodilians. EQ—not to be confused with IQ—is the ratio of actual brain weight to the expected brain weight given an animal's size and type. The expected brain weight for dinosaurs is based on measurements of living reptiles. EQ gives a general indication of brain development and therefore of an animal's intelligence. An EQ of more than 1 shows that an animal has a brain weight above average for its class, while an EQ below 1 shows the reverse.

EGGS AND PARENTAL CARE

As far as is known, all dinosaurs reproduced by laying eggs. Fossilized nests show that some were careful parents and looked after both their eggs and their young.

People have unearthed fossilized dinosaur eggs for centuries without realizing what they were. The first to be correctly identified were in France, just over 150 years ago. Since then many different types have been found, often exactly as they were laid. Dinosaur eggs were surprisingly small. The largest discovered is only about twice the length of an ostrich egg. They could not be larger, because the thick shells would have stopped the embryos inside from getting enough oxygen, and the baby dinosaurs would have been unable to break the shell when they hatched.

Dinosaur eggs came in a wide variety of shapes. Some of them looked like overstuffed sausages; others were round. Their shells could be pitted or smooth.
1 *Modern-day hen's egg— 3in.(7.5cm)long*
2 Maiasaura *egg— 6 in. (15cm) long*
3 Protoceratops *egg— 8 in. (20cm) long*
4 Hypselosaurus *egg— 12 in. (30cm) long*

DINOSAUR EGGS
Many of today's reptiles lay their eggs in shallow holes, which they scrape out in loose soil or mud. Fossilized nests, which have been discovered in many different parts of the world, suggest that most dinosaurs behaved in the same way. By scraping the ground with their feet, or perhaps their snouts, they excavated hollows or craters that could be over 3.3 ft. (1m) across. Like modern reptiles, the number of eggs laid by the dinosaurs varied. Some laid fewer than 10 eggs at a time, but some giant nests discovered recently in China contain 40 or more eggs.

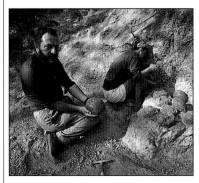

Complete dinosaur nests—like the one shown here—are a rare and exciting discovery. Most nests leave few remains, and for an entire nest to become fossilized before the young dinosaurs could hatch, something had to have gone badly wrong. This nest, which is being excavated by scientists in Argentina, was probably covered by a sudden sandstorm. The dinosaur embryos would have died from a lack of oxygen, allowing the whole egg clutch to be preserved.

INCUBATION
What happened after egg laying is more difficult to piece together. At one time paleontologists assumed that female dinosaurs covered their eggs and left them to develop on their own, but some fossils have shown that this may not always have been true. In the 1920s a fossil *Oviraptor* was found, apparently caught in the act of stealing eggs from a nest. However, more recent fossils (page 109) have shown *Oviraptor* sitting on its own eggs, probably to protect them and perhaps to keep them warm. If *Oviraptor* did incubate its eggs, it is unlikely to have been the only dinosaur that behaved in this way.

Some dinosaurs may have incubated their eggs by covering them with fresh vegetation. As the plants rotted they generated warmth like a compost heap. The warmth would

▷ *Dinosaur eggs were packed with nutrients, which would have made them a useful source of food for omnivores such as* Oviraptor. *Here, one has been caught trying to raid a* Protoceratops *nest, and the nest's owner has gone on the attack with its beaklike jaws.*

▽ *By nesting together, herd-forming species like* Maiasaura *had a better chance of fighting off nest raiders. Each female — perhaps helped by her mate—built a crater-shaped nest of mud up to 6.6 ft. (2m) wide. The female then laid about 20 eggs and covered the clutch with a mixture of foliage and sand. The eggs probably took about a month to hatch.*

have allowed the eggs to develop, even if the outside temperature was low.

LEAVING THE NEST
By examining the shells of empty eggs, researchers can figure out how young dinosaurs behaved immediately after they hatched. In many nests the shells are open at one end but largely intact. This suggests that the young moved out of their nest soon after hatching, or the empty shells would have been crushed by the young dinosaurs.

To leave the nest this early, these young animals must have been well developed. Their parents may have watched over them, but they were more likely to have been left to fend for themselves.

STAYING PUT
Other dinosaur nests tell a very different story. At a nest site in Montana crushed eggshells have been found with the fossilized remains of young nestlings. The nests were made by *Maiasaura*, a duck-billed dinosaur (page 104) that nested in groups. The recently hatched *Maiasaura* were still poorly developed, which makes it unlikely that they were about to leave the nest. They probably relied on their parents to bring them food. Once the young left the nest, they were protected by being part of a herd and by growing extremely rapidly. Even so, many young dinosaurs failed to survive their first year. This is why large families were an essential part of dinosaur life.

Carnivorous dinosaurs would have easily carried dead prey back to the nests. But plant food is harder to carry. *Maiasaura* probably brought plants back to its young, but other plant eaters may have fed their young with regurgitated semidigested food.

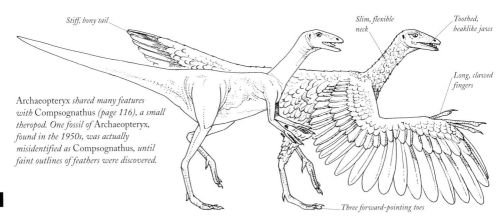

Longisquama's featherlike scales may have been used for gliding, but they are unlikely to have had any direct connection with the feathers evolved by birds.

THE ORIGIN OF BIRDS

MOST SCIENTISTS BELIEVE THAT BIRDS
EVOLVED FROM SMALL THEROPOD DINOSAURS.
THE KEY STEP WAS THE DEVELOPMENT OF
FEATHERS, TURNING ANIMALS THAT COULD
RUN OR CLIMB INTO ONES THAT COULD FLY.

The earliest true bird known to science is *Archaeopteryx*, which lived in the Late Jurassic Period, over 150 million years ago. Discovered in 1861, the fossil looked like a cross between a reptile and a bird, with a toothed beak, a long bony tail, and the unmistakable outline of feathers. In recent years other feathered reptiles have been found.

THE FIRST FEATHERS

Birds use feathers for two different things: to keep themselves warm and to fly. Feathers that are used for insulation are usually short and fluffy; those used for flight are much larger, with a curved surface, or vane. These two kinds of feathers are unlikely to have evolved at the same time. Insulating feathers most likely came first, and then, over millions of years, some developed into specialized feathers that could be used for flight.

No one knows when feathers first appeared. Some paleontologists have claimed that they can be seen in *Longisquama*, a reptile that dates back to Triassic times, but the majority of experts are not convinced. The best evidence for feather evolution comes from small theropods recently discovered in China. One of these, called *Sinosauropteryx*, had short downy plumage and a feathery crest running down its neck and back. It was a feathered dinosaur, but it would not have been able to fly.

INTO THE AIR

Sinosauropteryx lived slightly later than *Archaeopteryx*, so it could not have been its direct ancestor. However, its downy plumage shows what the forebears of flying birds may have looked like before they evolved fully feathered wings. But how did wings develop and, more importantly, why?

One theory is that the ancestors of birds evolved wings as an adaptation for hunting insects and other small animals. According to this idea these protobirds chased their

Stiff, bony tail

Slim, flexible neck

Toothed, beaklike jaws

Long, clawed fingers

Archaeopteryx *shared many features with* Compsognathus *(page 116), a small theropod. One fossil of* Archaeopteryx, *found in the 1950s, was actually misidentified as* Compsognathus, *until faint outlines of feathers were discovered.*

Three forward-pointing toes

prey across the ground, leaping into the air to catch small animals as they tried to escape. Over a long period of time they developed extra-large feathers on their front legs to help them stay balanced and also perhaps to help them scoop up their prey. The feathers gradually became longer as the muscles that worked the front legs became stronger. Eventually this created animals that could flap their way off the ground.

GLIDERS IN THE TREES?

This ground-based theory is supported by some features shown by *Archaeopteryx*, such as its strong legs. But most paleontologists believe that birds actually evolved from reptiles that lived not on the ground, but in trees. By evolving extra-large feathers, these animals would have developed the ability to glide so that they could travel through woodlands and forests without having to touch the ground. From this, flapping flight would gradually have developed.

Gliding is something that has cropped up many times in reptile evolution. It was used by *Coelurosauravus* (page 170) and a range of other tree-dwellers, and it can be seen in several species of lizards alive today. For supporters of the tree-based theory, this makes it all the more likely that birds began in a similar way.

LIGHT FOR FLIGHT

Gliding uses up very little energy, but flapping flight is strenuous. To stay airborne, early birds had to undergo some important

design changes that made them increasingly different from their dinosaur ancestors. Evolution cannot look ahead, so these changes were not preplanned. Instead, they built up slowly over a long period as birds spent more and more of their time in the air.

Many of these changes helped birds lose the weight that made it harder for them to stay aloft. Many of their bones fused, and their skeletons became lighter. Like their theropod ancestors, they had hollow, air-filled bones, but the air spaces became larger and more extensive, reaching most of the way down their wings and legs.

They also developed enlarged breastbones, which anchored the powerful chest muscles that were needed for flight, and a V-shaped furcula, or wishbone, that braced the chest during flight.

These changes proved to be a winning combination. Birds became increasingly common in Cretaceous times, and when the Age of Reptiles came to its cataclysmic end, they were the only dinosaur descendants that managed to survive.

▽ Avimimus *(far left) was a feathered theropod that could not fly.* Archaeopteryx *(center) was smaller and lighter with well-developed flight feathers.*

Pigeon

△ *Unlike* Archaeopteryx, *modern birds like this pigeon have no teeth, short tails, and—with a handful of exceptions, such as the hoatzin—they have no wing claws.*

Avimimus

Archaeopteryx

▷ Archaeopteryx *had assymmetrical or "lopsided" wing feathers, like those of modern birds. Feathers like these generate lift when air flows over them, and they are evidence that* Archaeopteryx *could fly.*

EARLY BIRDS

Despite the discovery of many fossils, there are still plenty of unanswered questions about how early birds evolved. Some researchers think that they may have split into two groups early in their history. According to this theory the first group contained *Archaeopteryx* and other long-tailed species; the second contained short-tailed birds—the direct ancestors of the ones alive today. Not all paleontologists are convinced, but one fact is certain: by Late Cretaceous times, birds were very successful and lived all over the Earth.

△ *Apart from its toothed beak,* Ichthyornis *looked like a modern tern, and it probably had a very similar way of life. The evidence for* Ichthyornis' *diet comes from large numbers of fish bones found near its fossilized remains.*

▷ Hesperornis *swam by paddling with its webbed feet while using its stubby wings to steer. Compared to flying birds, diving species like* Hesperornis *have fewer air-cavities in their bones. This helped them stay submerged.*

ARCHAEOPTERYX

Archaeopteryx is probably one of the most famous prehistoric animals known. Only six fossil specimens have been found—all from Solnhöfen in southern Germany—but in most of them the imprint of feathers can clearly be seen. *Archaeopteryx* was about the size of a crow, but had toothed jaws and a long, reptilelike tail. Its legs were long, and its wings had three claws at their elbows, which might have been used for climbing. Like today's birds, it probably reproduced by laying and incubating eggs, although no fossils of these have been found.

MAXIMUM LENGTH 13.8 in. (35cm)
TIME Late Jurassic
FOSSIL FINDS Europe (Germany)

▷ Archaeopteryx *is a classic example of an evolutionary link between two groups of animals. It was discovered just two years after Charles Darwin published his theory of evolution.*

ICHTHYORNIS

With a name meaning "fish bird," *Ichthyornis* was similar to some of the seabirds alive today, although it still had one primitive feature—a beak lined with sharp teeth. Unlike *Archaeopteryx*, the bony part of its tail was very short, and its wings did not have claws. Internally it had two other features that are found in all modern flying birds: many of its bones contained large air spaces, which helped reduce its overall weight, and it also had a narrow, forward-pointing flap called a keel that protruded from its breastbone. This flap, which is missing in *Archaeopteryx*, anchored the large chest muscles that powered its wings.

MAXIMUM LENGTH 14 in. (35cm)
TIME Late Cretaceous
FOSSIL FINDS North America (Kansas, Texas)

HESPERORNIS

The earliest true birds were flying species, but as birds evolved some species lost the power of flight. One of them was *Hesperornis*—a large, fish-eating diver with tiny wings and legs placed far back along its body, near its tail. On land *Hesperornis* may have lumbered along like a seal, but its streamlined shape and webbed feet made it fast and maneuverable underwater like today's grebes. Becoming flightless may seem like a step backward, but during bird evolution many other species have followed this path. They include many land-dwelling species, including the largest birds that have ever lived (page 213).

MAXIMUM LENGTH 5.7 ft. (1.75m)
TIME Late Cretaceous
FOSSIL FINDS North America (Kansas)

GIANT MEAT EATERS

During the Jurassic and Cretaceous periods, predatory theropods evolved along with their prey. Some species, such as *Deinonychus*, tackled large animals by hunting in packs, but others relied on their individual size and power to make a kill. These giant meat eaters were the superpredators of the reptile age, able to topple plant eaters that could weigh over 30 tons. *Tyrannosaurus* is by far the most famous among them, but recent discoveries have shown that in Cretaceous times other predatory theropods may have been larger.

PACK ATTACK

Launching a deadly ambush, a group of Deinonychus attack a plant-eating hypsilophodont several times their own size. For Cretaceous plant eaters packs of these small and highly agile hunters would have been just as dangerous as much larger predators that stalked prey on their own.

CARNOSAURS

AT ONE TIME ALL LARGE PREDATORY DINOSAURS WERE CLASSIFIED IN A GROUP CALLED THE CARNOSAURS, MEANING "FLESH REPTILES." SINCE THEN RESEARCH HAS SHOWN THAT GIANT MEAT EATERS WERE NOT NECESSARILY CLOSE RELATIVES.

Unlike the smaller theropods, which often used their claws to attack their prey, the largest meat eaters of the dinosaur world used their teeth to attack their victims. Their arms were often puny, but their skulls were huge—a feature that *Carcharodontosaurus* (page 160), shows in a particularly chilling way. For hunting, this kind of anatomy proved to be lethally effective, and it probably evolved separately in several different theropod groups.

▽ *This cladogram shows the possible links between tetanurans, or advanced theropods. Each branch forms a clade, which includes an ancestral species and its descendants.*

FAMILY FEATURES
At first glance giant theropods, such as *Allosaurus* and *Tyrannosaurus*, look very similar. All of them had powerful hind legs, small arms, and narrow skulls with immense, tooth-filled jaws. They may not have been as fast on their feet as paleontologists once supposed, and it is likely that some of them

were scavengers as well as hunters, but their reputation as the ultimate terrestrial killers is still well deserved.

It seems only logical that these massively built hunters were as closely related as, for example, tigers and lions are today. But for paleontologists trying to work out the evolutionary history of dinosaurs outward similarities can cause problems. Animals often develop similar adaptations if they have similar lifestyles through convergent evolution. If they are already similar to begin with, convergence can make true family relationships extremely difficult to unravel. This is true of large theropods.

UNRAVELING THE PAST
To get a true picture of how closely different species are related, paleontologists and biologists use a system called cladistics. This involves comparing animals in detail and seeing how many derived features they share. A derived feature is one that develops in an ancestral species and that is then handed on to all of its descendants. Because ancestors have ancestors themselves, derived features steadily build up as time goes by. The more derived features two species share, the more closely they must be related. This information can be used to construct a cladogram, a chart that shows the branches in evolution that divide one group of species from another.

The cladogram on this page shows one idea of how all the advanced theropods might have been related. The allosaurs and tyrannosaurs are far apart and belong to two separate "clades": the carnosaurs, a group that contains some of the largest theropods, and the coelurosaurs, which contains some of the smallest. Through convergent evolution

TETANURANS   CARNOSAURS   COELUROSAURS

Megalosaurs | Allosaurs | Carcharo-dontosaurs | Coelurus | Compsognathus | Bird mimics | Segnosaurs | Oviraptor | Dromaeosaurs | Tyrannosaurs

tyrannosaurs developed giant bodies and tiny arms, just like the allosaurs, which had appeared 50 million years earlier.

LIMITS TO GROWTH

Like the plant-eating sauropods (page 84), giant theropods enjoyed some obvious advantages because of their size. Weighing up to six or seven tons, and with bodies up to 46 ft. (14m) long, they would have developed a nearly unstoppable momentum as they slammed into prey. As sauropods increased in size these hunters did as well, although the increase happened at different times in different groups, with the megalosaurs being the first to enter the heavyweight class.

But if large size was such an asset, why did theropods stop growing at seven tons, when plant-eating dinosaurs evolved bodies that were perhaps ten times heavier? The main reason is that, unlike plant eaters, predators rely on speed and agility to survive. Compared to smaller theropods, animals like *Allosaurus* were already slow and lumbering, and it is likely that if they had evolved much larger bodies, they would not have been able to function as predators that pursued their prey.

▽ *Large theropods like* Tyrannosaurus *evolved extreme differences in size between the front and back limbs. Their heads were the largest of all the dinosaurs, apart from some ceratopsians.* Tyrannosaurus *may have ambushed animals rather than chasing them. It may also have obtained a proportion of its food from carrion, which is an efficient form of nutrition.*

GIANT MEAT EATERS

MEGALOSAURS AND SEGNOSAURS

The megalosaurs were the earliest of the giant bipedal hunters. Megalosaurs had small front legs with three-fingered hands, massively built skulls, and in some cases horns or crests. Segnosaurs, also known as therizinosaurs, are known only from fragmentary remains. They were unrelated to megalosaurs, and experts have had great difficulty deciding where they fit into the dinosaur world. Some believe they were plant-eating sauropods, but others think they were highly specialized large theropods.

DILOPHOSAURUS

The earliest known megalosaur, *Dilophosaurus* was an agile hunter, despite weighing up to half a ton. Its most conspicuous feature was its double crest, which was positioned over its forehead and muzzle with a central furrow running down its length. Its function is unclear. It may have been used in courtship displays and is likely to have been larger in males than in females. The remains of three *Dilophosaurus* found together in Arizona suggest that this species may have hunted in packs. Some scientists have concluded from its long, thin teeth that *Dilophosaurus* was more likely to have used its clawed hands, rather than its teeth, to grab its prey and tear it apart.

MAXIMUM LENGTH	19.7 ft. (6m)
TIME	Early Jurassic
FOSSIL FINDS	North America (Arizona), Asia (China)

△ Dilophosaurus' *double head crest was partly hollow, so it is unlikely that it was used for self-defense. It may have been for display and unique to males.*

▷ Eustreptospondylus *was first mistaken for* Megalosaurus, *since the two animals were similar in many ways. However, it was about 6.5 ft. (2m) shorter, with a much smaller body weight.*

EUSTREPTOSPONDYLUS

Only one specimen of *Eustreptospondylus* has ever been found. Unusual for a land animal it was discovered in marine sediments, leading scientists to conclude that its carcass was washed out to sea. It may have reached the sea by a river, but it is possible that it lived on the shore, perhaps scavenging food from the remains of animals left stranded by the tide. Although incomplete, the fossil is still the best-preserved carnosaur yet found in Europe. It had a typical megalosaur build, with large back legs, three-fingered hands, and a head without a crest. Some of the bones show signs of not being fully developed, which makes it likely that it was not fully grown when it died.

MAXIMUM LENGTH	23 ft. (7m)
TIME	Mid Jurassic to Late Cretaceous
FOSSIL FINDS	Europe (England)

MEGALOSAURUS

Standing 10 ft. (3m) tall and weighing about a ton, *Megalosaurus*, meaning "great lizard" was an animal that lived up to its name. A *Megalosaurus* thighbone, found in England in 1676, was the first dinosaur bone to come to the attention of European scientists. At the time no one correctly guessed what it was, and over 150 years passed before Richard Owen, the pioneering anatomist and paleontologist, included *Megalosaurus* in a new category of extinct reptiles—the dinosaurs. Since then *Megalosaurus* remains have been found in several different countries, although none of the remains are complete. However, they show that it was one of the largest predators of the Jurassic, with a head around 3 ft. (1m) long. Fossilized trackways found in southern England show that it had a pigeon-toed gait and held its a feature of *Nanshiungosaurus* and its relatives. One species, called *Alxasaurus*, had finger claws that were up to 27.6 in. (70cm) long, making them probably the largest of any dinosaur.

| **MAXIMUM LENGTH** 16.4 ft. (5m) |
| **TIME** Mid to Late Cretaceous |
| **FOSSIL FINDS** Asia (China) |

PROCERATOSAURUS
The most unusual feature of *Proceratosaurus* was the horn on the top of its snout. This was thought to be evidence that it was a forerunner of the ceratosaurs (page 116), which is how it got its name. It is often classified as a megalosaur, but its place is open to doubt because the only remains found so far have been part of the skull and jaw. Apart from its horn, *Proceratosaurus* seems to have been a typical Mid Jurassic hunter, although a fairly small one with a maximum weight of perhaps 220 lb. (100kg).

| **MAXIMUM LENGTH** 13.1 ft. (4m) |
| **TIME** Mid Jurassic |
| **FOSSIL FINDS** Europe (U.K.) |

◁ Megalosaurus *was a successful prototype version of the giant bipedal predator. The same body form was seen among various groups of theropods right until the Age of Reptiles ended.*

◁ Proceratosaurus *is known from a single skull, which makes it difficult to judge exactly how it looked. This reconstruction shows it as a typical theropod, with small front legs.*

▽ *Looking more like a sauropod than a theropod,* Nanshiungosaurus *is a mystifying animal. It may have led an amphibious existence, feeding on fish, but its large size, long neck, and small head make it just as likely that it was a grazer.*

tail off the ground when moving quickly. It was probably a fairly rapid runner, although it was not built for a long chase.

| **MAXIMUM LENGTH** 29.5 ft. (9m) |
| **TIME** Jurassic |
| **FOSSIL FINDS** Europe (France, U.K.), Africa (Morocco) |

ERLIKOSAURUS
Erlikosaurus belonged to the segnosaur, or therizinosaur, family—an obscure group of less than a dozen known species, all from central Asia or the Far East. Although segnosaurs are generally classified as theropods, *Erlikosaurus*'s skull—the only segnosaur example discovered so far—looks unlike those of other predatory dinosaurs, with small teeth overall but an upper jaw that ends in a toothless beak. It had unusually large claws and probably stood on two legs. From studies of its teeth and skeleton, it seems possible that *Erlikosaurus* and other segnosaurs may have been fish eaters.

| **MAXIMUM LENGTH** 19.7 ft. (6m) |
| **TIME** Mid Cretaceous |
| **FOSSIL FINDS** Asia (Mongolia) |

NANSHIUNGOSAURUS
Like *Erlikosaurus*, this animal was also a segnosaur, but knowledge about it is based on a handful of very incomplete remains. Nothing is known about its head, because its skull has not been found, but it had a long neck and tail. Its front legs were well developed, and it may have moved on all fours. Enlarged finger claws seem to have been

GIANT MEAT EATERS

ALLOSAURS

ppearing 50 million years before the tyrannosaurs, the allosaurs may have included the largest carnivores ever to have lived on land. Found throughout the world, they were bipedal predators, with immense heads, very large back legs, but relatively short arms with three-fingered hands. No dinosaur—no matter how large—would have been able to withstand allosaur packs.

▽ *An* Allosaurus *attacks a* Diplodocus *several times its own size.* Allosaurus *may have hunted individually—on their own they would have been fearsome—or in packs.*

CARCHARODONTOSAURUS

Meaning "shark-toothed lizard," *Carcharodontosaurus* was first discovered in the 1920s. These remains were destroyed during World War II, but some new ones have only recently been unearthed (pages 160–161). This massively built hunter (and possible scavenger) may have weighed as much as eight tons, and had teeth up to 8 in. (20cm) long. Its skull measured about 5.2 ft. (1.6m) from front to back, and it is possible that the entire animal may have been larger than *Tyrannosaurus* (page 144), even though its brain was only about half the size.

MAXIMUM LENGTH 44.3 ft. (13.5m)

TIME Early Cretaceous

FOSSIL FINDS North Africa

ALLOSAURUS

Allosaurus was a common and widespread predator 150 million years ago. It hunted or scavenged for a living, and weighed up to three tons. Scientists are still debating how a predator this large would have moved or whether it would have been able to chase and catch fast-moving prey. Despite its powerful hind legs, it is unlikely that it would have been able to run faster than 18 mph (30km/h), and skeletal injuries in some *Allosaurus* remains suggest that it was often injured while hunting —either in falls or by its prey fighting back.

MAXIMUM LENGTH 39.5 ft. (12m)

TIME Late Jurassic

FOSSIL FINDS North America (western U.S.A.), Australia

NEOVENATOR

Discovered on England's Isle of Wight in 1978 but not excavated until the 1980s, *Neovenator*, meaning "new hunter," was a smaller and more agile predator than its cousin *Allosaurus*. The single fossil found so far shows that *Neovenator* has a strongly curved forehead and large nostrils, indicating a good sense of smell. During Cretaceous times it was probably the largest flesh-eating dinosaur in what is now northern Europe.

MAXIMUM LENGTH 42.6 ft. (13m)

TIME Early Cretaceous

FOSSIL FINDS Europe (England)

GIGANOTOSAURUS

Found in 1994 by an amateur paleontologist in Patagonia, *Giganotosaurus* may have been the largest predatory dinosaur ever. Its skull alone was nearly as long as a man is tall, and its body was as long as a bus. Estimates of its weight vary, with the highest figure— about eight tons—putting it among the real heavyweights of the theropod world. Unlike

△ *Striding across a marshy landscape,* Neovenator *sniffs the air for prey. This recently discovered allosaur had a muzzle shaped like a giant beak.*

Tyrannosaurus, Giganotosaurus had a relatively narrow head and teeth that were shaped for slicing through flesh, rather than for breaking bones. Its name means "giant southern lizard."

MAXIMUM LENGTH 42.64 ft. (13m)

TIME Late Cretaceous

FOSSIL FINDS South America (Argentina)

◁ *With its right shoulder seriously injured, the* Apatosaurus *risks crashing to the ground. If it does, it cannot escape, and the* Allosaurus *can make an easy kill.*

GIANT MEAT EATERS

◁ Two young Albertosaurus *race past a* Daspletosaurus *that has waded into water to eat a carcass. If the* Daspletosaurus *had been on land, the smaller animals would not have risked venturing so close.*

DASPLETOSAURUS
Only a handful of specimens of this dinosaur have been found, but its fossilized remains suggest that it may have been a direct ancestor of *Tyrannosaurus*. It probably weighed up to three tons, and would have been about 16.5 ft. (5m) tall. Like other tyrannosaurs, *Daspletosaurus* had an extra set of ribs called gastralia between its true ribs and its pelvis. These helped support its intestines and may have protected them when resting on the ground.

MAXIMUM LENGTH	26.5 ft. (8m)
TIME	Late Cretaceous
FOSSIL FINDS	North America (Alberta)

TYRANNOSAURS

Although they existed for only 15 million years, the tyrannosaurs are among the most fascinating and awe-inspiring animals from the dinosaur age. Their huge heads were armed with immense, serrated teeth, and they stood on pillarlike back legs that could be twice as tall as an adult man. Their front legs were even smaller than those of the allosaurs, and they ended in two-fingered hands not much larger than our own. Tyrannosaurs were undoubtedly meat eaters and probably lived mainly by hunting. They may also have scavenged for dead remains.

ALBERTOSAURUS
Weighing about three tons, *Albertosaurus* was small compared to its relatives, but still much larger than any predatory land animal alive today. It had the typical tyrannosaur build, with an outsized head, long hind legs, and a muscular tail that helped it balance. Each of its jaws had a single row of serrated teeth, which were gradually shed and replaced throughout its lifetime. It shared its habitat with plant eaters such as hadrosaurs (pages 104–107) and ankylosaurs (pages 164–165), which would also have been its prey.

▽ For tyrannosaurs life was a constant balancing act. As it strides along this Tarbosaurus *holds its tail high so that it acts as a counterbalance for its enormous head.*

TARBOSAURUS
This Asian tyrannosaur looks very much like *Tyrannosaurus*, but had a longer skull and was not so heavily built. Like *Tyrannosaurus*, it was unlikely to have survived solely by hunting and probably scavenged dead remains. It lived in Asia, where it would have been the largest land predator. Fossil remains of *Tarbosaurus* were first discovered in 1948 and since then experts have been divided on exactly where it fits into the tyrannosaur family. Because it is so similar to *Tyrannosaurus*, some experts think that it might actually be the same animal.

MAXIMUM LENGTH	46 ft. (14m)
TIME	Late Cretaceous
FOSSIL FINDS	Asia (Mongolia)

MAXIMUM LENGTH	26.5 ft. (8m)
TIME	Late Cretaceous
FOSSIL FINDS	North America (U.S.A., Canada)

▽ *With a menacing lunge of its head, a* Tyrannosaurus *threatens a* Troodon *that has just stolen part of its meal. The subject of the feast is a hadrosaur, which has died from natural causes. Remains like these probably made up an important part of* Tyrannosaurus' *diet. Like scavengers today,* Tyrannosaurus *would have found this type of food partly by smell and partly by looking to see where other scavengers had gathered.*

TYRANNOSAURUS

After *Carcharadontosaurus* (page 142), this huge animal was probably the largest land-based predator that has ever lived on Earth. Several superbly preserved fossil skeletons have been found, most notably "Sue" (page 147), which was discovered in 1990. These fossils show that *Tyrannosaurus* weighed up to seven tons and towered up to 20 ft. (6m) high. It took strides nearly 16.5 ft. (5m) long—farther than most long-jumps—and dealt with its food using 6 in. (15cm)-long teeth with serrated edges like steak knives. Some scientists have suggested that it was too large to pursue its prey in the open, because its tiny arms could not have broken its fall if it tripped and fell. Instead, it may have hunted by lurking among trees, launching an attack when its prey was close.

MAXIMUM LENGTH 46 ft. (14m)

TIME Late Cretaceous

FOSSIL FINDS North America (U.S.A., Canada), Asia (Mongolia)

ALIORAMUS

Most tyrannosaurs had deep skulls, and jaws that were flattened from side to side. *Alioramus* and its relatives were different, because their skulls had elongated snouts with weaker jaws. *Alioramus* also had about six bony knobs located between its nostrils and eyes. These knobs were too small to have been weapons, and it is possible that they played a part in courtship, like the "horns" some lizards have today. If this is true, they may have been present only in the males.

MAXIMUM LENGTH 16.5 ft. (6m)

TIME Late Cretaceous

FOSSIL FINDS Asia (Mongolia)

FOSSIL HUNTING IN NORTH AMERICA

THE FIRST DINOSAUR FOSSILS WERE FOUND IN EUROPE, BUT NORTH AMERICA IS THE PLACE WHERE "DINOMANIA" REALLY GOT UNDERWAY —PARTLY AS A RESULT OF A BITTER FEUD BETWEEN TWO LEADING PALEONTOLOGISTS.

Dry places are particularly good for finding fossils. Over millions of years wind and rain scour the surface of the ground, revealing fossils entombed in the underlying rock. This tree trunk is one of hundreds in Arizona's Petrified Forest National Park. This particular trunk has broken into sections as the rock that supported it has slowly crumbled away.

In 1858 the zoologist Joseph Leidy described the first dinosaur skeleton found in North America as *Hadrosaurus*. But during the late 1800s two much more forceful characters dominated the fossil-hunting stage: Edward Drinker Cope (1840–97) and Othniel Charles Marsh (1831–99). They discovered huge numbers of fossils, and their rivalry ignited public interest in North America's fascinating prehistoric life.

COLLECTING THE PAST

By the time Cope and Marsh died, they had accumulated an extraordinary variety of fossil remains. These included the first reconstruction of a giant plant-eating sauropod—*Apatosaurus* (known at the time as *Brontosaurus*)— and a wide array of others, including predators such as allosaurs and tyrannosaurs, as well as the horned dinosaurs, or ceratopsids, which were unique to North America. They also helped trace the path that evolution had followed. Marsh, for

△▷ *Edward Drinker Cope (above) and Othniel Charles Marsh (right) were pioneering North American paleontologists.*

example, assembled a complete series of fossil horses, showing how these animals had slowly adapted to life on North America's open plains.

TREASURE TROVES

Because of its size and varied geography North America is a paleontologist's paradise. Many of the best finds have been made in the Badlands and deserts of the midwestern U.S.A., where ancient sedimentary rocks have been slowly eroded by rivers, rain, and wind. Some of these sites have produced an enormous number of fossils. At Ghost Ranch in New Mexico, for example, the remains of over 1,000 *Coelophysis*—a small bipedal predator—are convincing evidence that these agile animals hunted in packs. Another site, the Red Deer River in Alberta, Canada, has produced more types of dinosaurs than any equivalent area in the world. Farther west—and further back in time—Canada was also the site of one of the most important fossil formations revealing early animal life: the Burgess Shale (page 32–35).

Not all North American fossil finds consist of remains that were once buried in rock. The famous La Brea tar pits, in Los Angeles, are deposits of sticky tar that has seeped up from natural springs since prehistoric times. From these treacherous pools the fossilized remains of thousands of trapped animals have been recovered (page 212).

RECENT DISCOVERIES

North America is famous for giant fossils, and in recent years there have been spectacular discoveries. One of the most exciting came in 1990, when the remains of a gigantic

△ *Soft sedimentary rocks are a prime source of fossils. These rocks in Arizona were laid down during the Triassic.*

Tyrannosaurus rex were found in South Dakota. The fossil—named Sue after its finder Sue Hendrickson—is now displayed in the Field Museum, Chicago, and is the largest and most complete *Tyrannosaurus* on display anywhere in the world. Unlike previous finds, Sue's skeleton includes a wishbone, or furcula—evidence that supports the widespread belief that birds evolved from predatory dinosaurs.

Some finds are accidental. In 1979 two hikers in New Mexico came across the fossilized tail of *Seismosaurus*. The tail led paleontologists to the rest of this plant eater's skeleton, which is still being unearthed.

△ *Excavating fossils is a delicate business. A wooden frame is used to protect the pelvis of a Tyrannosaurus before it is winched away from the surrounding bedrock.*

◁ *The completed mount of Sue's fossilized skeleton is displayed at the Field Museum in Chicago. This massive animal weighed about 6.5 tons and was nearly 42.7 ft. (13m) long.*

△ *Paleontonlogists work on the fossilized skeleton of a* Tyrannosaurus, *cleaning and stabilizing the remains before they are removed from the site where the have lain for over 60 million years.*

WERE DINOSAURS WARM-BLOODED?

BECAUSE DINOSAURS WERE REPTILES IT IS EASY TO IMAGINE THAT THEIR BODIES WORKED LIKE MODERN REPTILES'. BUT IN ONE KEY AREA THEY MAY HAVE BEEN DISTINCTLY DIFFERENT.

At one time, scientists assumed that dinosaurs were cold-blooded, which means that their temperature depended on their surroundings. But in the early 1970s an American biologist, Robert Bakker (page 84), argued that they might have been warm-blooded, like mammals and birds. This controversial theory has radically altered ideas about dinosaur biology.

Lizards are cold-blooded. Their temperature rises as the day warms and then falls at night.

Walruses are warm-blooded. Their body temperature always remains at 95°F (35°C).

WARMTH FROM WITHIN

Living vertebrates (animals with backbones) can be divided into two overall groups. Animals in the first group—amphibians, fish, and reptiles—are cold-blooded, or ectothermic. Their body temperature rises and falls according to the temperature around them. Birds and mammals, on the other hand, are warm-blooded, or endothermic. An inbuilt thermostat keeps their body temperature almost constant— and usually much higher than that of their surroundings. Warm-blooded animals generate more heat by breaking down more food, and they retain it by having an insulating layer of feathers, fat, or fur.

These two different systems have some far-reaching effects on the way animals live, because bodies work more efficiently at high temperatures. When it is hot, cold-blooded animals are also hot, and they can move quickly. But when it becomes cool, the same animals become slow and sluggish. In really cold conditions they have difficulty moving at all. Warm-blooded animals stay warm whatever the conditions are outside, so birds and mammals can remain active and busy during the coldest winters; some of them are even comfortable on polar ice.

WRAPPING UP

Dinosaur remains do contain some clues that hint at a warm-blooded lifestyle. For many paleontologists one of the most convincing is feathery insulation— something that has only been seen in the very recent past. The first feathered dinosaur, *Sinosauropteryx*, was discovered in northeast China in 1996, revealing patches of feathery filaments around its fossilized skeleton. In 2000 an even clearer example of primitive plumage—this time in a dromaeosaur—was unearthed in the same region (page 111). Neither of these Chinese dinosaurs could fly, and the only conceivable function for their feathers was to retain body heat. Both were small predatory theropods, and if they had feathers, it is quite likely that other theropods did as well. They were not the only insulated reptiles of prehistoric times. Some pterosaurs, such as

Sordes (page 174), seem to have had the equivalent of close-cropped fur.

Another factor that points to warm-bloodedness was their way of life. Like other small theropods, *Sinosauropteryx* had a relatively large brain, and its skeleton shows that it would have been an agile and fleet-footed hunter. This kind of lifestyle would have called for rapid reactions—a characteristic feature of warm-blooded animals.

EVIDENCE IN BONE

Some experts also believe that signs of warm-bloodedness can be seen in dinosaur skeletons. In the 1970s Robert Bakker pointed out that when looked at under a microscope, dinosaur bones show signs of sustained rapid growth. This feature is common in warm-blooded animals, but rarer in cold-blooded ones, except in times when there is a particularly good supply of food.

But many paleontologists today find this evidence doubtful, and recent research into dinosaur breathing has prompted different conclusions. The paleontologists looked at dinosaur noses with X-ray scanners, searching for turbinal bones inside the nasal cavity. In birds and mammals these bones form a complicated collection of paper-thin scrolls that allow warmth and moisture to be collected and recycled from outgoing air. But if dinosaurs were cold-blooded, their

breath would also have been cold, so there would have been no warmth to recycle and probably no turbinal bones. The results so far show that dinosaurs did not have them.

DINOSAUR HEARTS

If dinosaurs were warm-blooded, their circulatory systems would have been modified to produce a higher rate of oxygen flow. They would have needed larger hearts than their cold-blooded relatives, and their blood would almost certainly have flowed in a figure-eight circuit. This double circulation system allows oxygen-rich blood to be pumped at high pressure and high speed.

Unfortunately, soft organs, such as dinosaur hearts, hardly ever fossilize, but in 2000 the remains of what looked like a heart were found in a fossil of *Thescelosaurus*, a small plant-eating hypsilophodont. Using medical scanning techniques, researchers concluded that it did have a double circulation system, meaning that it could have been warm-blooded.

◁ *The photograph (far left) shows growth rings in dinosaur bone. Growth rings like these are usually found in cold-blooded animals, and they show spurts of growth that occur during warm conditions, when there is plenty of food.*

◁ *Dinosaurs also have fibrolamellar bone (center), which is found in warm-blooded animals. This kind of bone grows quickly, and is not usually found in cold-blooded animals, although there are some exceptions to this rule.*

DOUBLE CIRCULATION SYSTEM

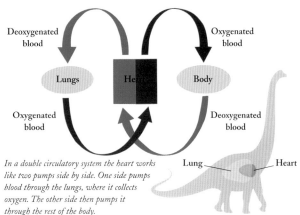

Deoxygenated blood — Oxygenated blood

Lungs — Heart — Body

Oxygenated blood — Deoxygenated blood

Lung — Heart

In a double circulatory system the heart works like two pumps side by side. One side pumps blood through the lungs, where it collects oxygen. The other side then pumps it through the rest of the body.

△ A warm-blooded predator needs about ten times as much food as a cold-blooded one, so 100 antelope could keep one lion, or 10 crocodiles, fed for a year.

▽ Warm-blooded hunters need a high intake of food to keep their bodies working, and to make up for heat loss.

ENERGY FROM FOOD

In the debate about whether dinosaurs were warm-blooded, the search for anatomical clues continues. But paleontologists also have another line of evidence—the relative numbers of predators and their prey.

Cold-blooded predators, which include all of today's reptiles, can survive on a small amount of food. Crocodiles, for example, can go for weeks between meals, because they need only a small amount of energy to keep their bodies running, and some snakes can last over a year. Warm-blooded

predators, on the other hand, use up about ten times as much energy simply running their bodies and keeping them warm, which means that they need to take in about ten times as much food per kilogram (2.2 lb.) of body weight. A lion can survive without eating for a few days, but if this hungry period stretches to much more than a week, it runs the serious risk of starving to death. For smaller warm-blooded animals things become critical even more rapidly, because their body warmth quickly drains away.

This difference means that the same numbers of prey can support ten times as many cold-blooded hunters as warm-blooded ones. Assuming that hunters and their prey fossilize at the same rate (which may or may not be true), paleontologists should be able to tell if a predatory dinosaur was warm-blooded simply by counting fossils, and doing some simple arithmetic.

At present, this work on prehistoric ecology is still underway. Some researchers claim to have found a warm-blooded ratio, but the overall picture is far from clear.

MIX AND MATCH

Faced with this confusing and sometimes contradictory evidence, paleontologists have come to a variety of conclusions. Some think that all dinosaurs were warm-blooded, while others believe that they were cold-blooded, like modern reptiles. But a growing number are convinced that different groups of dinosaurs worked in different ways.

According to this idea, small highly active predators, such as *Sinosauropteryx*, were fully warm-blooded, like birds, while some of the smaller plant eaters may have been cold-blooded, like modern reptiles. But the largest dinosaurs—particularly the sauropods—may have been somewhere in between, simply because they were so big. Like giant fermentation tanks on legs, these animals would have absorbed heat energy as their internal microbes broke down their food, but their massive bulk would have meant that this heat would have been very slow to drain away. They would have been "lukewarm-blooded"—a curious situation that has no equivalent in animals alive today.

ARMORED DINOSAURS

In the early stages of dinosaur evolution, plant-eating species often relied on their great size to protect them from predators. But during the Jurassic Period, different ways of protecting herbivores from attack evolved. One of these was body armor, a defensive system that allowed plant eaters to stand their ground. Most armored dinosaurs belonged to the ornithischian, or bird-hipped, branch of the dinosaur world. They included animals with massive head shields and gigantic horns, as well as ones that carried their own armor plating on their backs.

DINOSAUR DEFENSES

FOR PLANT-EATING DINOSAURS, RESISTING
ATTACK RATHER THAN RUNNING AWAY WAS
A HIGH-RISK STRATEGY. IN A WORLD FULL
OF PREDATORS THEY NEEDED THE BEST
DEFENSES THAT EVOLUTION COULD PROVIDE.

It is hard to imagine what it feels like to be approached by a hungry carnivore weighing six or seven tons. In normal circumstances most plant-eating dinosaurs did their very best to prevent this from happening by being constantly alert for danger and being ready to walk or run away. But for armored dinosaurs different instincts applied. These animals evolved a strategy that meant standing their ground. Their bodies were designed to withstand a direct assault, but to increase their chances of survival, many of them tried to land the first blow by going on the attack.

FOSSIL EVIDENCE

Dinosaur defenses are not always what they seem. Stegosaurus had a row of bony plates along its back, which were once thought to be armor against attack. However, detailed examination of fossilized plates—like the one shown here—has revealed that they were made of relatively soft bone. Instead of being a form of armor, they are more likely to have been used to control body temperature.

JAWS AND CLAWS

Unlike predatory theropods, most plant-eating dinosaurs were unable to do much damage with their teeth. This was either because they did not have any or because their teeth were shaped for collecting and crushing plants, rather than for stabbing flesh. Some armored species had toothless beaks that could deliver a dangerous bite (page 155), but jaws played little part in plant eaters' self-defense. Feet and claws were another matter. Many sauropods could rear up on their hind legs to stamp on an attacker— something that was made even more effective by a single sharp thumb claw on each front foot. Although they were much smaller, many ornithopods also had these claws, and because they often moved on only their hind legs, they would have been able to carry out hand-to-hand combat. These thumb claws were especially large in iguanodonts (page 100).

WHIPS AND CLUBS
But with some plant eaters the part that a predator had to watch out for was the tail. The 33-ft. (10-m)-long tail of an adult *Diplodocus* had the same sort of strength and flexibility as tire rubber reinforced by strands of steel wire. If it was given a sudden flick, the tip would reach supersonic speeds, wrapping around an enemy's body like a whip. A well-aimed blow against a predator's eyes or legs would leave it temporarily blinded or reeling on the ground.

Some sauropods, such as *Shunosaurus* (page 75), had tails with bony tips, which turned them into clubs. The real specialists at this form of defense were the ankylosaurs (page 165). Their tails were not particularly long by dinosaur standards, but they carried a more substantial weight. In *Euoplocephalus*, one of the largest species, the tail could probably reach a speed of over 30 mph (50km/h) by the end of a 180-degree swing, landing with enough force to inflict a skull-cracking blow.

SPINES AND HORNS
Clubbing the enemy was one way to fight back—stabbing it was another. Stegosaurs and nodosaurs both used this kind of defense, one group fielding spines on their tails and the other having them on their shoulders. It is not always easy to distinguish true weapons from ornaments (pages 162-163), but a sideways slant is often a clue that a spine could be used in earnest—vertical ones

were more likely to be for show.

Ceratopsians, which include *Triceratops* and its relatives, often had giant head shields and horns projecting from their muzzles and brows. These were probably used partly for impressing rivals and partly for self-defense.

ARMOR PLATING
If all else failed and a predator continued its attack, armored dinosaurs relied on their body plating to save them. This consisted of flat pieces or raised nodules of bone, which developed in the skin rather than being attached directly to the skeleton. Bony growths like this, called osteoderms, also formed the ankylosaurs' clubs. Interestingly, osteoderms are one of the oldest forms of self-defense in the vertebrate world, dating back to the first armored fish, 400 million years ago. Unfortunately, osteoderms—and the spines attached to them—usually become scattered when an animal dies, so it is often difficult to decide exactly how they would have been arranged in life. However, they were usually separated by small areas of skin, which allowed the armored layer to bend. Many armored dinosaurs had well-protected backs but relatively vulnerable undersides—a weak point that their enemies would have exploited if they had the opportunity.

△ *These three tails show different adaptations for defense. In Ankylosaurus (left) the tail ends in a body club.* Stegosaurus' *tail (center) is armed with spikes.* Diplodocus' *tail (right) had neither, but was extremely strong and could be slapped at an enemy like a whip.*

◁ *A* Stegosaurus *fossil from the Morrison Formation, in Wyoming, shows what look like defensive plates. The true function of these plates may actually have been very different.*

◁ *Crouching down to protect its vulnerable underside (far left), a* Euoplocephalus *lashes out at a* Tyrannosaurus *with its tail club. To be really effective, the blow needed to be well aimed —not easy to do because the animal was inevitably facing the other way.*

◁ Leptoceratops *would probably have been able to move on either two or four legs. Its front feet had five clawed, prehensile fingers for grasping vegetation and pulling it toward its beak.*

3.3 ft. (1m) high at the shoulder and probably had a lifespan of 10 to 15 years.

MAXIMUM LENGTH 8.2 ft. (2.5m)

TIME Early Cretaceous

FOSSIL FINDS Asia (China, Mongolia, Thailand)

CERATOPSIDS

O ften known as horned dinosaurs, most members of this family were distinguished by armor-plated skulls and formidable horns. Their armor would have been used for defending themselves against predators and perhaps in courtship, much as rhinoceroses use theirs today. The ceratopsids were one of the last families of dinosaurs to evolve before the great extinction 66 million years ago. They were plant eaters and ranged from the size of a large dog to larger than a bull elephant. They almost certainly foraged in herds and lived across the Northern Hemisphere.

PSITTACOSAURUS
Named "parrot lizard" because of its parrotlike beak, *Psittacosaurus* walked on two legs and was once classified as an early iguanodont. However, it is now thought to have been a primitive ceratopsid. It lacked the horns and frills of true horned dinosaurs, but it did have a ridge of bone at the top of its skull to which its jaw muscles were attached, and small horny projections on its cheeks. *Psittacosaurus* stood about

▽ Psittacosaurus *ate cycads and other tough plants, and it balanced itself with its tail.*

LEPTOCERATOPS
This small dinosaur represents a halfway stage between the parrot dinosaurs, such as *Psittacosaurus*, and the later horned dinosaurs. Like *Psittacosaurus*, it had a parrotlike beak, although with some teeth in the upper jaw. However, the fringed projection at the back of the skull is more evident, without being as exaggerated as it was in later ceratopsids. Unlike its later relatives, it did not have any horns. With its well-developed back legs, *Leptoceratops* was a good runner—an essential feature for a plant eater with no other way of defending itself. It probably ate on all fours, but reared up when it needed to move at any speed.

MAXIMUM LENGTH 9 ft. (2.7m)

TIME Late Cretaceous

FOSSIL FINDS Asia (Mongolia), North America, Australia

MICROCERATOPS
The midget of the ceratopsid family, *Microceratops* was lightly built and probably quick on its feet, judging from its long, athletically built hind legs. However, it would almost certainly have grazed on all fours, keeping an eye out for potential predators and running away if one was spotted. The back of its skull had the raised fringe typical of this dinosaur family.

MAXIMUM LENGTH 31.5 ft. (80cm)

TIME Late Cretaceous

FOSSIL FINDS Asia (China, Mongolia)

BAGACERATOPS

Bagaceratops represents another step along, or divergence from, the evolutionary line for the ceratopsids. It was small but heavily built, with a solid body and stout legs, and it would have moved on all fours. It had the beginnings of a skull crest, with bony ridges leading up from its sharp, birdlike beak. It also had a blunt, stubby horn on the top of its nose and earlike horny projections on each cheek. It would have used its beak to tear off vegetation and its cheek teeth to grind it up. Well-preserved fossils of *Bagaceratops* have been found. From their posture it seems some may belong to animals that were in underground nests when they died.

MAXIMUM LENGTH   3.3 ft. (1m)
TIME   Late Cretaceous
FOSSIL FINDS   Asia (Mongolia)

PROTOCERATOPS

Some excellent fossil finds have given paleontologists a good picture of

what *Protoceratops* looked like and how it lived. It was a heavily built creature, weighing about 440 lb. (200kg), although it stood less than 3.3 ft. (1m) tall. It normally moved on all fours, but it may have been able to raise itself up and run on two. It had a pronounced shieldlike projection at the back of its head, which anchored some of the muscles that worked its powerful beak. When this dinosaur was discovered, in the 1920s, paleontologists also found nests and fossilized eggs. The eggs had remarkably thin shells and were laid in groups of over a dozen in spirals in the sand.

MAXIMUM LENGTH   9 ft. (2.7m)
TIME   Late Cretaceous
FOSSIL FINDS   Asia (Mongolia, China)

▽ *The fossilized remains of a fight to the death between a* Protoceratops *and a* Velociraptor *were found in 1971.* Velociraptor *had vicious claws to slash its prey, but despite being a plant eater,* Protoceratops *was able to hit back with its powerful beak. The desperate duel seems to have ended in a stalemate, leaving both dinosaurs mortally wounded. Their remains were probably engulfed by sand.*

ARMORED DINOSAURS

STYRACOSAURUS

The most formidably armed of the horned dinosaurs, *Styracosaurus* fully lived up to its name, which means "spiked lizard." It was actually far larger than any lizard alive today, with a single 2-ft. (60-cm)-long horn on the tip of its nose and a ring of equally impressive spikes around its head shield. It weighed about three tons, and it probably defended itself like a modern-day rhinoceros, using its horns and spikes to inflict serious injuries. Studies of this dinosaur's body shape and fossilized tracks indicate that it ran on all fours at speeds of up to 20 mph (32km/h). A find of about 100 fossilized specimens in Arizona makes it look very likely that *Styracosaurus* lived in herds.

The dinosaurs probably ate cycads and palms, grinding the tough leaves with their cheek teeth.

MAXIMUM LENGTH 18 ft. (5.5m)

TIME Late Cretaceous

FOSSIL FINDS North America (Alberta, Arizona, Montana)

PACHYRHINOSAURUS

Scientists are unsure whether or not this ceratopsid had a nose horn because the fossil evidence consists of about a dozen incomplete skulls. The skulls have a thick ridge of bone between the eyes. This may have formed the base of a horn that later fell away, or it may have been a weapon in its own right. However, both sexes certainly had a large, frilled head shield, which was armed with horns and spikes. *Pachyrhinosaurus* weighed over 2.5 tons, and its

▽ During their relatively short history ceratopsids developed an amazing variety of head shields and horns. From the left the trio shown below are Styracosaurus, Pachyrhinosaurus, *and the massively built* Triceratops. *These animals' shields and horns had a dual purpose —they were used to fend off predators, but they were also used in real or mock fights with rivals. The horns and frills may also have been used to help them cool down when necessary.*

arched back was almost twice the height
of an adult human being.

MAXIMUM LENGTH 23 ft. (7m)

TIME Late Cretaceous

FOSSIL FINDS North America (Alaska, Alberta)

TRICERATOPS

The most famous of the horned dinosaurs,
Triceratops gets its name from its three-
horned head. It was the giant of its family,
weighing up to ten tons. The two horns on
its brow were 3.3 ft. (1m) or more in length,
while its entire skull was up to 10 ft. (3m)
long, making it one of the largest of the
dinosaurs. Its skull shield was remarkable
because of its size and because it consisted
of a solid sheet of bone. Hundreds of fossils
show that this huge plant eater roamed
North America in large herds. Some skulls
show major injuries, suggesting that these
animals engaged in fierce contests, probably
over mates. *Triceratops* was one of the last
of its line, evolving a few million years
before the dinosaurs disappeared.

MAXIMUM LENGTH 30 ft. (9m)

TIME Late Cretaceous

FOSSIL FINDS Western North America

△ *Like other ceratopsids,
Anchiceratops was a
variable animal, with no
two individuals having
exactly the same shield
and horn shape. Some
scientists think that these
differences would have
allowed these dinosaurs
to recognize each other
as they mingled in herds.*

ANCHICERATOPS

Considerably smaller than *Triceratops*, this
animal had a long and narrow head shield
with a serrated edge of backward-pointing
spines. Its shield also had a pronounced
central dividing ridge. *Anchiceratops* was a
swamp dweller and lived on lush vegetation,
gathering it up with its parrotlike beak.
It could weigh over five tons and probably
spent much of its time wading through
shallow water and wet mud.

MAXIMUM LENGTH 20 ft. (6m)

TIME Late Cretaceous

FOSSIL FINDS North America (Alberta)

CENTROSAURUS

Looking like a gigantic rhinoceros—
although from a totally different line of
the animal world—*Centrosaurus* was a heavy,
powerful, thick-set animal with a large horn
on top of its beaklike snout. Unlike many
other ceratopsids, it had a relatively short
head shield, although it was edged with
toothlike horns. The frill was not made
of solid bone, but had two openings,
reducing its weight. In Canada a find
of about 50 specimens close together
points to their being herd animals.

MAXIMUM LENGTH 20 ft. (6m)

TIME Late Cretaceous

FOSSIL FINDS North America (Alberta,
Montana)

ARMORED DINOSAURS

STEGOSAURS

S tegosaurs were slow-moving plant eaters with a double row of bony plates or spines protruding from their backs. These plates were attached to their skin, rather than their skeletons, making it difficult to establish exactly how they were positioned in life. Opinions differ about their purpose; they may have been used for self-defense, but they could also have played a part in heat regulation, helping warm up or cool down the animal's blood. If so, the plates may have been able to blush—something that could have been used as part of a mating ritual or as a warning signal. Stegosaurs were also armed with vicious spikes on their tails, which would have been wielded like a medieval weapon to stab their enemies.

STEGOSAURUS

Stegosaurus weighed about three tons and was the largest member of its family. It had a strangely proportioned body, with its hind legs much larger than its front ones, giving it a massively humped back. Its remarkably small head was held low and housed a tiny brain, which was not much larger than a walnut. Like other stegosaurs, it had a beaklike snout, and chewing teeth at the back of its mouth. *Stegosaurus* probably fed on all fours, although some experts think it could have reared up to reach its food.

MAXIMUM LENGTH 29.5 ft. (9m)

TIME Late Jurassic

FOSSIL FINDS Western North America, Europe (U.K.)

▷ *One of the oldest known stegosaurs,* Huayangosaurus *was also one of the smallest, standing only about 6 ft. (1.8m) at the hips— roughly the height of a man—and weighing just over one ton. It may have been the ancestor of later members of the stegosaur family.*

◁ *The five animals shown here give an idea of how stegosaur armor varied.* Tuojiangosaurus *(top left) and* Stegosaurus *(top right) had two rows of broad, flat plates. The plates look impressive, but many paleontologists think they were actually too thin to have been used in self-defense.* Dacentrurus *(bottom left),* Lexovisaurus *(bottom center), and* Kentrosaurus *(bottom right) had narrower plates graded into spikes on their tails. These five animals shared several features typical of their family—elephantlike legs, an arched back, and a relatively tiny head.*

HUAYANGOSAURUS

Like the rest of the family, *Huayangosaurus* was equipped with a paired row of pointed back plates and a further elongated and hornlike pair on its hips. Its tail was armed with two pairs of pointed horns. Unusually for a stegosaur, it had teeth in its beak, rather than just in its cheeks. *Huayangosaurus* is one of several species that have been unearthed in China, making this region the best part of the world for stegosaur remains.

MAXIMUM LENGTH   13 ft. (4m)
TIME   Mid Jurassic
FOSSIL FINDS   China

TUOJIANGOSAURUS

A good picture of this dinosaur comes from the discovery of two sets of fossilized remains found in China. It had pairs of V-shaped plates running along its spine, which were largest in the middle of its back and decreased in size toward its neck and tail. Just like *Stegosaurus*, it had two pairs of long, spiky horns on its tail and a steeply arched back. At its tallest point—over its hips—it was about 6.6 ft. (2m) high.

MAXIMUM LENGTH   23 ft. (7m)
TIME   Late Jurassic
FOSSIL FINDS   China

KENTROSAURUS

First discovered in the early 1900s, during the German fossil-hunting expeditions to Tanzania (page 160), *Kentrosaurus* is one of Africa's best-known stegosaurs, with dozens of additional specimens being unearthed in recent times. Although similar in shape to *Stegosaurus*, *Kentrosaurus* was much smaller. The pairs of plates on its back gave way to spiky horns, about 2 ft. (60cm) long, from midway down its back to the tip of its tail. It was believed to have had a long spike protruding sideways from each of its hips, or perhaps from each of its shoulders. These

spikes would have been useful in self-defense. Like other stegosaurs, it had relatively small teeth for a plant eater and may have swallowed stones to help it grind up its food (page 78).

MAXIMUM LENGTH   16.4 ft. (5m)
TIME   Late Jurassic
FOSSIL FINDS   Africa (Tanzania)

LEXOVISAURUS

Named after an ancient tribe from France, where some of the earliest remains were found, *Lexovisaurus* was a typical stegosaur, with pairs of narrow pointed plates down its back, as well as an additional pair of spikes, up to 4 ft. (1.2m) long, thought to have been located on its shoulders. Weighing up to two tons, it was probably faster than some of the larger stegosaurs and may have been able to run at speeds of up to 19 mph (30km/h).

MAXIMUM LENGTH   16.4 ft. (5m)
TIME   Mid Jurassic
FOSSIL FINDS   Europe (England, France)

DACENTRURUS

One of the smaller stegosaurs and also one of the earliest, *Dacentrurus* weighed about one ton and was well armed with sharply pointed back and tail plates up to 18 in. (45cm) long. Its remains have been found in several locations in western Europe, and they include what may have been one of its eggs.

MAXIMUM LENGTH   14.8 ft. (4.5m)
TIME   Mid Jurassic
FOSSIL FINDS   Europe (England, France, Portugal)

FOSSIL HUNTING IN AFRICA

AFTER SOME SPECTACULAR DISCOVERIES DURING THE LAST 100 YEARS, AFRICA IS A KEY DESTINATION FOR PALEONTOLOGISTS. FAMOUS FOR FOSSILS OF HUMAN ANCESTORS, ITS PREHISTORIC INHABITANTS INCLUDED THE LARGEST LAND PREDATORS EVER.

Fossil collecting in Africa began on a truly grand scale with the discovery of an immense "dinosaur graveyard" in Tanzania in 1907. Since the 1920s East and South Africa have produced finds that help us to map out human evolution, and recently major dinosaur finds have been made on the edges of the Sahara Desert and in Madagascar.

Paul Sereno, seen here during his 1993 expedition to Niger, has been one of the most successful fossil hunters of recent years. As well as discovering Afrovenator *and rediscovering* Carcharodontosaurus, *he has made some major breakthroughs in the study of early dinosaurs in South America. His finds here include* Eoraptor *and the most complete specimens so far collected of* Herrerasaurus.

a museum in southern Germany, but during World War II the building was damaged by Allied bombs, and its unique fossils were destroyed.

For the next five decades, it remained on the list of dinosaurs that had been found and then lost. That was the situation in 1996, when a team from the University of Chicago, led by paleontologist Paul Sereno, carried out a prospecting trip in Morocco's Atlas

▽ *Seen next to the extraordinarily large skull of* Carcharodontosaurus, *a human skull looks like little more than a bite-sized snack.*

THE HUNTER-KILLERS
Ask anyone to name a giant predatory dinosaur, and the chances are that they will think of *Tyrannosaurus rex*. Far less well known, although probably even larger, was an immense allosaur that lived in North Africa in Early Cretaceous times. Called *Carcharodontosaurus*, which literally means "shark-toothed lizard," this awe-inspiring predator was first discovered in the 1920s, when European paleontologists found parts of its skull and a small number of other bones. These remains were eventually taken to

△ Afrovenator— *"African hunter"—was an allosaur that lived in the Early Cretaceous. It was up to 29.5 ft. (9 m) long and weighed up to two tons.*

Mountains. Working on a ridge of eroded sandstone, they extracted a skull measuring 5.2 ft. (1.6m) long: *Carcharodontosaurus* had been rediscovered, and the new specimen was even larger than the one that had vanished during World War II. For Paul Sereno this discovery was both a first and a second, because he had already found another African allosaur—which he named *Afrovenator*—during an expedition to Niger in 1993.

Off the coast of Africa, Madagascar is also a scene of great interest in the dinosaur world. In 1999 remains of primitive plant-eating dinosaurs were found to be over 230 million years old, making them the most ancient species yet discovered.

THE FOSSILS OF TENDAGURU HILL

Paleontologists in Africa often work in remote locations, but they do have the benefit of modern transportation. Things were not so easy in the early 1900s when the German naturalist Eberhard Fraas traveled through Tanzania—then known as Tanganyika—following up information about fossil finds at a site called Tendaguru Hill. On arrival Fraas found that Tendaguru contained a vast array of remains. Between 1909 and 1913 German paleontologists carried out four expeditions to the area and collected over 200 tons of fossils. These were coated in plaster, packed up, and then carried all the way to the coast to be shipped back to Europe.

Among this extraordinary haul were the remains of a large range of plant eaters, including stegosaurs, hypsilophodonts, and diplodocids. But in terms of size the most impressive finds were several partial *Brachiosaurus* skeletons, including—unusually for a sauropod—an almost complete skull. When these eventually arrived in Germany, a complete *Brachiosaurus* skeleton was assembled, creating the largest articulated dinosaur fossil in the world. The skeleton is still housed in Berlin's Humboldt Museum.

HUMAN ORIGINS

One visitor to Tendaguru, after the German excavations were over, was the British anthropologist Louis Leakey. At the time of Leakey's visit most anthropologists believed that human evolution had begun in Asia—an idea that American fossil-hunting

expeditions hoped to prove when they visited the Gobi Desert (page 108). But during his long career, spent largely in Tanzania and Kenya, Louis Leakey and his wife, Mary, helped show that this was not true. Among their fossil finds was *Homo habilis*, a humanlike primate that was a direct ancestor of our own species and lived about two million years ago.

Following Louis Leakey's death in 1972 his son Richard continued the family tradition, making several important finds.

◁ Standing next to the remains of a Brachiosaurus, these Tanzanian laborers were some of the hundreds who excavated and carried fossils during the German expeditions to Tendaguru Hill in the early 1900s.

◁ The Tendaguru Brachiosaurus—the world's largest dinosaur on exhibit—is at the Humboldt Museum in Berlin. When this skeleton was prepared, Brachiosaurus was the tallest dinosaur known, but the number one position has since been taken by Sauroposeidon.

◁ Here a group of American and British paleontologists are at work, cleaning sauropod remains in Niger. Once exposed to the surface, fossils like these slowly fracture as they become warm and expand in the desert sunshine, then cool and contract after dark. Some of the resulting fragments can be seen on the ground.

WEAPONS AND ORNAMENTS

IN THE DINOSAUR WORLD SOME BODY PARTS, SUCH AS HORNS AND SPINES, EVOLVED AS MUCH FOR IMPRESSING RIVALS AS FOR FENDING OFF PREDATORS.

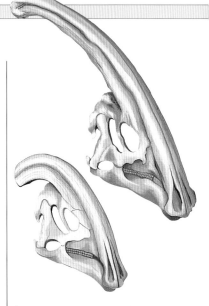

A t first glance the huge horns of a *Triceratops* look as though they were designed for one thing only: keeping carnivores at bay. The same is true of their head shields and of the spines, lumps, and bumps that many armored dinosaurs possessed. But studies of living animals show that structures like these are not always what they seem. In modern mammals horns and antlers are often used by males as badges of rank, as well as for self-defense.

SEXUAL SELECTION

In the living world animals evolve because the ones best adapted for survival have the most young, which inherit their characteristics. This is called natural selection. But in many species another kind of selection is at work as well— sexual selection. It occurs when females decide which males to choose as mates. Imagine a species of bird in which males have red tails. If the females find red tails attractive, the males with the biggest and reddest tails will stand the best chance of mating. Those males will father more young, and the proportion of males with large red tails will slowly increase.

◁ *From relatively modest beginnings, shown here by* Protoceratops *(top), the head shields of ceratopsians became increasingly elaborate.* Styracosaurus *(middle) had holes in its spine-edged frill, but in* Triceratops *(left) the frill was solid and extremely heavy.*

△ *The crests of hadrosaurs are typical examples of structures that evolved through sexual selection. This shows two* Parasaurolophus *skulls; the male's crest is longer than the female's.*

Tails will get larger and redder, making males increasingly different from their mates.

What is true of tails is also true of any other feature that females find impressive, whether it is bright plumage, large horns, or the strength and skill to push rivals out of the way. Sexual selection can help exaggerate any of these as time goes by.

Sexual selection is something that paleontologists have to bear in mind when looking at dinosaur armor and weapons. For example, the elaborate head shields of *Triceratops* and its relatives almost certainly started out as a clear-cut form of defense. But over millions of years they became suspiciously large in males and highly elaborate. They also varied enormously from one species to another. To experts in animal evolution this suggests one thing: sexual selection was at work. As these animals evolved it slowly turned their head shields into ornaments as well as armor, helping the males to win mates.

Sometimes these ornaments were simply shown off, making their owner look more striking and desirable. The crests of some hadrosaurs, for example, probably functioned in this way. But fossil remains show that head shields and horns of ceratopsids were used in ritual combat between rival males.

LOCKING HORNS

At the beginning of the breeding season *Triceratops* and its relatives probably behaved like many grassland animals today, with males sparring with each other for the right

that had this kind of drawback. A *Triceratops* head shield, for example, was an enormous and extremely heavy "attraction" that would have taken a large amount of energy to grow, and even more to carry around. To a lesser extent the thickened brain cases of dome-headed dinosaurs, or pachycephalosaurs, fell into the same category. But one of the best examples of an animal with burdensome body parts is the Irish elk, a prehistoric deer

▽ *In* Triceratops *the head shield and horns were status symbols that were shown off in male-to-male confrontations. However, when turned against predators, they made effective weapons. Here a mature male fights off a* Tyrannosaurus.

to mate. One of the key features of this kind of fighting is that it looks more dangerous than it really is. The two rivals square up to each other in a threatening way, but when they clash, they do so in a fashion that prevents either of them becoming seriously injured. Like today's buffalo and antelopes, ceratopsids had large air spaces in the front of their skulls. This helped cushion the impact of a head-on clash, protecting their brains from damage.

However, injuries did sometimes occur. Many *Triceratops* skulls show shallow nicks in their surface—evidence of painful gouges where an opponent's horns hit home.

GOING TO EXTREMES

An interesting feature of sexual selection is that it can make some body parts so large that they become a handicap. Dinosaurs and other prehistoric animals showed features

from the Pleistocene Epoch (page 211). Males had antlers over 10 ft. (3m) wide, which weighed nearly 110 lb. (50kg). Antlers this large were so cumbersome that they were almost useless as weapons, but amazingly—as in today's deer—they were shed and regrown each year.

▽ *Rhinoceroses use their horns in the same way as dinosaurs. With their horns locked together, these males are unlikely to do each other harm, but one will yield to the other.*

NODOSAURS AND ANKYLOSAURS

Ankylosaurids first appeared in the Late Jurassic, but their heyday was during the Cretaceous. First to evolve were the nodosaurs, which spread across the Northern Hemisphere. They were heavily built, slow-moving plant eaters equipped with body armor of horns and bony plates. Toward the end of the Cretaceous the nodosaurs gave way to the ankylosaurs proper, which had even tougher armor and a bony club at the end of their tail.

△ Nodosaurus *(top),*
Hylaeosaurus *(middle),*
and Silvisaurus *(bottom)*
were all typical nodosaurs
and had an extensive
protective body armor
of horny plates and spikes
running over their backs.
Only their legs and
undersides lacked this
protection, but incomplete
fossils mean that their
exact appearance is still
a matter of conjecture.

HYLAEOSAURUS

Hylaeosaurus was first discovered in about 1830 by the famous British paleontologist Gideon Mantell. It was only the third dinosaur to be identified, and only a few isolated fragments of its skeleton have come to light since. As a result its exact appearance is difficult to establish, but it is likely to have shared a range of typical nodosaur features, including armor plating, perhaps backed up by rows of horns projecting sideways from its flanks and along its tail. Like other nodosaurs, its front legs were probably shorter than its hind legs,

giving it a humped profile, and they would have been stoutly built to carry the weight of its armor.

MAXIMUM LENGTH	19.7 ft. (6m)
TIME	Early Cretaceous
FOSSIL FINDS	Europe (England, France)

SILVISAURUS

Like *Hylaeosaurus*, this was an early nodosaur with a range of primitive features, including small, pointed teeth in its upper jaw—in contrast with later species, which typically had toothless beaks. It also had a relatively long neck, which makes it possible that it browsed on tall shrubs as well as eating plants closer to the ground. It was armored with large bony plates and also with spikes, but incomplete fossils make it difficult to tell how these were arranged on the living animal.

MAXIMUM LENGTH	13 ft. (4m)
TIME	Early Cretaceous
FOSSIL FINDS	North America (Kansas)

NODOSAURUS

With an arched back covered in bands of small bony plates, stretching from behind its neck right down its tail, *Nodosaurus*—"lumpy lizard"—looked like a huge prehistoric armadillo. No skulls have yet been found, but its head was likely to have been small, with fairly narrow jaws. Like all ankylosaurids, it fed on low-growing plants and had leaf-shaped teeth. Its heavy build and small brain were typical of an animal that relied on armor to avoid attack, and its lifestyle and diet make it probable that it lived in herds.

MAXIMUM LENGTH	19.7 ft. (6m)
TIME	Late Cretaceous
FOSSIL FINDS	North America (Kansas, Wyoming)

EDMONTONIA

Edmontonia was one of the largest nodosaurs. Several almost-complete fossil skeletons have been found, and they show that it was built even more solidly than a rhinoceros. A band of bony plates extended all the way down its tail, and there were additional plates over its neck and skull. The two vertebrae that joined its head to its spine were fused together. This means that it would have had difficulty bending its neck. Once it reached adulthood, *Edmontonia* was so well-armored that it was unlikely to be attacked. It had several pairs of giant spikes protruding from its shoulders, which would have been an effective deterrent against predators. It lived in the same time and place as *Euoplocephalus*, but its narrower jaws imply that it had a different diet, reducing direct competition between the two.

MAXIMUM LENGTH 23 ft. (7m)

TIME Late Cretaceous

FOSSIL FINDS North America (Alaska, Alberta, Montana)

EUOPLOCEPHALUS

With body armor extending even in front of its eyelids and a tail ending in a heavy club, *Euoplocephalus* was a typical ankylosaur. It had a large head with protective spikes, and further spikes and nodules arranged in rows down its back and the base of its tail. Over 40 fossil finds have been made so far. These including several skulls, which show that it had a broad, toothless muzzle—one that would have been good at cropping swathes of low-growing plants. *Euoplocephalus* probably weighed about two tons, and although it was solidly built, its tail club suggests that it was quite nimble on its feet in the event of an attack by a predator.

MAXIMUM LENGTH 23 ft. (7m)

TIME Late Cretaceous

FOSSIL FINDS North America (Alberta, Montana)

ANKYLOSAURUS

Largest of the true ankylosaurs and almost the last of its line, *Ankylosaurus* was a massively built plant eater. It weighed up to four tons, but its club weighed over 110 lb. (50kg) and could be swung quickly to smash a predator's teeth or skull. It had armor plating embedded in its skin and the rows of spikes and raised nodules that characterize ankylosaurs. It may have been a herding animal, like many of its relatives, but its size means it would have been safe feeding on its own.

MAXIMUM LENGTH 32.8 ft. (10m)

TIME Late Cretaceous

FOSSIL FINDS North America (Alberta, Montana)

△ Euoplocephalus *(top), with its distinctive club-ended tail, and* Edmontonia *(bottom) coexisted in Late Cretaceous North America. Although they had the same general build, differences in their jaw structures suggest that they fed on different plants.*

◁ *Weighing as much as one of today's elephants, but with its own built-in weaponry and armor,* Ankylosaurus *was one of the best-protected plant eaters during the Age of the Reptiles, but it failed to survive when the Cretaceous Period came to an end.*

ARMORED DINOSAURS

DOME-HEADED DINOSAURS

In the dinosaur world a large head was not necessarily a sign of great intelligence. This is particularly true with the pachycephalosaurs, or bone-headed dinosaurs. These remarkable animals get their name from their reinforced brain case, which in some cases was over 8 in. (20cm) thick. Scientists believe that male bone-headed dinosaurs used their skulls in head-to-head clashes in the same way sheep or goats do today. Alternatively, they may have used them as battering rams to butt rivals in the side.

▽ Homalocephale *(top) and* Stegoceras *(bottom) were both small, bipedal, grazing dinosaurs with thickened tops to their skulls.* Homalocephale *had a flat top to its skull, and* Stegoceras *had a dome. Both lived in herds and used speed and agility to escape predators.*

HOMALOCEPHALE

Homalocephale's head had a thick, flat top of bone with bony protrusions around the edge like a crown. The thick skull bones were flexible and relatively porous. Some experts think that this is evidence against the head-butting theory, because a skull like this would not have been able to withstand a massive impact. Certainly no evidence of skull damage has been discovered. *Homalocephale* had small, leaf-shaped teeth, which indicates that it would have lived on a diet of plants, fruit, and seeds.

MAXIMUM LENGTH	10 ft. (3m)
TIME	Late Cretaceous
FOSSIL FINDS	Asia (Mongolia)

STEGOCERAS

In size, body shape, and behavior *Stegoceras* was probably very like *Homalocephale*. It too was a small, bipedal plant eater with a steeply sloping snout, and serrated teeth shaped for chewing low-growing plants. The most obvious difference was its head—a raised dome adorned with a prominent crown of bony growths, the largest of which was at the back of the skull. The dome probably got bigger as the animal reached maturity, and it seems to have been more pronounced in males. For males a large head would have been a sign of importance in the same way that large tusks are a badge of rank in bull elephants. *Stegoceras* would have been a fast runner, and like other bone heads, it lived in herds. Although it ran on two legs, it probably dropped onto all fours to feed.

MAXIMUM LENGTH	6.6 ft. (2m)
TIME	Late Cretaceous
FOSSIL FINDS	North America (Alberta, Montana)

166

DOME-HEADED DINOSAURS

PRENOCEPHALE

In 1974 a superbly preserved skull of *Prenocephale* was found in Mongolia. It had a large, bulbous head with a knobbly ridge running around the edge and looked like a small-scale *Pachycephalosaurus*. *Prenocephale* probably lived by browsing on leaves and fruit and, like its relatives, almost certainly lived in herds. It shared another family feature: a mesh of bonelike tendons in the rear half of its tail, which would have held its tail rigid.

MAXIMUM LENGTH 8.2 ft. (2.5m)

TIME Late Cretaceous

FOSSIL FINDS Asia (Mongolia), western North America

PACHYCEPHALOSAURUS

The biggest of the bone heads, this dinosaur weighed nearly half a ton. It had a very large skull topped with a solid dome up to 10 in. (25cm) thick. Running around the outside of its head, at the base of the dome, was a ring of bony knobs. *Pachycephalosaurus* had tiny teeth for its size. Like other bone heads, it probably had a good sense of smell, which would have been useful for detecting predators. As the only fossil finds have been skull remains, scientists have had to guess what the rest of its body looked like. This dome-headed giant was one of the last of its line, surviving until the mass extinction that wiped out all of the dinosaurs 66 million years ago.

MAXIMUM LENGTH 15 ft. (4.6m)

TIME Late Cretaceous

FOSSIL FINDS Western North America

▽ △ Pachycephalosaurus *would have used its "bone head" to win in clashes with male rivals.*

DINOSAUR DROPPINGS

WITH THEIR OFTEN HUGE APPETITES, DINOSAURS PRODUCED IMMENSE AMOUNTS OF DROPPINGS. SOME HAVE SURVIVED AS FOSSILS, GIVING PALEONTOLOGISTS A DIRECT INSIGHT INTO WHAT DINOSAURS ATE.

Coprolites, or fossilized droppings, are discovered less frequently than fossilized bones. One reason for this is that they have an irregular shape, which means that even expert eyes find them difficult to spot. Another factor is that droppings are considerably softer than bones, which gives them less of a chance of being preserved. Rain washes them away, and scavenging animals, such as insects, often break them apart. Only occasionally does genuine dino dung does come to light, millions of years after it dropped to the ground.

REMAINS OF A KILL
In 1995, a group of scientists working in Saskatchewan, took a stroll from a site where a *Tyrannosaurus* was being excavated. One of the team noticed some pale round objects that were slowly being eroded from a layer of hard mud. These came from a giant dinosaur coprolite, the largest that has ever been found. Roughly cyclindrical, it measured about 17.7 in. (45cm) long and up to 6.3 in. (16cm) across, and when fresh, probably weighed about 5.5 lb. (2.5kg).

The fossil was taken back to the lab, where paper-thin slices were shaved off and viewed under a microscope. These revealed pieces of broken bone that had been partially digested. By looking at the pattern of blood vessels inside the bone fragments, researchers were able to

△ Fossilized droppings are often difficult to identify. The one on the left came from a dinosaur, and the one on the right may have been produced by a marine reptile.

tell that the victim was a young dinosaur and probably a plant eater. The animal that produced the coprolite, on the other hand, was undoubtedly a carnivore, the most likely candidate being *Tyrannosaurus* itself.

DUNG AND DIET
Plant-eating dinosaurs outnumbered meat eaters and ate more food. Some herbivores had only modest food requirements, but giant sauropods, such as *Argentinosaurus*, probably consumed about three or four tons of food a week. This translates into about one ton of droppings—an enormous potential source of evidence about dinosaur diets.

Unfortunately, compared to carnivores, plant eaters' droppings fossilized less frequently, mainly because they contained no hard fragments of bone. The few sauropod droppings that have been found include specimens from Utah, which look like squashed basketballs up to 15.7 in. (40cm) across. Their shape is explained by the fact that they originally contained water and hit the ground from a height of many feet. Some of these coprolites contain pieces of conifer stems.

At the other end of the scale, geologists in England have discovered large numbers of coin-sized coprolites, thought to have been produced by a plant-eating dinosaur. What the droppings lacked in size, they made up for in numbers. One deposit contained nearly 300 of these pellets, and a close examination showed that they contained the undigested remains of cycad leaves, a common ingredient of dinosaur diets.

DINO DUNG AS RAW MATERIAL
Some coprolites of plant-eating dinosaurs are riddled with fossilized burrows, each up to the thickness of a finger. These burrows were created by dung beetles, which mined the giant droppings as a source of food. Just like dung beetles today, some would have shaped pieces of the dung into balls and rolled them away to make nurseries for their young. By dismantling and scattering piles of dung, these scavenging insects helped to return nutrients to the soil—nutrients that plants in Mesozoic times needed to grow.

REPTILES IN THE AIR

Before birds evolved, reptiles were the only backboned animals that had successfully taken up life in the air. Initially reptiles were gliders rather than true fliers, using specialized scales or skinflaps to cushion their fall as they leaped from tree to tree. But by the end of the Triassic a completely new group of flying reptiles evolved, equipped with muscle-powered wings. These were the pterosaurs, a collection of quick-witted and sometimes gigantic aviators that soared and flapped their way through the skies. They flourished for over 150 million years and left a great treasury of fossils.

WINGS OF SKIN

GLIDING OR FLYING REPTILES EVOLVED ON
AT LEAST FOUR SEPARATE OCCASIONS IN THE
DISTANT PAST. THE MOST SUCCESSFUL BY FAR
WERE THE PTEROSAURS, WHICH TOOK TO
THE AIR ON WINGS MADE OF SKIN.

The first flying reptiles appeared toward the end of
the Permian Period, over 240 million years ago. These
early aviators were all gliders, speeding between trees
on winglike flaps that they opened just before takeoff. They
included *Coelurosauravus*, which had foldaway wing flaps
along its sides, and *Longisquama* (page 62), a Triassic animal
with elongated scales down its back. One of the strangest,
a tiny animal called *Sharovipteryx* (page 60), had two pairs
of flaps. But none of these animals could stay airborne
for more than a few seconds, because their wings
could not be flapped up and down.

▽ Coelurosauravus
was an early glider from
the Late Permian. About
15.7 in. (40cm) long, it
had elongated ribs that
could hinge outward
to form a pair of skin-
covered wings. Some of
today's lizards glide in
exactly the same way.

FIRST FLAPPERS

With the evolution of the pterosaurs in the
Late Triassic, reptiles stopped being simple
gliders and developed real mastery of the
skies. Pterosaurs are sometimes confused
with dinosaurs, and although they were
a distinct group, they did share the same
direct ancestors. Not only did they appear
at the same time as the dinosaurs, they also
became extinct at the same time. Until the

Many pterosaurs fed on fish or squid, catching
prey by swimming close to the water's surface.
If they crashed, their remains sank to the
bottom, where they stood a good chance of
becoming fossilized. This Pterodactylus *fossil*
is a typical example and shows the entire
skeleton in superb detail. By contrast, species
that lived over land, such as Quetzalcoatlus,
left a meager amount of fossil evidence.

global disaster that brought the Age of
Reptiles to an end, pterosaurs were by far
the largest animals that could fly. Unlike
gliding reptiles, they could flap their wings
to stay airborne, and they may even have
been as maneuverable as today's birds.

DESIGN FOR FLIGHT

Few fossils of the earliest pterosaurs exist,
but later forms, particularly from near the
end of the Jurassic, have left a wealth of
well-preserved remains. They show that
pterosaurs had very specialized arms
featuring an immensely elongated fourth
finger, often as long as the rest of the limb.
When the wing was extended, this finger
stretched open a double-sided membrane
of skin, which ran in a triangle between
three points: the shoulder, the wingtip,

and a region near the hind leg. A second and much smaller membrane formed a forward part of the wing. It also started at the shoulder, but ran in front of the main arm bones to a point near the wrist, creating a straight edge in front of the elbow. The remaining fingers were far shorter and clustered together at the wing's leading edge. They were probably used for walking and climbing, and perhaps tearing up food.

Unlike a bird's feathers, which consist of dead cells, a pterosaur's wing membranes were made of living tissue. They were reinforced by tough but elastic fibers, and they contained a network of blood vessels to keep them alive. Compared to feathers, they were simple structures and did not need lots of preening to keep them in good condition. But although minor damage could be repaired, a major tear was likely to be permanent, and therefore potentially fatal.

Apart from their wings pterosaurs showed other physical modifications. Their skeletons were light, with a reduced number of bones, and the rib cage was deep but short. Early species, the rhamphorhynchoids, had long tails. Later ones, the pterodactyls, had tails that were reduced to

a short stub. In these pterosaurs the head was often longer than the rest of the body.

ENERGY FOR FLIGHT

The shape of their beaks, together with the fossilized remains of meals, shows that pterosaurs were carnivorous and fed on a range of animals from

insects to fish or scavenged on remains. Strangely, once flowering plants evolved, pterosaurs do not seem to have branched out into eating fruit and seeds, although these are both packed with energy.

Giant pterosaurs, such as *Arambourgiana* (page 178), were experts at soaring, a highly efficient way of flying that uses very little muscle power. But smaller species would have needed to put a lot of effort into flapping, one of several reasons why paleontologists think that most petrosaurs, or perhaps all of them, were warm-blooded.

◁ Different tail lengths make it easy to tell rhamphorhynchoids and pterodactyls apart.

◁ The largest pterosaurs had a wingspan larger than a hang glider; the smallest were not much larger than a starling when fully grown.

▽ Pterosaur wings consisted of a double-sided sheet of skin reinforced by tough fibers. As in birds, most of the bones contained air cavities to minimize weight.

1 Quetzalcoatlus
2 Pteranodon
3 Dsungaripterus
4 Dimorphodon
5 Pterdactylus
6 Sordes

1
2
3
4
5
6

REPTILES IN THE AIR

LONG-TAILED PTEROSAURS

The long-tailed pterosaurs were the first reptiles capable of true powered flight. They appeared in the Late Triassic Period and were widespread in the Jurassic. Like the pterodactyls, which eventually replaced them, they had leathery wings held open by a lengthened fourth finger, but they also had some more primitive features. These included sharply pointed teeth and slender tails that often ended in a diamond-shaped vane. Many of these pterosaurs fed on fish, but they probably did not spend time in the water. Instead they did all their hunting on the wing.

▽ *Clinging to rocks with wing claws and feet, two* Dimorphodon *bask in the morning sunshine while another flies off to feed. Like other pterosaurs,* Dimorphodon *would have used a lot of energy in flight. It was probably warm-blooded and insulated by furlike scales.*

DIMORPHODON

Fossils of this animal were first found in 1828 by the British collector Mary Anning (page 198), and for over a century it remained the most primitive pterosaur known to science. With its bulky, puffinlike beak, *Dimorphodon* was one of the most distinctive long-tailed pterosaurs. Its head was almost as large as the central section of its body, but it was lighter than it looked, because the skull contained large spaces separated by thin struts of bone. Its front teeth were long and protruded from its beak, but the teeth farther back were much smaller. Its wings were equipped with three large, clawed fingers, and its tail was long but probably very stiff, because

it was reinforced by parallel rods of bone. Opinions are divided about how *Dimorphodon* lived and why it had such a large beak. It may have fed on fish or small land animals, but its beak may have acted partly as display, in the same way that toucans' beaks do today.

WINGSPAN	4.6 ft. (1.4m)
TIME	Early Jurassic
FOSSIL FINDS	Europe (England)

SCAPHOGNATHUS

This long-beaked pterosaur is one of several species that have been found in the Solnhöfen limestone of southern Germany— a geological formation famous as the source of *Archaeopteryx* fossils (page 134). It had the large, protruding teeth typical of long-tailed pterosaurs and short wings. Its tail ended in a diamond-shaped vane—another feature common in early pterosaurs, which would have helped improve its stability when flying. *Scaphognathus'* jaws would have allowed it to catch fish or insects, but there is no evidence whether or not it fed over water or on land.

WINGSPAN	35.4 in. (90cm)
TIME	Late Jurassic
FOSSIL FINDS	Europe (Germany)

ANUROGNATHUS

Anurognathus literally means "without tail or jaws"—an understandable, if misleading, description of this unusual pterosaur. Known from just one specimen found in Germany in the 1920s, it had a tail that was no more than a stump and a short, blunt head with only a few small teeth. Its legs and feet, however, were well developed. One possible explanation for these features is that the fossil is of a young animal, which would have changed shape as it became an adult. Another possibility is that *Anurognathus* was a lightweight hunter of dragonflies and other insects and may have used dinosaurs as living launchpads to dart after its prey.

WINGSPAN 19.7 in. (50cm)

TIME Late Jurassic

FOSSIL FINDS Europe (Germany)

RHAMPHORHYNCHUS

Rhamphorhynchus is the best-known of the long-tailed pterosaurs, because of some superbly preserved fossils in the Solnhöfen limestone of southern Germany. Several species have been identified, but they all have long, pointed jaws armed with large, crisscrossing teeth. Their wingspan was among the largest of all tailed pterosaurs, but their legs were disproportionately short, suggesting that they were not very agile on the ground. The Solnhöfen fossils show outlines of the wings along with the vane-tipped tail, which was often longer than

the rest of the body. *Rhamphorhynchus'* jaws were slightly upturned at their tips, and they would have made a very effective fish trap. To feed, the animal probably skimmed close to the surface, with the lower half of its beak slicing through the water. If the beak made contact with a fish, it would have snapped shut instantly—a fishing technique still used by some birds today. Some *Rhamphorhynchus* fossils show the remains of fish in the stomach in various stages of digestion.

WINGSPAN 5.7 ft. (1.75m)

TIME Late Jurassic

FOSSIL FINDS Africa (Tanzania), Europe (England, Germany)

PREONDACTYLUS

Preondactylus is one of the earliest known pterosaurs. It had several primitive features, including long legs and a short skull, but it was a capable flier, skimming over lakes and lagoons to catch fish. One fossil consists of a jumble of bones apparently regurgitated by a large fish; it may have been swallowed after it crash-landed.

WINGSPAN 5 ft. (1.5m)

TIME Late Triassic

FOSSIL FINDS Europe (Italy)

◁ *With a fish clamped in its tooth-filled beak, a* Rhamphorhynchus *flies off to feed. Small fish would have been swallowed whole. Larger ones would be taken to a safe place and then torn apart— as shown by the animal in the background. Unlike today's birds, pterosaurs could hold their catch with their wing claws while they tore it apart with their teeth.*

▽ *Swinging its feet forward and cupping its wings, a* Preondactylus *comes in to land. For pterosaurs—just as for birds—good eyesight and coordination were essential for flight. Studies of pterosaur skulls showed that these animals had well-developed brains, allowing them to carry out precise maneuvers in midair.*

REPTILES IN THE AIR

EUDIMORPHODON

Fossils of this animal show a number of interesting details of pterosaur anatomy. Like most other long-tailed species, it had a long beak with large teeth at the front and smaller teeth at the sides. Its large eyes were protected by a circle of thin bony plates called a sclerotic ring, and it had thickened neck vertebrae to support the weight of its head. It also had gastralia, or stomach ribs, so its rib cage enclosed almost the whole of its underside. *Eudimorphodon* was a fish eater and is among the earliest pterosaurs known from the fossil record.

WINGSPAN   3.3 ft. (1m)

TIME   Late Triassic

FOSSIL FINDS   Europe (Italy)

BATRACHOGNATHUS

Like *Rhamphorhynchus*, this pterosaur had a deep, blunt beak. This, together with its small size, makes it likely that it fed on insects. Its skull was about 2 in. (5cm) long and contained large spaces, covered by skin, that helped reduce weight. Fossils show that, like many of its relatives, this species had a uropatagium—a flap of skin stretching between its legs and tail—as well as the flaps that formed its wings. Many of today's bats have a similar skin flap helping them fly.

WINGSPAN   19.7 in. (50cm)

TIME   Late Jurassic

FOSSIL FINDS   Asia (Kazakhstan)

SORDES

When the remains of this animal were first discovered, in the 1960s, it looked very much like a standard pterosaur. But under close examination the fossil showed one astonishing feature—signs of what look like a coat of fur. As with bats, the fur seems to have covered the animal's head and most of its body, but not its wings or tail. Many paleontologists take this as evidence that pterosaurs were warm-blooded—a theory that may explain their highly active way of life. If this is true, it is likely that many pterosaurs had "fur," although it is rarely seen in fossil remains. Apart from its remarkable coat, *Sordes* had large eyes and a long, narrow beak with large, protruding teeth. As with *Batrachognathus*, its small size suggests that it fed on insects rather than fish.

WINGSPAN   2 ft. (60cm)

TIME   Late Jurassic

FOSSIL FINDS   Asia (Kazakhstan)

▽ Sordes *(top and left), had a batlike shape, with a flap of skin connecting its hind legs to the base of its tail. Its furry scales may have been a common feature in pterosaurs, but so far it is the only species that shows this clearly in fossils.*

▽ Batrachognathus *(bottom right) had well-developed wing claws useful for clinging to vegetation when it landed to swallow its catch.*

◁ Circling over a lagoon, a small flock of
Dsungaripterus soar upward on rising air. Although
they fed along the seashore, these pterosaurs would have
visited freshwater to drink and to bathe.

DSUNGARIPTERUS

This unusual pterosaur—the first to
be discovered in China—had a beak with
a vertical crest at its base and an upturned
and sharply pointed tip. Its teeth were
short, strong, and effective at crushing
food rather than grasping it. From these
features it seems likely that *Dsungaripterus*
fed on mollusks and other hard-bodied
seashore animals, prizing them from rocks
and then crushing them in its jaws. Its long
legs would have been ideal for wading
among tide pools as it searched for food.

WINGSPAN 11.5 ft. (3.5m)
TIME Early Cretaceous
FOSSIL FINDS Asia (China)

ORNITHODESMUS

Ornithodesmus was one of several pterodactyls
that had wide, ducklike beaks. Its beak looks
heavy, but the tip was attached to the rest
of its skull by remarkably
narrow struts of bone, making
it far lighter than it appears.
It had short but effective
teeth at the tip of its beak,
making it likely that it
fed on fish. The name
Ornithodesmus is also
used for a species of
dinosaur; because this was named first, the
pterosaur will eventually be renamed.

WINGSPAN 16.4 ft. (5m)
TIME Early Cretaceous
FOSSIL FINDS Europe (England)

PTERODACTYLS

The pterodactyls were a group of pterosaurs
widespread in the Late Jurassic. By the Cretaceous
the long-tailed pterosaurs had died out, leaving the
pterodactyls as the only reptiles in the skies. They had very
short tails, and some were adorned with bizarre bony crests.
Some species were not much larger than pigeons, but others
were the largest flying animals
that have ever existed on Earth.

▷ A number
of pterosaurs had
flattened crests at
the tip of their beaks.
This is Criorhynchus,
which had a wingspan
of over 16.5 ft. (5m).
In flight, its trailing legs
acted as a counterbalance
for its head, and they
may have helped
it to steer.

▷ Seen from the
front, Ornithodesmus'
beak reveals its ducklike
shape. This kind of
beak may have helped
Ornithodesmus catch
fish in muddy water,
where it would have
used touch rather than
sight to find its prey.

ORNITHOCHEIRUS

Up to 13 ft. (4m) long and
with a wingspan three
times the size of the
largest flying bird alive
today, *Ornithocheirus* (page
182) was a spectacular airborne reptile.
Like other pterodactyls, it had a front-heavy
build, with a large head and neck, but only
the shortest trace of a tail. In many species
the beak was highly distinctive, with a vertical
crest at its tip. *Ornithocheirus* was not shaped
for flapping flight. It traveled by seeking out
thermals, or columns of warm, rising air.
Having reached the top of one thermal,
it could then glide down to the next. This
method of flight was highly energy-efficient.
Ornithocheirus could travel great distances with
little effort. It probably fed on squid and fish.

WINGSPAN 39.4 ft. (12m)
TIME Early Cretaceous
FOSSIL FINDS Europe (England), South America
(Brazil)

▷ *Added together,*
Pteranodon's beak and
crest were nearly 6.6 ft.
(2m) long—longer
than the rest of its body.
Despite its great size,
this pterosaur probably
weighed no more than
40 lb. (18kg), about
the same as the heaviest
flying birds alive today.
The species shown here
is Pteranodon longiceps.

▽ *Sweeping majestically*
over a herd of sauropods,
a flock of Quetzalcoatlus
sets off to find food. These
huge pterosaurs could
have migrated immense
distances and would
probably have been far
more widespread than the
few fossil finds suggest.

PTERANODON

The first remains of
Pteranodon were found in the
1870s, and for the next 100 years
it was the largest pterosaur known.
Its wingspan dwarfed that of most
other pterosaurs, but its most remarkable
feature was its huge and bizarrely-shaped
head, which had an extraordinary bony crest.
In one species, *Pteranodon sternbergi*, the
crest sticks up almost at right angles to the
beak, but in *Pteranodon longiceps* it sweeps
backward so that the beak and crest are
almost in line. This kind of crest would
have counterbalanced the beak, but it also
acted like an airplane's tail fin, keeping the
beak pointing into the oncoming air. The
stabilizing effect may have been an advantage,
but many other pterosaurs—including the
gigantic *Quetzalcoatlus* (below)—managed to
fly perfectly well without a crest. *Pteranodon*
probably caught fish by skimming close
to the waves. Like some of today's fishing
seabirds, it is unlikely to have landed on the
water because, with its immense wingspan, it
would have found it difficult to take off again.

WINGSPAN 29.52 ft. (9m)

TIME Late Cretaceous

FOSSIL FINDS Asia (Japan),
Europe (England), North
America (Kansas,
Oregon, South
Dakota)

QUETZALCOATLUS

Named after an Aztec god,
Quetzalcoatlus may have been
the largest flying animal ever to
have existed. Its claim to the top
spot is even stronger if—as some
palaeontologists suggest—*Arambourgiana*
(pages 178–179) is really a *Quetzalcoatlus*
that has been misidentified. The original
remains of *Quetzalcoatlus*, which were
unearthed in 1971, consist of wing bones
built on a gigantic scale. By comparing these
with complete skeletons of smaller species,
estimates of its wingspan have ranged as high
as 50 ft. (15m), although current figures are
generally smaller. Unlike most pterosaurs,
Quetzalcoatlus probably lived inland, and
it would have flown largely by soaring, like
a living glider. Its toothless beak suggests
that it was probably a scavenger, although
it may also have caught animals on the
ground (page 181).

WINGSPAN 39.4 ft. (12m)

TIME Late Cretaceous

FOSSIL FINDS North America (Texas)

TROPEOGNATHUS

This large South American
pterosaur had a vertical
crest above and
below the tip
of its beak, like
the one seen
in *Ornithocheirus*
(page 175). Its
beak was armed
with interlocking
teeth, showing that
it was a fish eater,
and it is possible
that the crest may

have helped it catch food. However, an alternative explanation is that the crest was used for display purposes during the animal's breeding season. If so, it probably varied in size between the sexes, although this has not been proven from fossil remains.

WINGSPAN 19.7 ft. (6m)

TIME Early Cretaceous

FOSSIL FINDS South America (Brazil)

ANHANGUERA

Like *Tropeognathus*, *Anhanguera* is known from remains found in northeastern Brazil. It had a typical fish eater's beak, with interlocking teeth, and its complete skull was about 19.7 in. (50cm) long. Like other pterodactyls, its backbone was shaped in an unusual way, with the largest vertebrae in the neck, tapering to the smallest ones in its stumpy tail. By comparison most terrestrial reptiles have their largest vertebrae in the central part of the body, where they carry the most weight. Pterodactyls needed their extra-large neck vertebrae to support their oversized heads.

WINGSPAN 13 ft. (4m)

TIME Early Cretaceous

FOSSIL FINDS South America (Brazil)

CEARADACTYLUS

Another fish eater from modern-day Brazil, *Cearadactylus* had about a dozen unusually long teeth at the tip of its beak, much smaller ones farther back in the jaws, and no teeth at all at the point where its beak hinged. This kind of anatomy, which was common among pterodactyls, meant that *Cearadactylus* could not chew its prey. Instead, it would have swallowed small fish whole or torn larger ones apart after landing with its catch.

WINGSPAN 13 ft. (4m)

TIME Early Cretaceous

FOSSIL FINDS South America (Brazil)

PTERODACTYLUS

The first specimen of this well-known reptile came to light in 1784, making this the earliest pterosaur to be discovered. Its name means "wing finger," and the word "pterodactyl" has often been used mistakenly for pterosaurs as a whole. *Pterodactylus* had a compact body with a small rib cage, long wings with three tiny clawed fingers, and a short tail. Its neck was well-developed to support its large head and beak—but it did not have a crest. *Pterodactylus* was a fish eater with relatively small teeth for grasping its slippery prey. Over a dozen species of *Pterodactylus* have been identified, varying slightly in their anatomy and size.

WINGSPAN 8.2 ft. (2.5m)

TIME Late Jurassic

FOSSIL FINDS Africa (Tanzania), Europe (England, France, Germany)

△ *On the ground most pterodactyls walked on all fours, although some of them could stride on their hind legs alone. Here a* Pterodactylus *shows how the wings folded back when not in use.*

▽ Tropeognathus *(top),* Cearadactylus *(middle), and* Anhanguera *(bottom) were three large pterodactyls found in Brazil. When these animals existed, South America and Africa were just beginning to drift apart as the Atlantic Ocean formed.*

GLIDING GIANTS

Gliding over a Late Cretaceous seascape, two Arambourgiana
*watch for fish swimming near the surface. These immense pterosaurs
are known from the slenderest fossil remains—a single neck vertebra
measuring 2 ft. (60cm) long, which was found in Jordan in 1943.
From this one bone paleontologists have deduced that* Arambourgiana
*probably had a wingspan of 39.5 ft. (12m), making it perhaps
the largest pterosaur of all time.*

How PTEROSAURS FED

WITH THEIR WARM-BLOODED BODIES, PTEROSAURS NEEDED A PLENTIFUL SUPPLY OF FOOD. MANY WERE FISHERS OR INSECT EATERS, BUT SOME HAD DISTINCT WAYS OF STAVING OFF HUNGER.

Fossilized pterosaur skulls provided plenty of evidence about their eating habits. Their beaks evolved to fit particular diets. Most seem to have fed over water, but land-based species had a smaller chance of being fossilized if they died.

△ *Rhamphorhyncus probably fed in the same way as skimmers— living seabirds that fish from the water's surface.*

LIVING STRAINERS

Of all the pterosaurs known from fossils, one stands out from all the rest. Called *Pterodaustro*, or "southern wing," it was originally found in Argentina and lived during the Early Cretaceous. Unusually for a pterosaur, *Pterodaustro*'s beak had a strong upward curve, but its strangest feature was a set of about 500 wiry teeth on either side of the lower jaw. These teeth pointed up like the bristles of a toothbrush, and they were so long that they could not fit inside the beak when the upper jaw was closed.

Pterodaustro used its teeth to strain food from shallow water. As water flowed past the bristles tiny animals and plants became trapped in them. The pterosaur would then close its beak so that it could swallow its catch—a feeding system remarkably like the one used by flamingos today.

As a rule fish-eating pterosaurs hunted from the air, skimming the surface, but rarely landing on the water. Some experts think that *Pterodaustro* also fed in this way, but another view is that it waded through the shallows with its wings folded back, sweeping its beak from side to side. If true, it would have been an ungainly sight.

◁ Pterodaustro *uses its bristle-filled beak to feed. The bristles— actually highly modified teeth—were up to 1.6 in. (4cm) long and were made of keratin, the same substance that forms hair and claws.*

△ *Starting from the top right and going counterclockwise, this four-stage sequence shows* Anhanguera *catching a fish. Its catch is small enough to be swallowed while flying—anything much larger than this would have to be taken back to land and ripped apart.*

GETTING A GRIP

Apart from *Pterodaustro*, pterosaurs had either widely spaced teeth or no teeth at all. Unusually for reptiles, the toothy species sometimes had several types of teeth, including large, single-pointed ones at the front of the jaws, and smaller ones with a number of points at the sides. This feature must have developed at an early stage in pterosaur evolution because it is visible in some of the oldest species, such as *Eudimorphodon* (page 184).

For pterosaurs that caught fish from the air, spotting prey and snatching it were the first two steps in a complex operation. Once a fish had been grabbed by the front teeth, it either had to be maneuvered into a headfirst position, so that it could be swallowed, or it had to be flicked from the front of the beak toward the back, so that it was secure for the journey back to land. This is where the small lateral teeth came in. Unlike the front teeth, they had a more powerful bite, and because they were short, the pterosaur could carry its victim without its beak gaping.

In some fossils the outlines of what look like throat pouches can be seen. These handy devices would have allowed pterosaurs to carry food back to land without any risk of it wriggling free.

FEEDING ON LAND

Fish eaters were not the only pterosaurs that had teeth. Smaller species based on land probably used their teeth to catch insects, both in the air and on the ground. At one time pterosaurs were thought to

▷ *Probing into soft mud, a* Pterodactylus *catches a worm. Like today's birds, pterodactyls had very good eyesight, moderate hearing, but probably a poor sense of smell. They would have found worms by sight, and perhaps by touch.*

be clumsy on land, moving with a scuttling walk, as many bats do today. More recent studies of pterosaur skeletons suggest that they might have been surprisingly agile. In some the rear legs were straight and strong, and with their wings folded back, their wing claws would have given them a tenacious grip.

At a time when giant plant-eating dinosaurs were common, this four-legged stance could have been put to good use. Some pterosaurs might have probed damp ground for insect grubs, but others probably followed dinosaur herds and watched for any insects as they fed. A dinosaur's back would have made a perfect platform for keeping an eye out for food, and with four sets of claws to keep them in position, pterosaurs would have been difficult to dislodge.

SOARING SCAVENGERS

During the Cretaceous the giants of the pterosaur world dispensed with teeth altogether. Instead, species such as *Pteranodon* and *Quetzalcoatlus* had massive, toothless beaks, sometimes over 3 ft. (1m) long. *Pteranodon* was a fish eater, but *Quetzalcoatlus* fossils come from rocks that formed inland. One theory is that *Quetzalcoatlus* lived like some of today's cranes and storks, striding across the ground or through shallow water, snatching any small animals it found. But it is more likely that it was not a hunter at all, but a scavenger. Its huge wings, combined with excellent eyesight, would have made it the supervulture of the Late Cretaceous, soaring high over open landscapes in search of dinosaur remains.

For a scavenging *Quetzalcoatlus* breaking through over an inch of dead dinosaur skin to reach the meat was a problem. Pterosaur teeth would not have been much help, but a daggerlike beak was perfect. With a few well-aimed blows, *Quetzalcoatlus* could have punctured the toughest of hides.

How PTEROSAURS BRED

FOR PTEROSAURS, RAISING YOUNG WAS A DEMANDING BUSINESS. INSTEAD OF LAYING EGGS AND THEN ABANDONING THEM—LIKE SOME DINOSAURS—THEY PROBABLY SPENT TIME CARING FOR THEIR YOUNG.

Fossils reveal little about the family life of pterosaurs, but there are a few clues about how they bred. One is that female pterosaurs generally had a narrow pelvis; this makes it unlikely that they gave birth to live young, unless the young were small and poorly developed. They are more likely to have laid eggs. They would have laid them in inaccessible places, such as cliffs and trees, away from predators.

▷ *Back from a fishing trip, an adult* Ornithocheirus *regurgitates food for one of its offspring.*

DELIVERING FOOD

If pterosaurs were warm-blooded, they would probably have incubated their eggs. The young hatchlings would have looked like miniature versions of their parents, but with shorter beaks and wings. They would not have been able to fly, which means that they would have depended on their parents for food. Some adult pterosaurs may have brought back pieces of food in their beaks, but for fishing species—which often wandered far out to sea—this would have been an inefficient method of delivery. Instead, they probably fed their nestlings on regurgitated and partly digested food, a system that allowed them to catch several fish before having to head back to shore.

For most pterosaurs the work of feeding and guarding the young is likely to have kept both parents fully occupied. Because they had to operate as a team, the two adults would have stayed together for the whole of the breeding season, or perhaps even for life.

FLYING LESSONS

Today's flying vertebrates—birds and bats—have to wait until they reach adult size, or very close to it, before they fly. A remarkable feature of pterosaurs is that the young seem to have begun flying when they were still a lot smaller than their parents. Evidence for this comes from fossils of *Pterodactylus*, which include some specimens less than 4 in. (10cm) long. These have well-developed wings; but some of their other features, such as the shape of their beak, show that they were juvenile animals.

This discovery has some intriguing implications for pterosaur family life. Young pterosaurs had to learn to fly, and most likely they were instructed by their parents. But even when they were fully at home in the air, they may still have been partly dependent on their parents for food. While the parents hunted for prey their youngsters may have flapped around them in a family flock until the time came when they could catch all their own food.

REPTILES IN THE SEA

A lthough reptiles evolved on land, many slowly abandoned terrestrial life and moved into the sea. During the Mesozoic Era these included dolphinlike ichthyosaurs, long-necked plesiosaurs, and a number of other predators, some almost as large as today's baleen whales and far more dangerous. Together they were the dominant marine animals, but their supremacy was not to last. The ichthyosaurs died out during the Cretaceous, and of the other animals featured in this chapter, only turtles survived into modern times.

ADAPTING TO LIFE IN WATER

FOR AIR-BREATHING, FOUR-LEGGED REPTILES, MOVING FROM LAND TO WATER MEANT SOME MAJOR CHANGES IN SHAPE AND ALSO IN BEHAVIOR. DIFFERENT GROUPS OF REPTILES MADE THE CHANGE IN DIFFERENT WAYS.

Because reptiles were so successful on land, it seems even more remarkable that so many kinds took up life in the sea. But evolution does not work in a set direction, and if a change brings advantages, that change is likely to be made. For marine reptiles the advantage was reduced competition for food—a factor that made life increasingly difficult on land. The ancestors of today's turtles were among the first to make the transition, followed by a variety of other groups. Interestingly, dinosaurs were not among them, although it is likely that most could swim.

▽ *The hand bones of an iguanodon (left) compared with those in the flipper of an ichthyosaur (right). Ichthyosaurs evolved large numbers of additional bones, which made their flippers more rigid.*

SHAPES FOR SWIMMING

For land animals gravity is a tiring fact of life, but air resistance is rarely a problem. In the sea things are the other way around. Here animals are buoyed up by the water around them, so they weigh little or nothing. But the moment they start to move, water resistance slows them down. The faster they swim, the more energy this resistance wastes.

The best way to minimize resistance is to have a streamlined body—something that all marine reptiles evolved at an early stage. Turtles developed flatter, smoother shells; pliosaurs had bodies with long heads and short

necks. The true specialists, however, were the fastest-moving of all prehistoric marine reptiles—the ichthyosaurs. With their beaklike snouts and barrel-shaped bodies, they could swim as fast as dolphins.

As well as different body shapes, marine reptiles also had different swimming styles (pages 194–195). But while some wriggled their way through the water and others sped along with their flippers or tails, almost all had one thing in common—a large number of phalanges, the bones that make up fingers and toes. Typical land-dwelling reptiles, such as lizards, have four phalanges in each finger or toe, the same number as humans. Marine reptiles could have as many as 17, and some had extra fingers and toes. All these bones were bound together by strong ligaments, turning their feet into reptilian fins.

This proliferation of finger and toe bones is known as hyperphalangy. Millions of years after most marine reptiles died out, exactly the same adaptation evolved in the cetaceans, the group of mammals that includes today's dolphins and whales.

COMING UP FOR AIR

Despite some far-reaching changes in shape, marine reptiles still needed to breathe air. In fact, this is one area in which evolution has never quite managed to turn back the clock in reptiles or in sea mammals. Instead of losing lungs, marine reptiles developed ways of breathing more easily at sea.

One of the first and simplest adaptations was nostrils high up on the head, equipped with flaps that allowed them to be closed. Another was a secondary palate—a flap at the back of the mouth that could shut off the windpipe, or trachea. This would have been vital because marine reptiles did not have lips, so they could not keep water out of their mouths while they were submerged. The palate prevented water from flowing down the windpipe and into their lungs.

With the help of these two modifications they could take a breath at the surface and then dive down to search for prey. No one knows how long they could stay underwater, but today's crocodiles may provide a guide. When they are active, large species surface

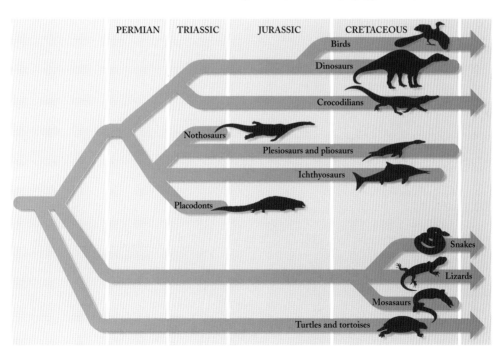

Young ichthyosaur
emerging tailfirst

roughly every five to ten minutes, but
they can rest underwater for several
hours. In prehistoric times
the deepest divers were the
ichthyosaurs, and some, such as
Ophthalmosaurus, may have been able to
stay underwater for an hour or more, but not
nearly as long if swimming at high speed.

EGGS OR LIVE BIRTH?
Apart from their need to breathe air,
ichthyosaurs were fully equipped for life at
sea. Fossils show that they gave birth to live
young, which meant that they never had to
return to land. But for other marine reptiles
in these distant times evidence about

reproduction is extremely thin on
the ground. No remains have ever been
found of young animals developing inside
their mothers or of embryos inside eggs.
As a result paleontologists can only guess
how these animals might have bred.

It is possible that smaller species
might have dragged themselves onto
land to lay eggs, as turtles do today. But
with giant species, such as the whale-sized
Liopleurodon (page 191), this is likely to
have been physically impossible. For this
reason most experts believe that animals
like this gave birth, instead of laying eggs.

◁ *This fossil shows
a female ichthyosaur
in the act of giving
birth. The young
animal is emerging
tailfirst, and its head
is partly hidden by
its mother's hind flippers.*

▽ *This family tree shows
how marine reptiles were
related to other reptiles
of the Mesozoic. Several
marine groups died out
well before the Age of
Reptiles ended.*

PERMIAN   TRIASSIC   JURASSIC   CRETACEOUS

Birds
Dinosaurs
Crocodilians
Nothosaurs
Plesiosaurs and pliosaurs
Ichthyosaurs
Placodonts
Snakes
Lizards
Mosasaurs
Turtles and tortoises

REPTILES IN THE SEA

NOTHOSAURS

MAXIMUM LENGTH   13 ft. (4m)
TIME   Mid Triassic
FOSSIL FINDS   Europe (Italy, Switzerland)

PISTOSAURUS
Unlike *Ceresiosaurus*, *Pistosaurus* had
some advanced features that made it even
better equipped for life in open water.

The nothosaurs, with the unrelated placodonts, were early marine reptiles that showed different degrees of adaptation to life in water. Some of them lived in lagoons and along shallow shores and spent much of their time on land, but others were sea creatures that may have wandered far into open water. A fossilized embryo found in Switzerland shows that some or perhaps all of these animals reproduced by laying eggs, a primitive characteristic that made them partly dependent on land.

Its flipperlike legs were smooth and elliptical—without any visible toes—and its backbone was relatively stiff, allowing it to move by paddling instead of by waving its tail. Its head was small and almost cylindrical, another adaptation that would have helped to reduce energy-wasting turbulence as it slipped through the water. *Pistosaurus* is classified in the same order as the nothosaurs, but in a family of its own. It could clearly have ranged far out to sea, but if it laid eggs, as other nothosaurs seem to have done, it would have had to return to land to breed.

MAXIMUM LENGTH   10 ft. (3m)
TIME   Mid Triassic
FOSSIL FINDS   Europe (France, Germany)

△ Pistosaurus
*had well-developed
flipperlike limbs,
although the outlines
of toes were probably
evident beneath the
surface of its skin. Its
tail was cylindrical
and did not have a fin.*

▽ Ceresiosaurus *had
a characteristic nothosaur
body, with a long neck,
finned tail, and well-
developed flippers with
distinct toes. It probably
hunted for fish in rocky
crevices on the seabed,
instead of in open water.*

CERESIOSAURUS
Ceresiosaurus was a typical nothosaur, with a slender, streamlined shape. It had a long, highly flexible tail and extra bones in its toes—a feature that evolved on many separate occasions in marine reptiles and mammals. Its head was relatively small, but its jaws were armed with small, sharp teeth—the hallmark of a fish eater. Opinions differ about how *Ceresiosaurus* swam. Instead of using only its tail, like the placodonts (see opposite), or its flippers, like the plesiosaurs (page 188), it may have used both, perhaps switching from one form of movement to the other as it adjusted its speed. Along with many other marine reptiles from the Triassic, its remains have been found in ancient marine sediments in the European Alps, an area which once formed part of the Tethys Sea.

LARIOSAURUS
Only about half the size of an otter, *Lariosaurus* was much smaller than some of its nothosaur relatives, although at the other extreme some nothosaurs were not much larger than a human hand. It had a lizardlike shape, with a short neck and toes. Its hind limbs still retained distinct toes and claws, although its feet would have been webbed.

It would probably have been amphibious, feeding in shallow water but spending much of its time resting on the shore. Because they had small bodies, animals like *Lariosaurus* would have been quickly chilled by cool seawater. As a result most of them were restricted to the tropics. Between swims they would have basked on rocks to warm themselves—like marine iguanas do today.

MAXIMUM LENGTH   2 ft. (60cm)

TIME Mid Triassic

FOSSIL FINDS Europe (Spain)

NOTHOSAURUS

Nothosaurus was a highly successful and widespread animal, appearing at the beginning of the Triassic Period and surviving, with relatively few changes, for over 30 million years. Several particularly well-preserved specimens have been found, clearly showing its webbed feet with five long toes.

lizardlike, with paddles that worked like a seal's flippers, allowing it to drag itself out onto land. Compared to the rest of its body, its head was small, perhaps allowing it to probe underwater crevices in search of fish to eat. There were several species of *Pachypleurosaurus*, and they varied a great deal in size. The smallest species were only about 2 ft. (60cm) long.

MAXIMUM LENGTH   8.2 ft. (2.5m)

TIME Mid Triassic

FOSSIL FINDS Europe (Italy, Switzerland)

Its front legs were shorter than its hind ones—a characteristic that is more useful for moving on land than it is for swimming at sea. This reptile had a sinuous, streamlined body, and spines on its vertebrae make it likely that its tail had a vertical fin. *Nothosaurus* was a fish eater, but its leg anatomy suggests that it spent a substantial amount of time on the shore, like modern seals do today.

MAXIMUM LENGTH   10 ft. (3m)

TIME Triassic

FOSSIL FINDS Asia (China, Russia), Europe (Germany, Italy, Switzerland), northern Africa

PACHYPLEUROSAURUS

At one time this animal and its relatives were thought by scientists to be nothosaurs, but they were probably close cousins, rather than members of the same family. *Pachypleurosaurus* itself was slim and

PLACODUS

Looking like a large, humpbacked lizard, *Placodus* was one of the earliest marine reptiles. It had webbed feet and a flattened tail, but apart from this, it showed few modifications for life in the water. Its head was short, and it had three different types of teeth: protruding incisors at the front of its jaws, rounded molars along the sides, and a set of six flattened molars on the roof of its mouth. This suggests that it fed on mollusks in shallow water, prizing them from rocks and crushing them in its jaws. *Placodus* belonged to a group of reptiles called placodonts, which were protected by reinforced skeletons or sometimes bony shells (page 202). The placodonts became extinct before the Triassic came to an end.

MAXIMUM LENGTH   6.6 ft. (2m)

TIME Early Triassic

FOSSIL FINDS Europe (France)

△ Nothosaurus *was one of the larger members of its family, with a seallike lifestyle. Because it was cold-blooded—like its relatives—its oxygen consumption would have been relatively low, allowing it to stay submerged for several minutes at a time. Its nostrils were positioned halfway down its muzzle and would have been closed by flaps of skin when it dived.*

PLESIOSAURS

Plesiosaurs first appeared in the Late Triassic, but had their heyday in the Jurassic. There were two basic forms: species with long necks and small heads, the true plesiosaurs; and species with short necks and large heads, the pliosaurs (page 190). Both types had four flipperlike fins, and they swam by beating these up and down like wings, instead of by waving their tails. All of them were oceangoing carnivores that returned to land only when they laid their eggs. Compared to early marine reptiles, some of them were enormous, even rivaling modern whales in size.

PLESIOSAURUS

Some of the earliest *Plesiosaurus* fossils were discovered by the English fossil collector Mary Anning in the 1820s (page 197). The specimens she found were well-preserved and remarkably complete—a result of rapid burial by a soft blanket of marine sediment, which prevented the remains from being disturbed. Her finds and many others show that there were several species of *Plesiosaurus*, all of them variations on the same successful design. They had narrow heads, slender necks and tails, and two pairs of paddles roughly equal in size. Their teeth were numerous, pointed, and slightly curved—a shape that evolved for catching fish, which would then be swallowed whole. *Plesiosaurus'* large paddles and sturdy build make it likely that it pursued its prey, instead of waiting for fish to come within range.

MAXIMUM LENGTH	9.8 ft. (3m)
TIME	Early Jurassic
FOSSIL FINDS	Europe (England, France, Germany)

RHOMALEOSAURUS

With its relatively long neck and large head, *Rhomaleosaurus* looked like a halfway stage between true plesiosaurs and the pliosaurs. Its classification is still a matter of debate, and at times it has been allotted to both these groups. Its lifestyle is more certain, because fossils clearly show a powerful body, two pairs of roughly equal paddles, and crocodile-like jaws, sometimes nearly 3.3 ft. (1m) long, armed with large, protruding teeth. Some recent research suggests that *Rhomaleosaurus* and its relatives may have swum with their jaws slightly ajar, allowing water to go in through the mouth and out through the nostrils. This unusual arrangement—a reversal of the normal water flow—would have allowed them to track prey by smell rather than by sight.

MAXIMUM LENGTH	23 ft. (7m)
TIME	Early Jurassic
FOSSIL FINDS	Europe (England, Germany)

CRYPTOCLIDUS

A large plesiosaur with a 6.6 ft (2m) long neck, *Cryptoclidus* had a number of evolutionary refinements for life at sea. Its flippers were much larger than those of earlier plesiosaurs, giving it more power underwater. Its teeth were long, pointed, and interlocking so that they formed a cagelike trap for fish, shrimp, and squid. Fossils of this animal are often very well preserved, and some of the best came from clay quarries in England at a time when clay was dug out by hand. This kind of quarrying is now carried out by machine, so complete fossil skeletons are much more rarely found today.

MAXIMUM LENGTH	26.2 ft. (8m)
TIME	Late Jurassic
FOSSIL FINDS	Asia (Russia), Europe (England, France)

MURAENOSAURUS

Muraenosaurus—"moray eel lizard"—belonged to a group of reptiles called elasmosaurs, renowned for

△ Plesiosaurus *would have fed by powering through the water with its paddles while using its flexible neck to lunge after fish and squid. Its head was triangular with a pointed snout— an efficient shape for slicing through the water.*

▷ Rhomaleosaurus *was the Early Jurassic equivalent of a killer whale, hunting fish and perhaps other reptiles with its well-armed jaws. Unlike small-headed plesiosaurs, it could have torn large animals to pieces by tossing them in the air.*

their very long necks. It was one of the early examples of the neck-stretching trend, which became increasingly exaggerated. It had up to 44 neck vertebrae, and altogether they accounted for over half its entire body length. Its head was relatively tiny—just 15.7 in. (40cm) long. It also had relatively small flippers for its size and a stubby tail. This combination of features suggests that *Muraenosaurus* was not an active hunter. Instead, it probably rested on the seabed in shallow water, where it could attack fish either from beneath the surface or from above it. To feed, it would have drawn its neck back into a curve and then suddenly straightened it to grab its prey. Its small head would also have allowed it to extract fish from crevices among rocks.

MAXIMUM LENGTH 19.7 ft. (6m)

TIME Late Jurassic

FOSSIL FINDS Europe (England, France)

ELASMOSAURUS
Living 100 million years after *Muraenosaurus*, this bizarre marine reptile was the last of the elasmosaur line. It had up to 71 neck vertebrae, contributing to a snakelike neck—19.7 ft. (6m) long. The central part of its body was also much larger than in *Muraenosaurus*. *Elasmosaurus'* feeding technique was probably similar to its earlier relatives, although its increased neck length would have given it a greater reach. The theory that it was a sit-and-wait predator has been bolstered by the discovery of gastroliths, or stomach stones, which it may have used as ballast.

MAXIMUM LENGTH 46 ft. (14m)

TIME Late Cretaceous

FOSSIL FINDS Asia (Japan), North America (Kansas, Wyoming)

◁ *Powered by its well-developed paddles,* Cryptoclidus *would have "flown" through the water.*

▽ Elasmosaurus *homes in on a school of fish. This plesiosaur is often portrayed as a sea monster, but its narrow head meant it could tackle only very small prey.*

PLIOSAURS

D escended from plesiosaurs, pliosaurs became the top marine predators from the Early Jurassic into the Cretaceous. With short necks, massive heads, and viciously armed jaws, they could attack animals almost their own size, ripping off chunks of flesh like today's sharks or killer whales. They probably hunted alone, and they may have relied partly on their sense of smell to track down food. In pliosaur evolution natural selection favored increasing size. After more than 60 million years the outcome of this process was *Liopleurodon*, perhaps the largest predator ever to have existed on the planet.

△ Kronosaurus' *head accounted for about a third of its entire body length, and its jaws ran almost the entire length of the skull, giving them a depth of nearly 10 ft. (3m). It had two other distinguishing features that set it apart from other pliosaurs: the top of the head was unusually flattened and the ribs were thicker.*

MACROPLATA

A relatively primitive pliosaur from the Early Jurassic, *Macroplata* still had features in common with its plesiosaur ancestors: a long neck with 29 vertebrae and a fairly small head. Two specimens from England, dated about 15 million years apart, highlight the trends in pliosaur evolution—the more recent species had a longer head, as well as a slightly larger body. In pliosaurs as a whole the limbs also became larger and stronger than those of plesiosaurs, allowing them to power through the water after their prey.

MAXIMUM LENGTH	16.4 ft. (5m)
TIME	Early Jurassic
FOSSIL FINDS	Europe (England)

SIMOLESTES

Simolestes was slightly larger than *Macroplata* and had a more typical pliosaur shape, with a short neck, massively built head, and large, paddlelike legs. Its neck contained only 20 vertebrae, far fewer than many plesiosaurs, but still more than pliosaurs of later times.

Its jaws had blunt ends, giving it a snub-nosed appearance, and the lower one was equipped with half a dozen extra-large teeth, which stabbed upward into prey. It would have killed small prey outright, but with larger animals it probably attacked and then circled at a distance, waiting for the moment when its victim was too weak to fight back. Sharks use the same technique.

MAXIMUM LENGTH	19.7 ft. (6m)
TIME	Mid Jurassic
FOSSIL FINDS	Asia (India), Europe (France)

PLIOSAURUS

First identified in the 1840s, the original pliosaur has proven difficult to classify. Many paleontologists believe that it is actually a form of *Liopleurodon* because their remains look so similar. Among the few differences are the teeth. *Liopleurodon*'s were round viewed in cross section, while *Pliosaurus*' were triangular. *Pliosaurus* had about 20 neck vertebrae, and its skull was up to 6.6 ft. (2m) long.

MAXIMUM LENGTH	39.4 ft. (12m)
TIME	Mid Jurassic
FOSSIL FINDS	Europe (England), South America (Argentina)

PELONEUSTES

A compact Late Jurassic pliosaur, *Peloneustes* shows the developing trend in the family for a larger head and shorter neck, as well as a more streamlined shape. Its hind paddles were slightly larger than its front ones—the reverse of the situation in many plesiosaurs. However, as in plesiosaurs, both pairs of flippers were used in swimming, although the rear pair are likely to have done more of the work. Each

flipper would have twisted as it beat up and down through the water, creating a backward thrust that drove the animal forward (page 194). The remains of suckers, preserved as fossils in *Peloneustes*' stomach, show that squid formed an important part of its diet. Its teeth were relatively small, making it unlikely that it attacked large prey.

MAXIMUM LENGTH   10 ft. (3m)

TIME   Late Jurassic

FOSSIL FINDS   Europe (Russia, U.K.)

LIOPLEURODON

Once it reached maturity, this colossal pliosaur was so large that it had no enemies apart from its own kind. Estimates of its length range from about 39.4 ft. (12m) to as much as 82 ft. (25m)—a figure that suggests it might have weighed over 100 tons. This is much larger than the sperm whale, which is the largest living predator that tracks down and attacks individual prey. *Liopleurodon* would have fed on any marine animal large enough to attract its attention. Although it was fully equipped for life in the open sea, it may also have swum into shallower water, where it could pick off

dinosaurs foraging near the shore. It relied mainly on vision and smell, lunging forward to make a kill with an array of widely spaced, daggerlike teeth. These were conical in shape and up to 1 ft. (30cm) long—twice the length of those of *Tyrannosaurus*. They projected from the front of its jaws, which hinged at a point close to the back of the skull—a distance of up to 13 ft. (4m). Given its size, *Liopleurodon* would have been able to travel immense distances, but little is known of its breeding behavior. On land it would have been as helpless as a beached whale, which suggests that it gave birth to live young instead of laying eggs.

MAXIMUM LENGTH   82 ft. (25m)

TIME   Late Jurassic

FOSSIL FINDS   Europe (France, Germany, U.K.)

KRONOSAURUS

The first pliosaur fossil finds in Australia were made in Queensland and date back to the 1880s. In 1990 cattle ranchers in the same area stumbled across another set of fossilized bones protruding from the ground like tree stumps. They turned out to belong to *Kronosaurus* or a similar animal and are among the most complete pliosaur remains currently known. Although *Kronosaurus* was only generally a little over half the size of *Liopleurodon*, it was still larger and heavier than most land-based predators of the Cretaceous, with a head measuring 8.2 ft. (2.5m).

MAXIMUM LENGTH   33 ft. (10m)

TIME   Early Cretaceous

FOSSIL FINDS   Australia (Queensland), South America (Colombia)

◁ Liopleurodon *was a terrifying marine predator of enormous size and power. Armed with murderous, projecting teeth and protected by platelike bones on its underside, it would have reigned supreme in the Jurassic seas.*

▽ *Although a midget compared to some of its relatives,* Peloneustes *was still a substantial predator, the size of a large modern dolphin. It would have been a fast and agile swimmer, powered by its four paddles. It caught fish and squid in its narrow, toothed mouth.*

REPTILES IN THE SEA

ICHTHYOSAURS

Ichthyosaurs, or "fish lizards," were the first reptiles that were fully adapted to life in the sea. Ichthyosaurs had streamlined bodies and flippers instead of legs, and most had crescent-shaped tails. Like all reptiles, they breathed air, using nostrils at the base of their snouts. Some fossilized ichthyosaurs died with embryos inside their bodies, or even while they were giving birth— dramatic proof that they did not lay eggs.

▷ *Like other ichthyosaurs,* Mixosaurus *had four pairs of flippers, and a single upright fin on its back. The fin would have helped to keep it on a straight course while its tail moved from side to side.*

MIXOSAURUS

Mixosaurus (meaning "mixed lizard") lived about 220 million years ago, when ichthyosaurs were already well-established. Although it was fully adapted to life at sea, it still had several primitive features. The most obvious one was its tail, which ended in a point, instead of having two vertical lobes. *Mixosaurus* fed on fish,

and its distribution—in warm, shallow seas worldwide—shows that it was very successful.

LENGTH	3.3 ft. (1m)
TIME	Mid Triassic
FOSSIL FINDS	Asia (China), Europe (France, Germany, Norway), North America (Alaska, Nevada), New Zealand

ICHTHYOSAURUS

Looking like a small dolphin, *Ichthyosaurus* is one of the best-known marine prehistoric reptiles, with hundreds of fossils having been found. A powerful swimmer, it could probably have reached speeds of 25 mph (40km/h), powered by its vertical two-lobed tail. Its snout was long and narrow and was armed with small but sharp teeth—ideal for gripping squid and other slippery animals.

LENGTH	6.6 ft. (2m)
TIME	Early Jurassic to early Cretaceous
FOSSIL FINDS	Europe (England, Germany), Greenland, North America (Alberta)

▷ *Compared to most ichthyosaurs, Shonisaurus was a vast and bulky animal. At one fossil site in Nevada the remains of more than 30 Shonisaurus have been found close together. This suggests that these giant reptiles lived in schools, like many of today's whales.*

▽ *With its streamlined body and long jaws, Temnodontosaurus was shaped for catching fast-moving prey. Fish made up most of its diet, but it also ate squid and other cephalopod molluscs. Their hard remains have been found inside Temnnodontosaurus skeletons.*

TEMNODONTOSAURUS

Also known as *Leptopterygius*, this large ichthyosaur had a long snout, a barrel-shaped body, and a powerful two-lobed tail. Most ichthyosaurs had good eyesight, but this one's eyes were the biggest of any known animal, alive or extinct. They measured up to 10 in. (26cm) across, and as in most ichthyosaurs, were surrounded by a ring of thin, overlapping bony plates, which helped to protect them during dives. *Leptopterygius*' large eyes may have been an adaptation for hunting at night.

LENGTH 29.5 ft. (9m)

TIME Late Jurassic

FOSSIL FINDS Europe (England, Germany)

SHONISAURUS

With a body as long as a bus, *Shonisaurus* is the largest ichthyosaur that has yet been discovered. It appeared relatively early in ichthyosaur evolution and had some unusual features that set it apart from its relatives. Among these were a deep, bulky body; long, equal-sized flippers; and teeth only in the front of its jaws. Its diet is uncertain, but its size alone means that it would have been a formidable predator, capable of tackling many other sea animals.

LENGTH 49 ft. (15m)

TIME Late Triassic

FOSSIL FINDS North America (Nevada)

▷ Ichthyosaurs, plesiosaurs, and turtles all had different swimming styles. Ichthyosaurs, the most fishlike of the three, swam with side-to-side undulations. Plesiosaurs used a complex swimming technique with two pairs of paddles moving in alternate directions. Turtles swim with their front legs, with very little push coming from the pair at the rear.

Ichthyosaur

Plesiosaur

SWIMMING STYLES

WHEN REPTILES TOOK UP LIFE IN WATER, THEY EVOLVED DIFFERENT METHODS OF SWIMMING. SOME SWAM LIKE FISH, BUT OTHERS MOVED IN WAYS THAT HAVE NO DIRECT EQUIVALENT IN LIVING ANIMALS.

Turtle

To swim, an animal has to push against the water around it. This backward push drives the animal forward in the same way that the push from a propeller moves a boat. Reptiles evolved swimming styles with modified versions of two different body parts: tails and limbs. Tail propulsion is the common swimming style in fish and was the method evolved by ichthyosaurs. Limb propulsion is used by seals and penguins, but reptiles evolved some versions of it that were uniquely their own.

POWER AT THE REAR
To swim efficiently, an animal has to push against the water with minimum turbulence. This creates a smooth water flow as the animal moves—the exact opposite of what happens when somebody splashes around as they learn to swim.

Tail propulsion is ideal for this, and it is no accident that most fish use their tails to swim instead of rowing with their other fins.

The earliest marine reptiles, such as *Placodus* (page 187), had long, webbed tails that they rippled from side to side in conjunction with the rest of their bodies. For animals that originated on land, this way of swimming needed relatively few physical changes, but it had the disadvantage of being fairly slow. Ichthyosaurs, on the other hand, evolved shorter, bladelike tails, much more like those of fish. Most of their body movement took place at the tail end, and their paddlelike limbs acted as rudders and stabilizers, keeping them on course. This swimming style is almost exactly the same as that used by the fastest fish today.

△ *In fish and ichthyosaurs the body and tail push against the water as they bend from side to side.*

△ *The side-to-side movements generate a force that drives the animal forward through the water.*

△ *In plesiosaurs the tip of each flipper follows a roughly elliptical path (assuming the animal is still).*

△ *The backward push comes during the downstroke. The flipper then twists to move upward edge-on.*

△ *Turtles move both sets of flippers together, but the front pair does the work.*

△ *The flippers work like oars, although they can also glide like wings.*

△ *To push the turtle forward, flippers move downward and backward.*

PADDLES AND FLIPPERS

In most other marine reptiles evolution followed a different course. These animals also developed paddlelike limbs, but instead of being fairly immobile, their limbs kept some of the movement they had on land. For some of these reptiles the tail helped in propulsion. In others, particularly turtles, it became so small that it played no part in swimming at all.

Evolution often exaggerates differences between front and back legs, and this is exactly what happened with turtles. Their forelimbs became longer and more powerful, beating up and down like a pair of wings to push the animal through the water. The back legs were much smaller and used mainly for steering and stability. But in plesiosaurs, the four paddles stayed roughly similar in size. Plesiosaurs probably swam with all four limbs working simultaneously, a highly unusual swimming style that has not been seen either before or since.

THE PLESIOSAUR PUZZLE

For stability plesiosaurs' two pairs of legs would most likely have beaten in opposite directions, but the exact path of each paddle is not easy to work out. They may have pushed horizontally (like oars), diagonally, or vertically up and down. From studies of plesiosaur skeletons the second theory is generally accepted as the most likely of the three. Each flipper generated a backward push as it came down and then twisted so that it could slide back into the up position with minimal resistance against the water. The upstroke was aided by the animal's spine, which bent rhythmically as it swam.

▽ *Plesiosaurs used their flippers for steering and braking as well as for building up speed. Here an* Elasmosaurus *carries out a sharp turn to pursue a school of fish.*

195

FAMILY GROUP
Guarded by their mother, two young Temnodontosaurus *swim past a rocky reef in search of food. Because female ichthyosaurs gave birth to live young, they had small families. The females probably looked after their offspring and showed them how to hunt.*

FOSSIL HUNTING IN EUROPE

EUROPE WAS THE BIRTHPLACE OF PALEONTOLOGY. EUROPEAN FOSSIL FINDS HAVE INCLUDED A NUMBER OF SIGNIFICANT FINDS, BEGINNING WITH THE DISCOVERY OF FOSSIL REPTILES OVER 250 YEARS AGO.

Fossils are common objects in some parts of Europe. During the medieval period they were thought to be the remains of animals that had perished in the biblical Great Flood—something that some people still believe today. But by the 1700s fossils of truly gigantic animals started to come to light, making scientists increasingly doubtful about the traditional version of the earth's history. They gradually realized that the earth was far older than previously thought, and that a wide range of animals had lived in the distant past, only to become extinct.

▷ *Carefully splitting open thin sheets of limestone, quarry workers in Germany reveal well-preserved fossils of Jurassic fish that have been entombed in limestone for over 150 million years.*

▷ *This is a fossil shrimp from the famous Solnhöfen limestone quarries in southern Germany. Because the rock particles are so fine, all the details of its body have been preserved. Solnhöfen has also yielded fossils of soft-bodied animals, such as jellyfish.*

BROUGHT TO THE SURFACE

In the early days of paleontology most fossils were discovered by accident, often by workers in Europe's quarries. One of the most spectacular of these early finds was the Beast of Maastricht—a giant crocodile-like skull that was found in a chalk quarry in the Netherlands in 1776. The Beast was actually a mosasaur (page 200), but scientists of the time imagined that it must belong

Born in 1799, Mary Anning was the world's first professional collector of fossils. Her home town, Lyme Regis, England, is flanked by seacliffs of Jurassic shale and mudstone, and it was here, in 1811, that she found the first known remains of an ichthyosaur, which had fallen out of the cliffs onto the shore. Thirteen years later she discovered another first: the almost complete fossil skeleton of a plesiosaur.

to an animal that still existed, probably either a crocodile or a whale.

The confusion over this animal was understandable, because the tooth-filled jaws of a mosasaur do look distinctly crocodilian.

But in 1784 an Italian naturalist published an account of an even more remarkable fossil that he had found in the Solnhöfen limestone quarries in southern Germany. Unlike the Maastricht mosasaur, this animal was small, but it looked unlike anything that scientists had ever seen or heard of before. Resembling a cross between a bat and a bird, it was actually a pterosaur—the first one to be studied in a systematic way. This fossil was the scientific equivalent of front-page news, and as interest in paleontology mushroomed quarry workers kept a sharp lookout for interesting specimens, which by now were fetching record prices.

During the early 1800s quarries like Solnhöfen generated a steady stream of fossil remains. At this time a young woman named Mary Anning became the first person to collect fossils for a living. Mary Anning lived on the coast of Dorset, England, in an area where fossil-filled cliffs are being steadily eroded by the sea. Her finds included an almost complete ichthyosaur, which was identified as an extinct marine reptile. The idea of extinction was becoming widely accepted, and this helped prepare the way for more momentous discoveries in the years that followed.

THE FIRST DINOSAURS

The first dinosaur fossil to be formally described was found in 1676 by the English museum curator Robert Plot. At the time Plot's discovery—the knee end of a giant thighbone—was thought to be from a large mammal, perhaps even a giant human being. Over 140 years passed before more remains of the animal were found in an English quarry. These fossils were examined by pioneering geologist William Buckland, who recognized that they belonged to a carnivorous reptile, which he named *Megalosaurus*. The following year another English geologist, Gideon Mantell, identified the remains of *Iguanodon*, again correctly deducing that they were from a reptile, rather than a mammal.

The name *Megalosaurus* means "giant lizard" and shows that even in the 1800s geologists were still trying to squeeze their newly discovered animals into known branches of the reptile world. But this situation was not to last for long. In 1841

the leading English anatomist Richard Owen showed that *Megalosaurus* and *Iguanodon* were different from living reptiles in many ways, even apart from their size. He proposed a new name for this extinct group of reptiles— "the dinosaurs."

MAMMALS AND PEOPLE

After this breakthrough European paleontology began to move quickly. The first fossil of *Archaeopteryx* was found at the Solnhöfen quarries in 1861, and as the 1800s drew to a close European fossil hunters began to send back fossils from other parts of the world. These formed the basis of magnificent museum collections in cities such as London, Paris, and Berlin. Paleontologists continued to unearth a wide range of reptiles in Europe, particularly marine forms such as ichthyosaurs and plesiosaurs, but their finds also included extinct mammals— mammoths, bears, and rhinoceroses—that flourished in Europe during ice age times.

In the last 150 years Europe has also been an important source of fossils and artifacts belonging to early humans, who spread northward through the continent after the move from Africa. The finds include the remains not only of our direct ancestors, but also those of Neanderthal man (page 216).

◁ *The crumbling cliffs of Lyme Regis, on the south coast of England, are a fossil hunter's paradise. Their layered rock, formed from seabed sediment in Jurassic times, contains the remains of a wide variety of animals— from ammonites to ichthyosaurs.*

△ *The Solnhöfen quarries in southern Germany produce limestone with an extremely fine grain. The rock was built up by tiny specks of sediment that settled in coral reef lagoons during the Late Jurassic. The quarries are famous for being the source of* Archaeopteryx *and half a dozen kinds of pterosaur, but they have also yielded many fish and over 100 kinds of fossils insect.*

MOSASAURS

△ Mosasaurus *and its relatives were alive when the ichthyosaurs had died out, making them among the largest marine reptiles in the Late Cretaceous.*

two pairs of widely saced, finlike paddles, containing many more toe bones than in its land-dwelling ancestors. Its tail was vertically flattened, and this—together with its wedge-shaped skull—made it look like a fish crossed with a crocodile. Like all mosasaurs, its jaws had a joint about halfway along their length, allowing them to extend sideways, and they were equipped with a battery of sharply pointed teeth. It probably fed on fish, squid, and turtles, but it also ate ammonites. This is known because fossilized ammonites have been discovered with bite marks that match *Mosasaurus'* teeth.

MAXIMUM LENGTH 33 ft. (10m)

TIME Late Cretaceous

FOSSIL FINDS Europe (Belgium, Holland), North America (South Dakota, Texas)

TYLOSAURUS
Similar in form to *Mosasaurus*, although slightly smaller, *Tylosaurus* would have been an equally formidable predator of the Late Cretaceous seas. Like *Mosasaurus*, it drove itself through the water with its tail, using its paddle-shaped flippers for steering and perhaps for stabilizing itself when it rested inshore. Its teeth were up to 2 in. (5cm) long and 1.2 in. (3cm)

M osasaurs were latecomers to the ranks of Mesozoic marine reptiles, appearing late in the Cretaceous Period and disappearing when it came to a close. Unlike other reptiles in the sea, they belonged to the same line of animals as today's monitor lizards. They had scaly, lizardlike skin, and they swam by rippling their long bodies, which ended in a flattened, fin-bearing tail. Some of them grew to a great size, and they had unusual jaws that could bend sideways to engulf and crush their prey.

▽ Tylosaurus *(below) had the sinuous shape, small limbs, and narrow head characteristic of the mosasaur family.*

▷ Platecarpus *(right) had a large number of finger and toe bones, a typical feature of marine reptiles.*

MOSASAURUS
Mosasaurus has a unique place in the study of prehistoric life. When the first skull was found in a Dutch quarry in 1776, it was assumed to belong to an unknown animal—perhaps a crocodile or whale—that was still alive somewhere on Earth. But as the decades went by without a living *Mosasaurus* being found, scientists began to grasp a crucial fact: animal life in the past included species that have become extinct. The creature that triggered this breakthrough was one of the deadliest marine predators of the Late Cretaceous. Its limbs had evolved into

wide at the base and would have constantly been replaced throughout its lifetime. Its eyes were surrounded by a sclerotic ring—a circle of small, flattened bones that acted as a protective shield in front of the eyeball. Like other mosasaurs, *Tylosaurus* lived in shallow seas. But although hundreds of mosasaur fossils have been found, unlike ichthyosaurs, none shows signs of carrying embryos. This makes it probable that most mosasaurs laid eggs, dragging themselves onto sandy beaches like turtles. Their flippers would have been ineffective on land, so they may have writhed their way up the shore.

MAXIMUM LENGTH 26.2 ft. (8m)

TIME Late Cretaceous

FOSSIL FINDS North America (Kansas, Texas), New Zealand

PLATECARPUS

Remains found on both sides of the Atlantic show that *Platecarpus* was a fairly common marine reptile in the Late Cretaceous. Although very small compared to other mosasaurs, it was about the same size as many of today's open-water sharks, and its long jaws would have made it an effective predator. It probably fed on fish and squid, but exactly how it hunted is unclear. It may have fed in the same way as modern seals, cruising through the shallows close to the shore and catching animals frightened by its approach.

MAXIMUM LENGTH 19.7 ft. (6m)

TIME Late Cretaceous

FOSSIL FINDS North America (Alabama, Colorado, Kansas, Mississippi; Manitoba, Northwest Territories), Europe (Belgium)

GLOBIDENS

When *Globidens* first came to light in Alabama in 1912, it was given its name because of its remarkable teeth. They had rounded crowns and looked like a row of golf balls set in the animal's jaws. Teeth like these were clearly useless for grasping fish or squid, and instead *Globidens* probably fed on mollusks and crustaceans, cracking open their shells and body cases with its jaws. Only a handful of *Globidens* skulls have been found—all in North America—but isolated teeth have been found in other parts of the world.

MAXIMUM LENGTH 19.7 ft. (6m)

TIME Late Cretaceous

FOSSIL FINDS North America (Alabama, Kansas, South Dakota)

PLOTOSAURUS

One of the largest of about 20 mosasaurs so far discovered, *Plotosaurus* had a long body and a snakelike tail with a flattened vertical fin. Its small flippers were widely spaced, making them ineffective for propulsion but good for steering and stability. Skin impressions found near some *Plotosaurus* fossils show that it was covered in small scales, like today's monitor lizards. With its sleek shape and sharp teeth, it would have been a major threat to fish and squid in shallow seas as the Cretaceous neared its end.

MAXIMUM LENGTH 33 ft. (10m)

TIME Late Cretaceous

FOSSIL FINDS North America (Kansas)

△ *With its jaws gaping open,* Globidens *(top) reveals a mouth full of bulbous and extremely hard teeth. The main teeth were up to 1.2 in. (3cm) across; the ones at the front of the jaw were smaller and peglike.*

△ Plotosaurus *(above) was so well adapted to marine life that it would have had difficulty moving on land. This suggests that it gave birth to live young, unlike some of its relatives.*

REPTILES IN THE SEA

SHELLED REPTILES

During the Mesozoic Era two different groups of marine reptiles evolved shells as a protection against predators. One group, the placodonts, were relatives of some of the earliest reptiles in the seas (page 197). They emerged in the Triassic but were extinct before it came to an end. The other group were the chelonians—animals that also appeared in the Triassic and were the ancestors of today's tortoises and turtles. Although they lived at different times, these two groups evolved similar adaptations to suit similar ways of life.

△ *With its streamlined shell and huge "wingspan," Archelon (top right) roamed vast distances throughout the seas of the Late Cretaceous.*

▷ *Placochelys (right) is a combination name that means "placodont-turtle"—a fitting description of this remarkably turtlelike animal.*

▽ *Henodus (below) had a rectangular shell. Its legs were relatively short and stumpy, suggesting that it spent most of its time crawling across the seabed.*

ARCHELON
Chelonians first appeared on land, and although tortoises remained there, turtles took up life in freshwater or the sea. By the late Cretaceous, one marine species—*Archelon*—became the largest sea turtle that has ever lived. It weighed about three tons and swam by beating its winglike front flippers, which were 14.8 ft. (4.5m) from tip to tip. Its shell was formed by an open lattice of struts, instead of a complete shield of bone, and it probably had a rubbery surface, like the shells of modern leatherback turtles. Like other chelonians, *Archelon*'s jaws formed a toothless beak, and it fed on jellyfish and other soft-bodied animals. Despite its great weight, it reproduced by hauling itself onto beaches and laying eggs.

MAXIMUM LENGTH	13 ft. (4m)
TIME	Late Cretaceous
FOSSIL FINDS	North America (Kansas, Dakota)

HENODUS
Long before *Archelon* appeared in the seas, *Henodus*, a placodont, had evolved a shell for self-defense. Unlike a turtle's shell, this one was made up of several hundred bony plates, which fit together like a mosaic. The edges of the shell were drawn out into a pair of rigid flaps, giving a flattened shape. *Henodus* had a blunt mouth without any teeth, and it ate mollusks and other slow-moving animals in shallow water.

MAXIMUM LENGTH	3.3 ft. (1m)
TIME	Late Triassic
FOSSIL FINDS	Europe (Germany)

PLACOCHELYS
The shell of this placodont was shallow and almost rectangular and was covered with a scattering of bony plates that made it harder to attack.

It had flat-toothed jaws, ending in a narrow beak that was ideal for prying mollusks from rocks. It had flattened legs that worked like flippers, and their size meant that it was probably a good swimmer. However, like all marine turtles, it could not pull its legs within its shell if it was attacked. *Placochelys* most likely reproduced by laying eggs, and it would have had no difficulty crawling out onto land.

MAXIMUM LENGTH	3 ft. (90cm)
TIME	Late Triassic
FOSSIL FINDS	Europe (Germany)

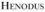

THE AGE OF
THE MAMMALS

During Earth's long history most of the changes involving animal life have been extremely slow. But 66 million years ago something happened that had an abrupt and disastrous effect on the world's dominant animals. The 150-million-year reign of dinosaurs came to an end, and many other reptiles, including pterosaurs and plesiosaurs, also disappeared. The surviving reptiles never completely recovered from this setback, but for mammals it brought new opportunities. The Mesozoic Era had ended, ushering in the Cenozoic—the era in which we live today.

THE END OF THE DINOSAURS

BEFORE THE AGE OF MAMMALS BEGAN SOME DINOSAUR FAMILIES HAD ALREADY BECOME EXTINCT. BUT WITHOUT THE CATASTROPHE THAT OCCURRED 66 MILLION YEARS AGO, DINOSAURS MIGHT STILL BE DOMINANT TODAY.

I n the earth's crust only the thinnest of lines separates the last rocks of the Age of Reptiles from the first ones formed during the Age of Mammals. But this geological turning point—known as the K-T boundary—has been studied by scientists in minute detail in places all over the world. The reason is that it holds the secret to what happened at the end of the Cretaceous Period, when as many as fifty percent of all the world's plant and animal species became extinct. Those studies point to one likely culprit: an object from outer space.

▷ *Terrified by the light released by a giant meteorite, a tyrannosaur reacts by running for its life. It has only seconds to live because the impact has already set off an atmospheric shock wave that will burst over the horizon, sweeping away almost anything that can be moved, from animals and plants to boulders weighing many tons.*

THE EVIDENCE

Dozens of theories have been put forward for the extinction of the dinosaurs, often without any evidence. But in the 1980s two American scientists, Luis Alvarez and his son Walter, published research showing that a massive meteorite up to 9 mi. (15km) across might have smashed into the earth, causing devastation on an unimaginable scale. Their evidence was the unusually high level of iridium that they found in the K-T boundary. Iridium is a chemical element and is normally ten times rarer than gold. The most likely explanation for the raised level, according to the Alvarez team, was that it had come from a giant meteorite that had vaporized on impact about 66.4 million years ago.

When they first proposed this idea, the site of the impact was unknown. But in the 1990s geologists investigated the remnants of a huge crater off Mexico's Yucatán Peninsula and found that its age almost exactly matched the time of this event. The crater is about 186 mi. (300km) across, indicating that the meteorite that made it would have sent shock waves right around the world.

THE IMPACT

Some scientists are not convinced by the meteorite theory and think that, as with the Permian extinction (page 66), the true causes might have been volcanic eruptions and other natural events. If a giant meteorite did crash into the earth, the results would have been incredibly destructive immediately after, as well as in the weeks and months that followed. In the second or so that it took to fall through the atmosphere, its outer surface would have melted, creating a burst of light brighter than thousands of suns. Once it struck the earth and vaporized, shock waves would have reverberated throughout the planet, triggering off landslides and earthquakes. Millions of tons of dust would have been blasted into the air, replacing the intense light of the impact itself with day after day of deep gloom. Choked by dust and deprived of light, plant plankton soon would have died in the sea, followed by plants on land. And without plants, animals would have had no food.

VICTIMS AND SURVIVORS

The few remaining species of sauropods would have soon died out, followed by other plant-eating dinosaurs. Predatory theropods might have been able to hold out for longer by scavenging, but the disintegration of food chains would have made life increasingly difficult. Eventually, after perhaps centuries or millennia, the last dinosaurs would have disappeared. Small animals fared better, perhaps because they were less exposed, but the checklist of survivors raises some puzzling questions. Why did pterosaurs vanish, while birds managed to pull through? What physical features allowed crocodiles to survive, while most other aquatic reptiles perished? More than 60 million years after the K-T event answers to these questions are still not known.

THE AGE OF MAMMALS

EARLY TERTIARY

The Tertiary Period (meaning "third") was given its name in the 1700s, when it was thought to be the third major interval in Earth's distant past. The Tertiary began after the Cretaceous mass extinction, and it continued until 1.6 million years ago, which means that it includes almost all of the Age of Mammals. During the Early Tertiary—often known as the Paleogene—some of the continents were close to the positions they occupy today, but Australia was still in the process of becoming an island, and North and South America were separated by the sea.

▷ Pakicetus *(top right) is the earliest known cetacean—the group of mammals that includes today's whales and dolphins. About 6.6 ft. (2m) long, it had long jaws with flesh-tearing teeth.*

▽ Pristichampus, *a land-dwelling crocodile, attacks a* Hyracotherium, *one of the earliest known members of the horse family.* Hyracotherium *stood just 8 in. (20cm) high at the shoulders.*

CHANGING DIETS

When the Tertiary Period began mammals had already existed for at least 150 million years, and two major lines—the placental mammals and the marsupials—were well established. However, during this long phase in their history neither of these lines played a major role in Earth's animal life. They were about the size of today's mice and voles, and they emerged under the cover of darkness to feed. Most of them ate insects, earthworms, and other small animals, cutting up their prey with tiny but sharp teeth.

With the disappearance of the dinosaurs and many other groups of animals, mammals were confronted with new opportunities on an extraordinary scale. Practically all of the large plant eaters had disappeared, leaving a huge and largely untapped source of food. There were no large meat eaters at all. From modest beginnings mammals went through an astounding surge of evolution. They eventually filled both these gaps, becoming the most important plant eaters and hunters on land and even spreading into the air and sea.

Some of the first large carnivorous mammals were the creodonts, a group of placental mammals that included species that looked like weasels, cats, and hyenas. Creodonts flourished for several million years, but became extinct before the Early Tertiary came to an end. Marsupial meat eaters were important predators in Australia and South America. But a group of placental, meat-eating mammals, the carnivores, became the leading predators in all other parts of the world.

Early Tertiary carnivores included the ancestors of all the main families of mammalian hunters, including cats, dogs, and mustelids (animals that include today's badgers, otters, and skunks). One feature that all these animals shared was a set of teeth shaped for gripping and slicing flesh. Their gripping teeth, or canines, were near the front of their jaws, ideally placed for stabbing into prey. As carnivores evolved, some species developed very long canines, a feature that reached its high point in the saber-toothed cats. These were equipped with two stabbing teeth up to 6 in. (15cm) long, which were flattened from side to side. True saber-toothed cats were all placentals, but some marsupials— for example, *Thylacosmilus* (page 208)— developed in a similar way, an example of convergent evolution.

THE RISE OF THE PLANT EATERS

For mammals that fed on insects the switch to eating plants was more complicated than the switch to hunting larger prey. They gradually evolved front incisors to harvest their food and grinding teeth or molars to reduce it to a pulp. More importantly, they developed complex digestive systems filled with microorganisms that helped them break down food. Many of these animals developed long legs and hooves, which meant they could run for safety if attacked.

During the Early Tertiary several lines of hooved placental mammals developed in different parts of the world. They included the early ancestors of today's elephants, as well as tapirs and rhinoceroses. Horses evolved in the Northern Hemisphere, but they were mirrored by convincing horse look-alikes, litopterns, which developed in isolation in South America. The most impressive of these plant eaters would have been the brontotheres, animals that looked like giant rhinoceroses with head shields and horns. One of the largest, *Brontotherium*, lived in North America, had a forked horn, and weighed up to two tons.

REPTILES AND BIRDS

Apart from the mammals, other survivors from the Cretaceous extinction made the most of new opportunities in a dinosaur-free world. Among them were the reptiles that emerged from the extinction unscathed: lizards and snakes, turtles and tortoises, and —largest of all—the crocodilians. Most crocodilians kept to their original watery habitats, but some, such as *Pristichampus*, abandoned this kind of life and took up hunting on land, running on powerful legs that ended in hooflike claws.

For birds the disappearance of pterosaurs meant less competition for fish. But on land the extinction of their immediate relatives— the predatory theropods—opened up some new and different ways of living. Giant, flightless hunters evolved, capable of running down other animals and tearing them apart with their beaks. One of the best-known examples of these feathered predators was *Diatryma*, which lived in North America and Europe about 50 million years ago. Standing about 6.6 ft. (2m) tall, it probably fed on mammals, but declined when predatory mammals became larger and more widespread. Similar birds survived for much longer in South America, perhaps because large predatory mammals were rare on this island continent, which was cut off from the rest of the world.

◁ *Crouched in shallow water,* Moeritherium *feeds on water plants. This portly, pig-sized animal was an early proboscidean—a relative of today's elephants and of extinct mammoths and mastodonts. Its ears, eyes, and nostrils were in a line along the top of its head, allowing it to float with most of its body submerged.*

▽ *With its long legs and powerful beak,* Diatryma *was well equipped for making sudden raids among herds of small grazing mammals. Small animals were swallowed whole, but larger ones were torn up by the hook at the beak's tip.*

THE AGE OF MAMMALS

LATE TERTIARY

The Late Tertiary, or Neogene, began about 23 million years ago. Life had fully recovered after the great Cretaceous extinction. Mammals continued to flourish and reached a peak of diversity as the global climate became cooler and drier. The continents were less scattered than they were in Early Tertiary times and, toward the end of this period a significant event occurred in the Western Hemisphere: North and South America became joined by a narrow isthmus of dry land.

▷ Hapalops *was a ground sloth that lived in South America about 20 million years ago. It was about 4 ft. (1.2m) long—a modest size compared to some of its later relatives, such as* Megatherium *(page 213).*

▽ *The South American marsupial, saber-toothed cat* Thylacosmilus *attacked its prey with a pair of enormous canine teeth. True placental cats evolved similar weapons independently— one well-known example is* Smilodon *(page 212).*

SEPARATION AND CONNECTION

Marsupial mammals first appeared during the Late Cretaceous Period, when many of the continents were still connected. Fossils show that they spread across Europe, North America, and South America and reached Australia in the Tertiary. Marsupials and placental mammals lived side by side, with marsupials proving just as successful as their relatives in the struggle to survive. But during the Tertiary Period, continental drift caused great changes in these two mammal lines. Some of the continents began to separate, carrying their mammals with them. Marsupials died out in Europe and North America, but in South America and Australia—now both isolated—they thrived.

Today Australia is well known for its marsupials, but South America had almost as many kinds in Tertiary times, including opossums—rodentlike insect eaters that spent their life in trees—and ground-based predators that looked like hyenas and bears. The largest of the South American predators were the saber-toothed, marsupial cats. One of these, *Thylacosmilus*, had the longest canine teeth of any hunting mammal.

In Australia marsupials remained in isolation until humans arrived, perhaps 60,000 years ago. There were no placental mammals to compete with, so they evolved into an extraordinary array of forms. In South America things were different partly because placental mammals also existed on the continent. But as the Tertiary neared its end the Central American land bridge allowed mammals from North and South America to mix. For some of South America's marsupials, particularly the opossums, this brought a chance to spread north, but for plant-eating species and placentals, it meant extra competition as hooved mammals, such as horses and deer, spread south.

UNLIKELY PARTNERS

During the Late Tertiary, as the world's climate grew drier, grassy plains became a major animal habitat for the first time. Plant-eating mammals gradually adapted to this, switching from a diet based on the leaves of trees and shrubs to one based on grass.

Grasses grow from the bottom up, rather than at their tips. As a result they can grow back if they are eaten down to the ground, whereas other plants, such as tree saplings, become stunted and die. By killing the plants with which grasses compete, mammalian grazers help grass spread.

This improbable partnership proved to be one of the great success stories in mammalian evolution, particularly in the interior of northern continents. In North America larger and faster horses evolved, as well as the antelope-like pronghorns. In Europe and Asia the main grazers were bovids, animals that include today's cattle and sheep.

OUT OF THE TREES
The Late Tertiary was an important time for primates, a group of mammals that adapted to life in trees. The earliest remains—just five teeth—date back to the Late Cretaceous. By the Early Tertiary ancestors of monkeys and apes make their first appearance in the fossil record. Primates had hands that could grip, forward-facing eyes, and large brains—features that helped them judge distances and jump from branch to branch.

Throughout the Tertiary primates in the Americas remained forest-dwellers, just as they are today. But in Europe, Africa, and Asia an increasing number of species took up life on the ground, probably because forests were giving way to grassland. These ground dwellers included the ancestors of today's baboons, as well as hominids—animals related to today's chimpanzees and gorillas, and also to us. Unlike monkeys, hominids did not have tails, and most could stand on their back feet to get a better view of their surroundings. This upright posture freed their hands for other tasks, such as carrying food or even making tools. It was a major development, and one that would have momentous consequences for the whole of the living world.

◁ Merychippus *was a Late Tertiary member of the horse family. About 3.3 ft. (1m) high at the shoulder, it was larger than* Hyracotherium *(page 206). And its weight was supported by just one toe on each foot, rather than three or four. As horses evolved all traces of their other toes disappeared.*

▽ *Keeping a careful watch for danger, a troop of* Ankarapithecus *forages on the ground.* Ankarapithecus *lived in the Near East about 10 million years ago— well before the split between the line that led to the great apes and the one that led to human beings.*

QUATERNARY

Upheavals caused by climate change have been a common feature in the history of life, but few periods have seen such abrupt swings as the last 1.6 million years. The Quaternary Period is divided into two geological epochs: the Pleistocene, which spanned the whole of the last Ice Age, and the Holocene, which began about 10,000 years ago, when the ice staged its most recent retreat. For land animals the Quaternary has been a challenging time.

▷ *The woolly mammoth evolved in Europe and Asia but spread to North America via the land bridge that formed across the Bering Sea (page 23). The hump on its head stored fat that acted as a food reserve.*

▽ *The European cave bear is one of several Ice Age species that are known from the fossilized remains of animals hibernating in caves underground.*

are almost certainly linked to variations in the earth's orbit around the sun. As well as changing average temperatures and ice cover, they have other effects on plant and animal habitats. One of these is a drop in sea level, caused by more water being locked up as ice. Another is a change in rainfall patterns, which can make some areas drier than they are in warmer times.

For plant life during the Pleistocene, climate changes were often problematic, particularly in the far north and south, where the ground was bulldozed by slowly moving ice. But for land animals falling sea levels sometimes proved useful, because they allowed species to cross land bridges to areas that they had not been able to reach before.

EBB AND FLOW

Ice ages are much more than periods of intense and long-lasting cold. During a typical ice age average temperatures swing up and down; with each steep drop, or glaciation, the world's polar ice caps advance, and glaciers creep farther down mountains in other parts of the world. During the warm intervals, or interglacials, the reverse happens, and the ice goes into retreat. We are currently experiencing an interglacial—one that started when the Holocene Epoch began.

Ice ages are impossible to predict, although they

MAMMOTHS AND MASTODONTS

At their maximum spread the ice caps of the Pleistocene stretched as far south as present-day New York and London. To the south of these giant ice sheets was tundra— a bleak and vast expanse of boggy grassland, crisscrossed by icy rivers carrying meltwater to the sea. It was a hostile landscape, but despite the cold, summer brought a rich supply of plant food. For warm-blooded mammals it was a good place to be.

The most celebrated of the Ice Age mammals were the mammoths and the mastodonts, two

◁ Unlike the woolly mammoth, the woolly rhinoceros did not manage to spread from Asia to North America, but it did have a wide distribution from the northern tundra to the grasslands farther south. As with modern rhinos, its horns evolved partly for impressing rivals and partly for self-defense.

were characteristic of Ice Age mammals, because large bodies can generate plenty of heat from their food, and thick fur helps retain it. Woolly rhinos lived in Europe and in Siberia and survived until the ice retreated at the end of the Pleistocene. Specimens have been found frozen in permafrost, but some have also been recovered from naturally occurring oil seeps in parts of central Europe.

Another Ice Age species, *Elasmotherium*, had what was probably the largest horn of any member of the rhino family. It was about the same size as a white rhino—the largest species alive today—but its horn was up to 6.6 ft. (2m) long, with a spreading base that covered almost all of its forehead and muzzle.

groups of animals belonging to the elephant line. The steppe mammoth, *Mammuthus trogontheri*, which lived in Europe about 500,000 years ago, was one of the first species to become adapted to severe cold by developing a coat of long, thick fur. Unlike today's elephants, it had a high-crowned head and sloping back, and in males the tusks were sometimes more than 16.4 ft. (5m) long. The more familiar woolly mammoth, *Mammuthus primigenius*, was a more compact animal, measuring less than 10 ft. (3m) high. Its tusks were also smaller, and it probably used them to scrape away snow as it searched for food. The American mastodont, *Mammut americanum*, looked similar and roamed the coniferous forests on the tundra's southern edge.

The steppe mammoth died out long ago, but the woolly mammoth and American mastodont survived into the relatively recent past. The mastodont is thought to have died out about 8,000 years ago, and the woolly mammoth clung on for another two millennia. Human hunters were probably responsible for making both species extinct.

ICE AGE RHINOS

The northern tundra was also home to the woolly rhinoceros, *Coelodonta antiquitatis*, another animal whose modern relatives live in much warmer parts of the world. Standing about 6.6 ft. (2m) high, it had a pair of solid horns made of matted hair—a family feature that distinguishes rhinos from other hooved mammals. Its thickset shape and long coat

SURVIVING THE WINTER

For plant eaters on the tundra, summer may have been a season of plenty, but winter was a testing time. Many grazing mammals migrated south, heading for forested regions where there was some shelter and food in the form of bark and buds. These included reindeer and the so-called Irish elk, whose remains have been found in many parts of northern Europe and Asia. Reindeer follow their traditional migration routes today, but the Irish elk is now extinct. In some remote parts of Europe the species may have lasted until 500 B.C.

Unlike grazing animals, ice age bears spent the winter in a dormant state, which meant that they did not have to search for food. In some caves in Europe, mud still carries scratch marks made by bears traveling to and from their hibernation dens.

▽ With its enormous antlers the male Irish elk would have been one of the most spectacular animals in Europe and northern Asia during Ice Age times. There were several species of these remarkable deer, all with extravagant antlers that were shed and regrown each year.

THE AGE OF MAMMALS

DEATH AT RANCHO LA BREA

Some of the most vivid evidence of life in Pleistocene times comes not from the far north, but from the heart of modern Los Angeles. This is the unlikely setting for one of the world's most remarkable fossil sites—the famous tar pits of Rancho La Brea. Here pools of sticky asphalt, or tar, existed in Ice Age times, creating traps for animals on a massive scale.

For much of the Late Pleistocene the climate of this part of California was cooler and wetter than it is today, and the well-watered landscape was home to a wide variety of animals, including mammoths, giant ground sloths, and saber-toothed tigers. The tar pits were often covered with the remains of dead plants, and in the winter animals could walk across the surface in complete safety, because the asphalt was cold and firm. But during the summer the asphalt absorbed the sun's heat and started to liquefy, like hot tar on the surface of a road. At this time of the year animals walking across what looked like solid ground could suddenly find themselves falling into sticky black pools,

with no hope of getting out. As they struggled to save themselves these trapped animals attracted predators and scavengers, which also became stuck.

After each summer's deadly toll winter rains covered the victims with sand and sediment, and the process of fossilization began. Unlike most fossils, the ones at Rancho La Brea consist of original bones, rather than ones that have been mineralized, or turned to stone. Impregnated with oily tar and cut off from oxygen in the air, they have escaped the normal processes of decay for over 10,000 years.

TREASURE IN THE TAR

Many of the tar pits have now been excavated, yielding fossils on a truly staggering scale. These Late Pleistocene treasure chests have disgorged the remains of nearly 60 mammal species, with over 2,000 skeletons of saber-toothed tigers alone. The largest victims were mammoths, and the smallest included flying insects that had made the mistake of settling on the surface of the tar, instead of flying on. Birds feature

▽ *In Ice Age California 20,000 years ago, an imperial mammoth lies in a tar pit while a saber-toothed tiger fights off scavengers that have already gathered in hopes of feeding on the mammoth's remains. The scavengers include storks, vultures, and the dire wolf—the largest known member of the dog family. Most of the animals in this scene became extinct about 10,000 years ago.*

▷ *The giant moa* Diornis maximus *was the largest of about two dozen species whose remains have been found in New Zealand. Until Polynesian settlers arrived about 1,000 years ago, it lived in a world entirely free of land mammals apart from bats. An adult giant moa could hold up to 5.5 lb. (2.5kg) of stones in its gizzard, helping it grind its food. Moas laid just a single egg.*

in the catch. Their fragile skeletons break easily, but in the tar pits they were well preserved. The only animals that managed to avoid this deadly trap were nocturnal species. This was because the surface of the tar hardened after sunset.

RULED BY BIRDS

Although mammals were the largest plant eaters of Ice Age times, some remote islands, such as Madagascar and New Zealand, had no large land mammals of their own. Their largest animals were flightless birds, which grew to colossal sizes. In Madagascar the biggest species were the elephant birds, some of which weighed almost half a ton. One species, *Aepyornis maximus*, laid the world's largest known bird egg (page 16). New Zealand's counterparts, known collectively as moas, included one species, *Dinornis maximus*, that measured up to 12 ft. (3.7m) high, making it the tallest bird ever.

Birds like these were able to evolve on remote islands because there were no predatory mammals to attack either them or their chicks. Most fed on seeds, berries, and shoots, and they ground up their food with gizzard stones, which were very like the gastroliths of dinosaurs (page 78). They survived the changes at the end of the last Ice Age, but sadly they were not able to survive the arrival of human beings, and their spears, bows and arrows, and dogs. Madagascar's last elephant bird probably died about 1,000 years ago, and the last of the moas is thought to have died out much more recently— perhaps as late as 1800.

▷ *The giant ground sloth* Megatherium *lived in South America during Ice Age times. Almost as large as a modern elephant, it could stand on its back legs to reach up into trees and hook down leafy branches with its long claws. Today's sloths belong to the same group of mammals, but rarely set foot on the ground.*

THE PLEISTOCENE EXTINCTION

One of the tantalizing features about Ice Age animals is that—in geological terms—they existed not that long ago. Few of them lasted as long as the moas, but a whole host of large mammals were still alive and well about 10,000 years ago. However, as the last glaciation came to an end hundreds of species abruptly died out. North America was one of the worst-affected regions, losing three fourths of all its large mammals, including many whose remains have been dug up at Rancho La Brea.

Why did this massive round of extinctions take place? Some paleontologists believe that it was triggered mainly by the sudden change in climate as the ice retreated and the world warmed up. According to this theory, rapid changes in plant life—such as the switch from tundra to forest—left many mammals without a source of food. But similar changes had happened in previous times, without the same widespread species loss. Many paleontologists point the finger at a very different cause: the rapid spread of human hunters. According to this theory, migrating humans targeted large animals, killing so many that natural food chains began to collapse, and animals were unable to recover.

THE AGE OF MAMMALS

HUMAN EVOLUTION

The origin of our own species is one of the most closely studied areas of prehistory. Although humans are unique in many ways, paleontologists have no doubt that we developed through evolution, just like all other inhabitants of the living world. Our closest living relatives are the great apes, but our own ancestors were humanlike animals called hominids, which split from the line leading to apes about 5 million years ago. Following that split, evolution produced a succession of hominid species, but today only one is left—ourselves.

△ Australopithecus afarensis *lived in Eastern Africa between about 3 and 4 million years ago. Adults stood about 4 ft. (1.2m) high, and had brains about one third the size of ours. Because they stood upright, their hands were free to use sticks and stones as tools, but unlike later hominids, there is no evidence that they shaped them for particular tasks.*

THE FIRST HOMINIDS

At one time experts believed that the ape and hominid lines parted up to 20 million years ago, meaning that this was the time when our last shared ancestor was alive. Since then human genes have been compared with those of other living primates. They show that our genes are remarkably similar to those of the great apes— particularly gorillas and chimpanzees. This connection has prompted some rethinking, and today most experts date the split between the apes and hominids at 4 to 5 million years ago.

At the beginning of the last century many paleontologists thought humans evolved in Asia, but today there is no doubt that Africa was the birthplace of the human line. The first known hominids belonged to the genus *Australopithecus*, which literally means "southern ape." With their long arms, short legs, and protruding jaws, australopithecines had many apelike characteristics, but even the earliest of them walked upright on their back legs more than 4 million years ago.

THE SOUTHERN APES

The first southern ape discovery was also one of the strangest. It was a child's skull found in a South African quarry in 1924. Raymond Dart, the anatomist who examined it, concluded that it belonged to an extinct species that linked humans and apes, which he named *Australopithecus africanus*. At the time many other scientists strongly disagreed, preferring the idea that humans evolved in Asia. But with further discoveries it became clear that Dart was correct and that the southern apes were very likely to have been among our ancestors.

Since the 1920s experts have identified at least six separate species of australopithecines from remains found at more than 20 sites in eastern and southern Africa. Most of these sites have been in Africa's Great Rift Valley, where periodic eruptions have engulfed hominids in volcanic ash. The remains often consist of no more than teeth or fragments of jaws. But in 1974 two American anthropologists stumbled across an amazing find—almost half a female skeleton belonging to a species called *Australopithecus afarensis*. Nicknamed Lucy, its owner lived nearly 3 million years ago. Trace fossils (page 19) have also been found. One of the most evocative, a trail consisting of three sets of footprints, was discovered in 1978. Left by two adults and a child, this family outing predated Lucy by about 500,000 years.

THE TOOLMAKERS

The last australopithecines died out between 1.6 and one million years ago. But long before they disappeared, they gave rise to a new group of hominids that lived alongside them for several hundred thousand years. These newcomers were our immediate ancestors and had much more humanlike

▷ *After a successful hunt a group of* Homo heidelbergensis *cut up a dead rhinoceros— a kill that will provide them with food for many days. This hominid was first found in Europe but originally evolved in Africa perhaps 250,000 years ago. Thought by some experts to be a form of* Homo erectus, *it probably gave rise to our own species.*

features. They are classified in the genus *Homo*, the small group of primates to which modern humans belong.

Unlike australopithecines, these anatomical humans were adept at making stone tools. One of the earliest species, *Homo habilis*, or "handy man," made simple tools by smashing stones to give them a sharp edge. *Homo erectus*, or "upright man," was a later species that evolved at about the time the australopithecines disappeared. It had a more skillful technique, using flakes chipped from stones, rather than the original stones themselves. These flakes were carefully shaped, creating spearheads and a wide range of other

implements. *Homo erectus* was not particularly good at inventing new designs, but as a stone toolmaker he (or she) would have been far more expert than almost anybody alive today.

No australopithecine remains have been found outside Africa, which makes it likely that the southern apes became extinct without spreading to other parts of the world. But *Homo erectus* was much more adventurous and spread throughout Europe and Asia, taking with it the art of toolmaking and also perhaps the knowledge of how to use fire. Shorter than modern humans and with a brain slightly smaller than ours, it was the most successful hominid so far, and our direct ancestor.

◁ *Peking man was a form of* Homo erectus *that lived in the Far East. Excavations at caves at Zhoukoudian, in northeast China, have revealed layers of ash near its remains, showing that this hominid knew how to use fire. Peking man probably lit fires from natural blazes and kept them going for weeks or months at a time.*

THE AGE OF MAMMALS

△ *A simple pebble tool (left) made by* Homo habilis *over two million years ago contrasts with a superbly crafted spearhead (right) made by prehistoric people called Cro-Magnons. The Cro-Magnons date back to about 35,000 years ago and lived in Europe and Asia.*

▽ *In this imaginary meeting somewhere in Ice Age Europe a group of Neanderthals (left) confront a hunting party of modern humans. Both sides are well armed, and events threaten to turn violent, because the Neanderthals sense that their home and livelihood are at stake. Whether scenes like this took place is not certain, but one fact is known— the Neanderthal species did not survive.*

MODERN HUMANS

Humans almost certainly evolved from *Homo erectus*, perhaps through the intermediate species *Homo heidelbergensis*, but there was no precise moment when modern humans suddenly stepped onto the prehistoric stage. Instead, our ancestors' features slowly changed, first going through an archaic form and then reaching a modern form indistinguishable from ourselves. The first modern humans probably appeared between 120,000 and 100,000 years ago. In geological terms this is remarkably recent, and it means that the family tree of modern humans stretches back no more than about 7,500 generations.

Modern humans are also thought to have evolved in Africa. Fossils show that they reached the Middle East by about 90,000 y.a. and the Far East by about 60,000 y.a. As a species, we have been spreading ever since.

EARLY MODERN HUMANS

In 1856, long before anything was known about hominids in Africa, workers in a German lime quarry found a collection of bones in the mud of a cave. The bones were heavily built and clearly very old, and among them was part of a skull with large brow ridges over the eyes. When these remains were examined by anatomical experts, many concluded that they belonged either to a subnormal human or an apelike animal.

Neanderthal man, as it came to be called, turned out to be one of the most extraordinary discoveries in the search for our ancestors. Known only in Europe and the Middle East, this hominid lived between about 120,000 and 35,000 years ago, at a time when modern humans had already made the move out of their African birthplace. At the end of this period the Neanderthals disappeared without trace.

Anthropologists are still not certain who the Neanderthals were and what happened to them. One theory is that they belonged to our own species and merged with modern human beings. A more likely possibility is that they were a separate species—one that lost out in the struggle for food and space and eventually became extinct.

SUCCESS STORY

If sheer numbers are a guide, humans are the most successful large animals that have ever lived. At present the human population totals about 6 billion, and it is expected to level off at about 11 billion at some point. Many factors have been responsible for our

success, including the invention of farming about 10,000 years ago and the rapid development of technology. However, first and foremost it is due to something that makes humans unique—the ability to communicate and to learn from other people's experience, as well as our own.

GLOSSARY

Adaptation A feature of an animal that helps it survive. Adaptations develop through evolution and may include physical features and different kinds of behavior.

Algae Simple plantlike organisms that grow by collecting energy from sunlight. Most algae live in water. Many are microscopic, but the largest, the seaweeds, can be many feet long.

Ammonoids Extinct mollusks with tentacles and spiral shells containing a row of separate chambers. Ammonoids lived in the sea and were distant relatives of today's octopuses and squid.

Anapsids Reptiles without any skull openings behind their eye sockets. Today's anapsids include tortoises and turtles.

Archosaurs The group of reptiles that includes pterosaurs and dinosaurs, as well as the crocodilians and the birds. Archosaurs are often known as the "ruling reptiles."

Arthropods A huge and highly successful group of invertebrate animals that have a flexible body case, or exoskeleton, and legs that bend at joints. Living arthropods include insects, arachnids, and crustaceans; extinct ones include trilobites and sea scorpions.

Bacteria The smallest, simplest, and most ancient living things on Earth. Bacteria live in a variety of habitats, including on and in living animals. Most are harmless, but some, called germs, can cause disease.

Bipedal Standing and moving on two legs instead of four.

Camouflage Protective coloration that allows an animal to blend in with its background. Plant eaters use camouflage to avoid predators; some predators are camouflaged to launch surprise attacks on prey.

Canine tooth A tooth with a single point, shaped for stabbing into prey. Enlarged canine teeth are a common feature in hunters such as saber-toothed tigers.

Carnivore Any animal that lives by eating other animals. The word "carnivore" is also used for a particular group of mammals that includes today's cats, dogs, and bears, together with their extinct ancestors.

Carnosaurs A group of giant, flesh-eating dinosaurs or theropods. Unlike smaller hunters, carnosaurs used teeth, not claws, to bring down prey.

Carrion The remains of dead animals.

Cenozoic Era The part of Earth's geological history that started after the extinction of the dinosaurs 66 million years ago and continues today.

Cetaceans Whales, dolphins, and their relatives. Cetaceans live in water, but they are air-breathing mammals, evolving from animals that lived on land.

Chelonians Tortoises, turtles, and their relatives. Chelonians are an ancient group of reptiles that have hardly changed in 250 million years.

Chordates Animals that have a reinforcing rod, or notochord, running the length of their bodies. Some are soft-bodied, but in most, the vertebrates, the notochord is enclosed inside a hard backbone, making up part of a complete internal skeleton.

Clade An ancestral species, together with all the other species that have evolved from it. Because the members of a clade share the same ancestor, they make up a complete and self-contained group in evolution. Dinosaurs and birds are examples of clades; fish are not, because they evolved from several different ancestors.

Cladogram A diagram that shows clades.

Cold-blooded See **Ectothermic**.

Continental drift The gradual movement of continents across the earth's surface. Continental drift is driven by heat from deep inside the earth, which keeps the solid crust on the move.

Convergent evolution The evolution of similar features in animals that share similar ways of life. Convergent evolution can make unrelated animals difficult to tell apart.

Coprolites Fossilized animal droppings.

Cyanobacteria Also known as Blue-green algae, it is bacteria that live in the same way as plants—by collecting the energy in sunlight.

Cycads Cone-bearing plants, resembling small palm trees, that were a common food of dinosaurs. Cycads still exist.

Diapsids Reptiles with two skull openings on either side of the head, behind the eye sockets. The diapsids include the dinosaurs, as well as the crocodilians, snakes, and lizards.

Ectothermic Having a body temperature that rises and falls with the temperature outside. Ectothermic animals include invertebrates, fish, amphibians, and living reptiles.

Endothermic Having a body temperature that stays warm and steady whatever the conditions outside. Living endothermic animals include mammals and birds; extinct ones included pterosaurs and some dinosaurs.

Estivating Spending hot or dry times of the year dormant, or asleep. When cooler times return, an estivating animal wakes up.

Evolution A gradual change in living things as each generation follows the one before it. Evolution allows animals to adapt to changes around them.

Exoskeleton A hard case that protects an animal's body from outside, instead of supporting it from within. Exoskeletons are a common feature in invertebrates; arthropods have exoskeletons made of separate plates, which meet at flexible joints.

Extinct No longer alive anywhere on Earth.

Fossil The preserved relics of living things. Some fossils are formed by animal remains, but others are traces, such as footprints, that animals leave behind.

Gastralia Extra ribs that protect the part of the body containing the stomach and the intestines.

Gastroliths Stones, swallowed by dinosaurs and other animals, used to help grind up food.

Gastropods Mollusks that have a coiled shell and a single suckerlike foot.

Gondwana A giant continent that formed part of Pangaea. Gondwana eventually broke up to form South America, Africa, India, Antarctica, and Australia.

Herbivore Any animal that lives by eating plants.

Hyperphalangy An evolutionary trend that increases the number of bones in an animal's feet. Hyperphalangy was a common feature of marine reptiles in prehistoric times.

Ichnologists Scientists who study fossilized footprints, tracks, and other trace fossils.

Ichthyosaurs A group of extinct marine reptiles that evolved fishlike bodies and narrow, tooth-filled "beaks."

Incisor tooth A tooth at the front of the jaw, used for cutting into food. Incisors usually have a single, straight cutting edge.

Invertebrates Animals that do not have a backbone or a bony skeleton. Invertebrates were the first animals to evolve, and they make up over 95 percent of all the animal species on Earth.

Laurasia A giant continent that once formed part of Pangaea. Laurasia broke up to form North America, Europe, and northern Asia.

Mesozoic Era The part of Earth's geological history that began 245 million years ago and ended when the dinosaurs became extinct.

Microorganisms Living things that can be seen only with the help of a microscope. They include bacteria, as well as other forms of life. For several billion years microorganisms were the only living things on Earth.

Molar tooth A tooth at the rear of the jaw, used for crushing and grinding food. Molars often have a flat surface with bumps or ridges that grind against each other.

Mollusks Invertebrates that have a soft body, which is often protected by a hard shell. Fossil mollusks are common, because their shells often fossilized when they settled on the seabed.

Nautiloids Extinct mollusks with tentacles and straight or spiral shells containing a row of separate chambers. Like ammonoids, nautiloids lived in the sea and were distant relatives of today's octopuses and squid.

Notochord A reinforcing rod that runs down an animal's body, allowing the animal to move by bending from side to side. Notochords are found only in chordates.

Ornithischians One of the two overall groups of dinosaurs, ornithischians had birdlike hip bones and were all plant eaters.

Ornithopods A group of ornithischian dinosaurs that included a range of small or medium-sized

plant eaters, such as iguanodonts and hadrosaurs.

Osteoderms Bony plates that form on the surface of the skin.

Paleontology The study of fossil remains.

Paleozoic Era The part of Earth's geological history that saw the development of the first hard-bodied animals, about 540 m.y.a. During this era living things made the transition from water to land.

Pangaea The supercontinent that existed during much of the Mesozoic Era, when reptiles ruled the land.

Placentals Mammals that give birth to well-developed young. The young develop inside their mother's womb, or uterus, and are fed through a spongy pad called a placenta, which is connected to their mother's blood supply.

Plankton Small or microscopic animals and plants that drift near the surface of the sea. Plankton is an important food for many marine animals.

Predators Animals that catch and eat other living animals—their prey. Unless they hunt in packs, predators are usually larger than their prey. They are always less common.

Pterodactyls A group of short-tailed pterosaurs, or flying reptiles. The pterodactyls included the largest flying animals that have ever existed.

Pterosaurs Flying reptiles that lived at the same time as the dinosaurs. Pterosaurs had leathery wings and bony beaks with or without teeth. Early forms had long tails.

Saurischians One of the two overall groups of dinosaurs. Saurischians had lizardlike hip bones, and they included predators as well as plant eaters. The largest and heaviest dinosaurs belonged to this group.

Sauropods Plant-eating dinosaurs with giant bodies,

long necks and tails, and relatively tiny heads. The sauropods included the largest land animals to have existed.

Scavenger An animal that feeds on dead remains.

Species A group of living things that share the same features and that can breed with each other in the wild. Each species has its own two-part scientific name—for example, *Tyrannosaurus rex*. The first part of the name indicates a genus, or collection of species, while the second part indicates one particular species in the genus.

Stromatolite A rocklike mound produced by microorganisms growing in shallow water. Fossilized stromatolites are among the oldest signs of life on Earth.

Synapsids Reptiles and other animals that have a single skull opening on either side of the head, behind the eye sockets. The synapsids include today's mammals and their ancestors, the therapsids.

Tetrapods Animals with backbones and four limbs. Most tetrapods use all their limbs for moving although some (humans and many dinosaurs) stand on their back legs alone.

Therapsids A group of extinct animals that had features somewhere inbetween reptiles and mammals. Also known as "mammal-like reptiles."

Theropods Predatory or omnivorous dinosaurs that usually walked on their back legs.

Trilobites A group of prehistoric arthropods named after the three lengthways lobes of their bodies. Trilobites lived in the sea and survived for over 250 million years.

Vertebrates Animals that have backbones. Vertebrates include fish, amphibians, reptiles, birds, and mammals.

Warm-blooded See **Endothermic.**

INDEX

Page numbers in **bold** refer to main sections.
Page numbers in *italic* refer to illustrations.

WEB SITES

www.dinodata.net
A giant compendium of facts and figures about dinosaurs

www.dinosauricon.com
One of the most comprehensive dinosaur sites on the web, with information on hundreds of genera

www.enchantedlearning.com/subjects/dinosaurs
A site that covers dinosaurs and other prehistoric animals, with up-to-the-minute news about excavations and discoveries

www.nhm.org
Web site of the Natural History Museum of Los Angeles County, California. Contains extensive information about prehistoric animals from the tar pits at Rancho La Brea, California

www.ucmp.berkeley.edu
Web site of the Museum of Paleontology at the University of California, Berkeley. Features a comprehensive guide to life at all stages in the Earth's past

www.ucmp.berkeley.edu/pin/pinentrance.html
An English-language web site that provides access to the Russian Paleontological Institute (PIN)—the world's largest fossil collection

www.fieldmuseum.org
Web site of the Field Museum, Chicago, Illinois, which features details of Sue—the world's most complete specimen of Tyrannosaurus rex

www.tyrrellmuseum.com
Web site of the Royal Tyrrell Museum of Palaeontology, Alberta, Canada. Contains a virtual tour of fossil exhibits, including the Burgess Shale

web.archive.org/web/20010330011544/www.pterosaurs.net/
The archive of one of the most comprehensive guides to pterosaurs on the web

ACKNOWLEDGMENTS

The publishers would like to thank the following for their contribution to this book:

Editorial assistance Sheila Clewley, Julie Ferris
Design assistance Mark Bristow
Picture reseach assistance Audrey Reynolds
Artbank assistance Wendy Allison, Steve Robinson

Photographs
Every effort has been made to trace the copyright holders of the photographs. The publishers apologize for any inconvenience caused.

(*t* = top; *c* = center; *b* = bottom; *l* = left; *r* = right)
Front cover: Bryan F. Peterson/Corbis; 3*c* Ardea London/Francois Gohier; 10*tr* Ardea London/Francois Gohier; 11*cl* Science Photo Library/Michael Abbey; *c* Science Photo Library/Sinclair Stammers; 12*tr* Ardea London; *cl* Geoscience Features Picture Library; 14*tl* NHPA/Daniel Heuclin; *clt* Ardea London/P Morris; *clb* Geoscience Features Picture Library; *bl* Geoscience Features Picture Library; 15 *br* The Natural History Museum, London, England/M Long; 16*tr* Ardea London/Masahiro Iijima; *cl* The Natural History Museum, London, England; 17*tr* Science Photo Library/Paul Zahl; *b* Novosti; 18*tr* Ardea London/Francois Gohier; *cl* Science Photo Library/Sinclair Stammers; 19*c* The Natural History Museum, London, England; 20*cl* Ardea London/Francois Gohier; *b* Geoscience Features Picture Library/Dinosaur Nat. Mon.; 21*tl* Geoscience Features Picture Library/Dinosaur Nat. Mon.; *tc* Geoscience Features Picture Library/Dinosaur Nat. Mon.; *tr* Geoscience Features Picture Library/Dinosaurs Nat. Mon.; *c* Geoscience Features Picture Library/Dinosaur Nat. Mon; *cr* Science Photo Library/Peter Menzel; 25*tc* /www.osf.uk.com/Phil Devries; TR Still Pictures/Bryan & Cherry Alexander; 30*tr* Science Photo Library/Louise K Broman; *bc* Frank Lane Picture Agency; *br* Ardea London; *br* Science Photo Library/Jim Amos; 56*c* Science Photo Library/Sinclair Stammers; 64*tr* NHPA/Dan Griggs; 78*tr* Corbis; 84*tr* Ardea London/Francois Gohier; *bl* Ardea London/Francois Grohier; 86*tr* The Field Museum/#GEO85673_2c; *bl* Science Photo Library/Carlos Goldin; 87*tc* Derek Hall; CR Science Photo Library; 103*tr* Ardea London; 108*tr* The Natural History Museum, London, England; *cl* Ardea London; *bc* Ardea London; 109*tr* Humboldt University, Berlin, Germany; *c* Frank Spooner Pictures; 110*tr* National Geographic Society/O. Louis Mazzatenta; *cl* Frank Spooner Pictures; *bc* Frank Spooner Pictures; 111*tr* National Geographic Society/O. Louis Mazzatenta; *b* The Natural History Museum, London, England; *c* Ardea London; 146*tr* Science Photo Library/Simon Fraser; *cl* The Natural History Museum, London, England; *bc* Science Photo Library; 147*tr* Geoscience Features Picture Library; *cr* Ardea London/Francois Gohier; *bc* Frank Spooner Pictures/J.M.Giboux; 148*c* Ardea London/Peter Steyn; *bc* BBC Natural History Unit Picture Library; 149*tl* Quarto/Dr Reed; 150*bl* Bruce Coleman Collection; 152*tr* Ardea London/Francois Gohier; 153*c* Ardea London/Francois Gohier; 160*tr* University of Chicago; *cl* University of Chicago; *br* University of Chicago; 161*tl* Humboldt University, Berlin, Germany; *tc* Humboldt University, Berlin, Germany; *c* The Natural History Museum, London, England; 162*l* Quarto; BR NHPA; 168*cl* Ardea London/P.J.Green; 170*tr* Ardea London; 171*tr* Quarto; *b* Quarto; 184*bl* Quarto; 194*tr* Quarto; 195*t* Quarto; 198*tr* The Natural History Museum, London, England; BC Geoscience Features Picture Library; 210*c* The Natural History Museum, London, England *bl* The Natural History Museum, London, England/M Long; 211*tl* The Natural History Museum, London, England/M Long; 213*tl* The Natural History Museum, London, England; 216*tl* Michael Holford; *tc* Michael Holford